D1093221

Dialectics of Improvement

Edinburgh Critical Studies in Romanticism
Series Editors: Ian Duncan and Penny Fielding

Available Titles
A Feminine Enlightenment: British Women Writers and the Philosophy of Progress, 1759–1820
JoEllen DeLucia
Reinventing Liberty: Nation, Commerce and the Historical Novel from Walpole to Scott
Fiona Price
The Politics of Romanticism: The Social Contract and Literature
Zoe Beenstock
Radical Romantics: Prophets, Pirates, and the Space Beyond Nation
Talissa J. Ford
Literature and Medicine in the Nineteenth-Century Periodical Press: Blackwood's Edinburgh Magazine, *1817–1858*
Megan Coyer
Discovering the Footsteps of Time: Geological Travel Writing in Scotland, 1700–1820
Tom Furniss
The Dissolution of Character in Late Romanticism
Jonas Cope
Commemorating Peterloo: Violence, Resilience, and Claim-making during the Romantic Era
Michael Demson and Regina Hewitt
Dialectics of Improvement: Scottish Romanticism, 1786–1831
Gerard Lee McKeever
Literary Manuscript Culture in Romantic Britain
Michelle Levy

Forthcoming Titles
Towards Romantic Periodical Studies: 12 Case Studies from Blackwood's Edinburgh Magazine
Nicholas Mason and Tom Mole
Romantic Environmental Sensibility: Nature, Class and Empire
Ve-Yin Tee
Scottish Romanticism and the Making of Collective Memory in the British Atlantic
Kenneth McNeil

Visit our website at: www.edinburghuniversitypress.com/series/ECSR

Dialectics of Improvement

Scottish Romanticism, 1786–1831

Gerard Lee McKeever

EDINBURGH
University Press

Edinburgh University Press is one of the leading university presses in the UK. We publish academic books and journals in our selected subject areas across the humanities and social sciences, combining cutting-edge scholarship with high editorial and production values to produce academic works of lasting importance. For more information visit our website: edinburghuniversitypress.com

Edinburgh University Press Ltd
The Tun – Holyrood Road
12(2f) Jackson's Entry
Edinburgh EH8 8PJ

Typeset in 11/14 Adobe Sabon by
IDSUK (DataConnection) Ltd, and
printed and bound in Great Britain.

A CIP record for this book is available from the British Library

ISBN 978 1 4744 4167 4 (hardback)
ISBN 978 1 4744 4169 8 (webready PDF)
ISBN 978 1 4744 4170 4 (epub)

Contents

Acknowledgements

A number of the ideas in this book originated in an AHRC-funded PhD completed at the University of Glasgow in 2014. That thesis was supervised by Dr Alex Benchimol and Professor Nigel Leask, and I am truly grateful for their continuing support of my work. I was employed by the 'Editing Robert Burns for the 21st Century' project at Glasgow for two years across 2015–16, and I would like to acknowledge the AHRC, as well as both Professor Gerard Carruthers and Professor Kirsteen McCue, for enabling me to develop my research during that period. Since 2017 I have been a British Academy Postdoctoral Fellow at Glasgow, which has been valuable to the completion of this volume. I am grateful to the series editors for their backing and advice with this as with other projects, as well as to EUP's anonymous reviewers for their hand in improving the work. Thanks to others who have commented on drafts: Dr Alex Benchimol, Professor Gerard Carruthers, Professor Colin Kidd, Professor Kirsteen McCue and Dr David Stewart. Thanks also to everyone involved in the activities of the Scottish Romanticism Research Group at Glasgow since 2010; to all my colleagues at Glasgow and elsewhere; and to all the students I have taught and learned from since 2012. Finally, thanks to my family for their love and encouragement, which have made this book possible.

An earlier version of material on John Galt in Chapter 4 appeared previously as, '"With wealth come wants": Scottish Romanticism as Improvement in the Fiction of John Galt', *Studies in Romanticism*, 55.1 (2016): 69–94; likewise, some of the thoughts on James Hogg in Chapter 2 appeared in preliminary form as '"All that I choose to tell you is this": Improvement Confronts the Supernatural in Hogg's Short Fictions', *Studies in Hogg and his World*, 25–6 (2015–16): 30–44. Thanks to the editors of both journals and, regarding *SiR*, the Trustees of Boston University, for permission to reproduce this work here.

For Annie and Ivy

Introduction

In its December 1786 issue, James Sibbald's *Edinburgh Magazine, or Literary Miscellany* reprinted an article with a familiar theme. Scotland, it explained, was in the midst of a profound experience of change. A vast, integrated system of cause and effect was making swift headway, since 'improvements of every kind make a more rapid progress, and are more discernible in countries though not entirely rude, yet but little cultivated' – just as 'loam or marle, or any other manure, operates more quickly and with greater effect on new than on old ground'. Signs of backwardness 'in agriculture, commerce, and the mechanical arts' were being erased in a nation once populated by the 'singular spectacle' of 'religious and learned barbarians'. At the same time, England's 'rural and bashful sister' was now acquiring 'all the arts and fashions of modish life'. The piece congratulated the Scottish aristocracy on their support of progress as 'improvement', proceeding to detail a whole variety of contexts in which this supreme narrative was apparent, from trade and infrastructure to law, politics and manners. This all combined to secure the axiom of 'a mutual action and reaction between industry, property, and a spirit of liberty', said to 'naturally support and promote each other'.[1]

Such improving latitude echoed a mainstream Enlightenment perspective with roots stretching back into the previous century. Yet visions of improvement were rarely without complications. Four and a half decades later, in January 1831, an uncredited reprint in a small Galloway periodical, the *Castle-Douglas Weekly Visitor and Literary Miscellany*, was articulating a very different view. 'In our endeavours towards the reformation of our manners and sentiments, we have erred in the same way as respecting our external circumstances', it lamented. 'Instead of correcting only what was amiss, and supplying what was defective, we have gone on indiscriminately reversing and changing, till what commenced in improvement had ended in deterioration.'[2]

The concept of improvement existed in the late eighteenth and early nineteenth centuries as a series of dialectical relationships encompassing both theory and practice, in a collision between – at its most basic – the old and the new, a key component of the culture of modernity. Sibbald had sourced the first item above from the Whig mouthpiece the *Political Herald, and Review*, and its panoramic historical optimism is indicative of a party-political disposition, just as the later article echoes a strain of Tory conservatism nurtured by publications such as *Blackwood's Edinburgh Magazine*, a favourite source of material for the *Weekly Visitor*.[3] Yet debate on improvement transcended party affiliation, just as it was not limited to the social elite or urban intelligentsia. These two reprinted articles register a much larger conversation that was circulating in the Romantic-era public sphere. Developing Benedict Anderson's well-known thesis in *Imagined Communities*, Meredith L. McGill has linked the practice of reprinting in periodicals to the act of imagining the national community, with reprints forging a common 'sense of simultaneity' inflected by local circumstances.[4] It is clear that to contemporaries in Scotland and further afield, the collective interest in improvement sometimes bordered on the condition of a craze.

In 1811 John and Leigh Hunt's *Examiner* reprinted 'A wag in the *Morning Chronicle*' enumerating a deranged catalogue of improvements for London, including plans to 'erect steam engines in every street', 'To prohibit Mr. Martin V. B. from shaving', and for 'St. Paul's to be moved into Warwick-lane'.[5] As this satire suggests, improvement had become a commonplace, an archetype. Yet it was not by that token either uniform or static. The sundry bent of the *Examiner* piece – entitled 'Improvements', plural – is significant. The plurality of improvement was not limited to the multiple areas of concern that might be addressed under the banner of Whig political economy, nor even to the distance between that position and a view of 'deterioration'. Rather, improvement existed in this period as a set of beliefs and practices concerned with progress, much of which bore attributes capable of being analogised, but which was also prone to contradiction and inconsistency. It was furthermore a situated discourse, beholden to time and place. Thus the Whig treatise above stresses the exceptionally 'high antiquity' of Scotland among nations preserving their 'ancient and original independence', granting improvement a patriotic resonance in a distinctive national iteration of what has become known as the 'Age of Improvement'.[6]

Two months before the *Edinburgh Magazine* carried the essay 'On improvements', it had published the first review of Robert Burns's Kilmarnock *Poems, Chiefly in the Scottish Dialect*. Sibbald's review would be eclipsed in the critical memory by the *Lounger* piece that Henry Mackenzie published in December 1786, but his warm appraisal set the tone for the reception of Burns, buying into the poet's avowal of rustic disadvantage to imagine 'some surly critic' bristling indignantly: 'Who are you, Mr Burns?' and 'At what university have you been educated?'[7] The ideal of 'refinement', this suggested, was very much a negotiable good. Such narratives were birthed by the progressive logic of improvement, which would continue to shape literary discourse across the following decades. It is well established that Burns's collected poems appeared during a period of social, political and economic change in Scotland. To take only the economic situation, rationalised farming methods in the agricultural Lowlands, including the consolidation of labour markets, along with the influx of imperial wealth around the Firth of Clyde,[8] had been among the forces acting to characterise bursts of 'economic growth little short of miraculous' from the mid-eighteenth century.[9] More generally, by 1829 Thomas Carlyle was moving to summarise an epochal 'grinding collision of the New with the Old'.[10] This book provides a consideration of four case studies in Scottish literature against this background, arguing that the 'dialectics of improvement' represented a principal fulcrum of literary meaning. Moving through the genres of poetry, short fiction, drama and the novel, it analyses what I contend are major literary-historical moments in the reimagining of improvement across the threshold of the nineteenth century.

Improvement emerges here as a conflicted set of ideas and contexts. In particular, *Dialectics of Improvement* spotlights narratives of commercial modernisation and their intersection with other trajectories of progress. Improvement contained many fraught junctures: a new road or a set of picturesque estate improvements might affect the cultural well-being of local communities and damage the environment. Further, as Joanna Baillie shows in her drama, the profit motive in improvement did not always map on to the cultivation of polite sentiment, and both of these sustained tricky overlaps with

Christian morality. In short, if innovation and tradition constitute the core of the subject, then rarely did either present a united front. Structurally, the idea of improvement depends on what has been improved or left behind. If improvement thus functions dialectically it can also be construed in dialogic terms, with improvement and the unimproved conjoined in an unavoidable symbiosis or symmetry. In historical terms, a variety of factors shaped the discourses of improvement across the turn of the nineteenth century, including a boom-and-bust economy, domestic class tensions and foreign war. Literature played a cogent role in this conversation and was modified in the process. Indeed, the case studies identified here represent some of the most important Scottish contributions to the debate taking place in the period over the form and function of the aesthetic. In them we find improvement shaping ideas about what literature is and what it can do.

Dialectics of improvement, then, helped to precipitate a series of innovations in Scottish literature between 1786 and 1831, including approaches to the politics and potential of the aesthetic itself. In making its case, this book builds upon recent work in studies of eighteenth- and early nineteenth-century Scotland, in which improvement has been gaining currency. The need for a study directly tackling the complexity of improvement in a range of literary contexts has become evident, though this book does not claim to be a comprehensive survey. Rather, its case studies isolate four distinctive aesthetic engagements shaped by genre and historical circumstances, individual reflections of a literary culture impregnated by the 'Age of Improvement' and thus by a central orthodoxy of Enlightenment thought. I address my decision to organise these under the rubric of a Scottish Romanticism below. However, this approach helps to extend the insight rehearsed by Saree Makdisi, that 'Romanticism can be partly understood as a diverse and heterogeneous series of engagements with modernization', building upon a complication of Enlightenment and Romanticism that has become particularly characteristic of work on the Scottish context. Makdisi describes a 'romantic critique' that is 'not merely a response' to, but 'a key constitutive element' of, modernisation.[11] I want to take that position a step further, articulating a Romanticism that has fully absorbed the dialectical form of improvement and thus cannot be said to exist merely in critical, symbiotic relation to modernisation, but rather offers an imaginative register in which modernity and its problematics can be diagnosed, marvelled at and acted upon.

Improvement was sufficiently important as a modality, trope and environmental condition to be viewed plausibly as a defining feature of literary production in late eighteenth- and early nineteenth-century Scotland. For John Galt, reflecting from the vantage of the 1820s, society had entered into a process of what seemed like endemic improvement. This historical spectacle manifested itself in conflicts between culture and capitalism, localism and cosmopolitanism, luxury and morality, enthusiasm and irony, within a society pulling in many directions at once. History as improvement was a source of both celebration and regret for Galt; he responded by cultivating a new form of novel that could embody and dissect it. His was one in a series of powerful literary responses to improvement by Scottish writers between 1786 and 1831, raising questions about progress that remain of acute relevance today. Reflecting in his autobiography on the transformation of the village of Inverkip in Renfrewshire, Galt wrote that

> The alteration was undoubtedly a great improvement, but the place seemed to me neither so picturesque nor primitive as the old town, and I could not refrain from lamenting the change, as one sighs over the grave of an old man.[12]

Improvement

There is a danger of overcomplicating a definition of improvement, which did literally mean making things better. Still, the nature of progress is a controversial subject. Improvement was capable of accommodating a variety of agendas, the culture around it including dissonant and outright hostile perspectives. Yet to establish its basic contours, we need to understand something of improvement's evolution. In *The Invention of Improvement*, Paul Slack finds what he calls a process of 'gradual and piecemeal change', involving 'an appreciation of material progress as a wholly beneficent process', emerging in seventeenth-century England. Slack's long-term assessment that 'English improvement could not be replicated elsewhere' is certainly not unproblematic, especially since he goes on to discuss the 'import' of improvement to Scotland. Nevertheless, he usefully observes, as many others have done, that the term has roots in the management of land, citing a 1613 dictionary definition entirely concerned with the raising of rents.[13] The metaphor of 'manure' used to describe a process of national improvement at the opening of this introduction is thus especially germane, and increasing the productivity of the land would remain integral to this model of growth. This genealogy of improvement helps explain its influence as a sign of modernity, given that land is a crucial material foundation for property, as in Adam Smith's famous analysis, and the source of the agricultural surplus that allows for a complex commercial society.[14] Indeed, to a significant group of thinkers, improvement is effectively the ideological root discourse of capitalism. This is the way Raymond Williams characterises improvement in *Keywords*: as securing 'the complex underlying connection between "making something better" and "making a profit out of something"'.[15] In the same vein, Peter Womack comments that 'The primary meaning of the word, etymologically and historically, is the narrowly economic one': 'it makes managing a stock so that it increases in value the universal type of beneficent change'.[16]

Nevertheless, we also need to pay attention to the moral as a cardinal facet of improvement together with the material. This could work in one of two principal ways. In the first, commerce and morality are aligned as twin arterials of improvement, parallel forms of exchange susceptible of refinement. Indeed, since the imaginative process of sociability ('sympathy') articulated in Smith's *Theory of Moral Sentiments* generates a complex web of moral calculations that supports civility, it forms something of an analogue to commercial exchange via the fiction of money, both reaching higher levels of abstraction and sophistication as societies grow more polite.[17] Of course, if the generation of wealth raises the standard of living and generates happiness, then commerce itself is an inherently moral activity. This basic alignment is associated with 'civilisation', which in eighteenth- and early nineteenth-century Britain remained a significantly Christian ideal, a providential worldview assuming the basic good of (Protestant) modernity.

It is primarily in this 'civilising' sense that improvement functioned for the range of texts and contexts associated with the Scottish Enlightenment, which for the purposes of this book affords an important pre- and parallel history to the intervention made by Romantic literature, a key thrust within a wider culture of improvement. Thus Christopher Berry describes 'a moral and normative core' in the Scottish Enlightenment's central 'account of commerce', which is tethered to improvement as a 'leitmotif'.[18] Stadial historiography presented a crucial vehicle for this position as a macroscopic analysis of improvement in action, detailing the progressive sophistication of society towards commercial modernity, with attendant moral benefits. Although Smith's *Lectures on Jurisprudence* (delivered 1762–63) are normally cited as the original source for stadial theory – at least in its 'four stages' guise – similar ideas were extant elsewhere. William Robertson's 1759 *History of Scotland*, for example, traces the country's emergence into the commercial present from a vague, distant past, leaving the reader in no doubt over the improving dynamic when he states that 'Truth begins to dawn in the second period'.[19] It might be observed that such narratives impose an artificial teleology, as capitalism dismisses alternatives to itself as merely its own infant germs. Equally, we will return below to the spatial implications of this discourse in Scotland, which was environmentally conducive to such a conception of history as national *Bildung*. However, it is sufficient for now to establish the role of improvement as the ur-narrative of the Enlightenment's progressive view of society, facilitating an extension of both profit and politeness into the basic tendencies of civilisation properly managed (with the collapse of Rome providing a dogged reminder of the non-inevitability and potentially cyclical nature of improvement).

Still, while critics such as Sarah Tarlow are correct to identify the commercial and the moral becoming 'knitted together' in the concept of improvement, this is far from the whole story.[20] Adam Ferguson's 1767 *Essay on the History of Civil Society* is a well-known expression of the hesitation within Enlightenment thought on improvement, seen as potentially endangering the ideal of a patriotic citizenry and producing in its stead passive, effeminate subjects (corrupted by 'luxury').[21] Such critiques existed alongside what David Spadafora calls 'the old idea of historical decline or decay', the jeremiad tradition influencing new cultural forms including eighteenth-century primitivism.[22] Ferguson also shared with Smith concerns about the effects of the division of labour in a complex market society, and while he was not finally convinced *against* improvement, in what

Berry calls a 'balance-sheet approach' to the subject, the dialectical tensions are clear.[23] In one sense it was the very sophistication of commercial modernity that was the problem, as signalled in David Hume's writing on the dangers of debt and paper money, openly abstract fictions, a subject later taken up by William Cobbett.[24] Certainly the traditional Enlightenment canon affords roots for a view that proves a consistent theme in the case studies in this book and indeed within Romanticism broadly conceived: that modernisation threatens both moral and cultural stability, unravelling ideas of tradition and generating social atomisation.

However, that conflict or rather set of conflicts does not describe the only potential misalignment of the moral and the material in improvement. We also need to account for mutually contradictory forms *of* improvement. This is a point that has been largely missed or passed over in the existing literature.[25] For example, moral improvement and spiritual growth could emerge in direct confrontation with commercial modernisation and the culture of politeness, as is the case in my study of Joanna Baillie in Chapter 3. Improvement at large was not a unified ideal: T. C. Smout illustrates how improving the landscape to make it more productive could be at odds with tasteful improvements and the pursuit of leisure (the 'use' and 'delight' dichotomy).[26] It is for such reasons that the improving field should always be conceived as a matrix of ideas about progress, many but not all of which cohere.

There are a great many nuances to the subject of improvement. For example, while its association with commercial modernisation instils a diachronic component within the discourse, the hierarchy of refinement could also be construed in synchronic, class-based terms. Equally, while improvement might be parodied as an excessive, maniacal doctrine of change, as in the *Examiner* piece above, it was more often conceived by its proponents as a force of 'moderation' between ultra-conservative and radical viewpoints, or between ruthless profiteering and economic stagnation – a kind of Whiggish middle way. The progressive rhetoric of improvement was also often even more non-linear than a dialectical model necessarily implies, as interested in renewal as in onward motion. This is illustrated, for example, by the improving framework discussed in Chapter 1, in which improvement is imbued with a 'simple' Presbyterian timbre, becoming partly a form of '*revolution*'. However, what is most critical here is the plural structure of improvement as both theory and practice, occasioning a complex set of negotiations with the real or imagined state of things – with the unimproved.

While dialectical complexity had always been true of improvement, it can be argued that the tenor of debate sharpened in the later eighteenth and early nineteenth centuries, as the culture evolved and as dissent from improving dogma became more pronounced. Fredrik Jonsson's analysis of attempts to improve the economic condition of the Highlands, for example, suggests a kind of ideological fatigue at the end of the eighteenth century; while other recent work has pinpointed the 1820s as a moment of crisis, at least in literature.[27] Economic downturns such as that of the mid-1820s, or indeed the impact of the poor harvests of 1783–84, were liable to nurture critical thought on improvement. And in political terms, the revolutionary 1790s turned Paineite radicalism into a spectre of the dangers of improvement to many conservatives in Britain, for whom attempts to challenge the established order were hubristic betrayals of tradition. Improvement was not dead at any point in this period – not even moribund – but it was hotly contested. In generic terms, the works of political economy, history and moral philosophy in which key aspects of the culture were articulated were themselves not uniform. Yet it is reasonable to suggest a particular efficacy for imaginative literature in allowing space for the form and implications of improvement to be freely contemplated.[28]

Still, if improvement was a decisive presence in Scottish culture between 1786 and 1831, then its model expression was a different kind of text. John Sinclair's first *Statistical Account of Scotland*, published in instalments across the 1790s, embodies much of the culture of improvement for the case studies that follow. Sinclair was not bashful about his project, writing in the advertisement to his second volume that 'there is no work, now extant, which throws such light upon the actual state of human society, or furnishes so many useful hints, of the most likely means of promoting its happiness and improvement'.[29] Having circulated 'Queries' to parish ministers across Scotland, he outlined in his first introduction an original intention, 'to have drawn up from their returns a general Statistical view of North Britain'. Yet the clergy's submissions displayed 'such merit and ability' that Sinclair was convinced to edit and

publish them at length.[30] What followed amply demonstrates both
the sweep and complexity of improvement. Ranging from 'Climate
and diseases' and 'Total real and valued rent' to the 'Character of
the people', Sinclair's list of 'Queries' indicates the manifold (perhaps
unlimited) realms susceptible of being managed towards improvement, just as the idiosyncratic parish reports also bear out what
I have called improvement's plurality.[31] Extensive detail throughout
on agricultural and manufacturing output confirms the centrality of
commercial modernisation to improvement, while the Revd Thomas
Henderson is fairly typical in finding concomitant 'proof of the civilization of the people', noting in his report for 'Dry'sdale' that even
though 'dramming sometimes does prevail, especially about the market times, there has not been a fight or quarrel worth mentioning for
these 11 years past'.[32] Yet improvement was always a matter of negotiation. In some of the reports alcohol consumption proves a cause
for real concern about the path of recent history. The Revd Thomas
Martin writes of Langholm parish that,

> Of all the inventions of modern luxury, none have contributed more
> to destroy that spirit of contentment and industry, that sobriety and
> decency of manners, which, not 20 years ago, so peculiarly charac-
> terized the peasantry of Scotland, than the unlimited introduction of
> distilleries.

Whisky, for some of the *Account* ministers, was a luxurious debasement sabotaging industry, a liquid evil of modernity at odds with
their vocation's duty to instil moral and spiritual improvement. In
that sense, what Martin calls the 'Pandora's box' of drunkenness
registers – as does the *Account* in general – the uneven prospect of
history as improvement, reflecting a complex dialectics that would
play out in the aesthetic innovations of Scottish Romanticism.[33]

Improvements

Critical interest in improvement across the eighteenth and nineteenth
centuries is heading towards a high-water mark in Scottish studies,
where a number of influential recent contributions have emphasised

aspects of the concept. Yet neither the history nor the study of improvement are a Scottish preserve. Richard Drayton, for example, invokes improvement as the legitimising principle of British imperialism on a global scale, with the scientific discipline of botany helping to generate an ideology of benevolent domination; while Toby Barnard finds improvement's 'larger benefits' being 'invoked to salve uneasy consciences' in seventeenth- and eighteenth-century Ireland.[34] Such work is indicative of a broad and growing recognition of improvement's hermeneutic potential. With an eye firmly on the Scottish milieu here, attention to the diversity of the literature will further clarify a term that was applied variously to field drainage, elocution lessons, a taste for landscape scenery and the macrohistory of Western civilisation.

Christopher Berry's 2013 *Idea of Commercial Society* captures the role of improvement as the narrative underpinning the Scottish Enlightenment's vision of a liberal modernity, in which market forces have thrown off the shackles of the feudal past. Berry describes an application of 'the utilitarian Baconian commitment to improve the human lot' through the exercise of scientific reason and a 'deliberate' realisation of 'a natural history track from concrete to abstract, from simple to complex, from rude to cultivated'.[35] The basic entanglement of improvement with commercial modernisation has long been a dominant feature of work on the subject. It is nicely complicated in Fredrik Jonsson's *Enlightenment's Frontier*, where the management of the forfeited Highland estates following the 1745 Jacobite rebellion helps to turn the region into 'a laboratory of the Scottish Enlightenment'.[36] Jonsson tracks a long struggle between broadly liberal and conservative views of regional development, between a faith in the efficacy of the free market and more interventionist economics. This is closely aligned with natural history:

> The defence of global commerce pioneered in the Enlightenment was inextricably tied to the improvement of the natural order [. . .] Was the market sufficient to order nature, or did the complexity of the natural order require the intervention of environmental expertise?[37]

In a sense, then, what Jonsson finds is an awakening to contextual limitations on improvement as a form of *laissez-faire* wealth creation, but it is also a debate on the substance of improvement itself, between, for instance, the 'conservative natural theology' of the naturalist John Walker and the radical liberalism of James Anderson.[38] His study usefully exemplifies the dialectical struggles occasioned by improvement – not only between competing blueprints of improvement, but also between humankind and the natural world.

An explicit concern with the land accounts for a rich seam of work on improvement, galvanised by T. M. Devine's account of agricultural revolution in the Scottish Lowlands, most notably in his 1994 study *The Transformation of Rural Scotland*.[39] Devine drew attention to a shift 'from peasant to capitalist agriculture' furthered by a 'new intellectual orthodoxy' that evolved in the eighteenth century and was disseminated in texts such as the *Statistical Account*.[40] While helping to build an evidential basis for the supposed Scottish 'Age of Improvement', this work also drew attention to improvement's mosaic of relatively covert processes across a Lowland experience of market orientation generally lacking the obvious 'clearance' component that made Highland history conspicuous. It is an area of study that has been absorbed into work on Scottish literature via Nigel Leask's *Robert Burns and Pastoral*, which rehearses the familiar unmasking of Burns as naive peasant bard to present him as a 'well educated but undercapitalized tenant farmer'. Leask's book explores how an 'aspirational ideology of improvement' rooted in but not limited to agriculture informed the poet's literary output.[41] Its basic position, addressed in Chapter 1 of this book, is notable for a sensitivity to improvement's twin theoretical and practical components, combining methods for refined manure recipes, crop rotations and indeed wage labour with a system of polite cultural ideals around (not against) which Burns could generate poetic meaning.

Elsewhere, T. C. Smout's long-term view of a contest over exactly how (and to what end) to 'improve' the land in the area he calls 'Northern Britain' has been mentioned above; while Eric Gidal's *Ossianic Unconformities* reflects another effort to directly tie together poetry, landscape and improvement.[42] Just as Leask seeks to reinscribe Burns's pastoralism within the reality of eighteenth-century agriculture, Gidal opposes a view of James Macpherson's Ossian poems as extra-historical romance, seeing them instead as 'complex records' of 'cultural progress, economic development, and political subjugation'. He links their achievement, and that of a motley variety of texts they inspired, to the trailblazing Enlightenment geology of James Hutton, which destabilised both time and place in a manner that resonated for a society undergoing rapid modernisation. Drawing together a manifold experience of modernisation and early industrialisation to find 'Scotland at the forefront of the carbon age', Gidal's view of improvement renders the literary text 'a memorial record of a vanishing moment within the landscape of industrial modernity and a product of the urbanized communicative networks facilitating the shaping of that new terrain'.[43] It is a useful way of framing what is a recurring dynamic in the present book, in which literature maintains a complex, ironic relationship to the spectacle of modernisation, as at once its product and memorial, just as it can function as both source and critique for narratives of improvement.

While *Dialectics of Improvement* locates the commercial as the foundational aspect of improvement, this must be balanced alongside the category of the moral, which John Dwyer contests was the dominant cultural imperative of late eighteenth-century Scotland.[44] Along these lines, work by Nicholas Phillipson did much to establish the pursuit of politeness as a defining characteristic of the Scottish Enlightenment and consequently of improvement. Phillipson writes: 'Throughout the eighteenth century Scottish intellectual life, and that of Edinburgh in particular, was to be meshed into a complex and constantly changing network of clubs and societies devoted to the improvement of manners, economic efficiency, learning and letters.'[45] The motif of improvement can highlight the theoretical nature of the distinction between commerce and morality. However, it is clear that politeness took on a particular significance in long eighteenth-century Scotland, whether or not we follow Phillipson's argument that the post-Union environment saw the emergence of a 'para-parliamentary' public sphere, in which 'the pursuit of literature had been established as an acceptable alternative to political participation'.[46] For her part, Janet Sorensen unpacks 'polite language' as an unstable identifier of political Britishness in Scotland and a bellwether for improvement's dialectic.[47] I want to briefly postpone addressing the national question that looms within improvement, however, to develop the moral theme a little further by introducing the tense relationships that exist around secular politeness.

Colin Kidd offers one means of approach in a recent essay analysing ecclesiastical satire in the eighteenth century, unearthing a 'pungent' attack by the Auld Licht minister John Witherspoon on his

Moderate-party opponents, whom Witherspoon portrayed in 1753 as 'embarrassed' by Calvinism. Kidd glosses his ridicule thus:

> Not only were the Moderates grasping hypocrites who cynically sub-scribed to the Church's Calvinist Creed, the Westminster Confession of Faith, while lacking inward belief in its core doctrines, but they also considered themselves – somewhat preposterously – to be men of the world, and as such preferred politeness to displays of piety.[48]

The overlap between the Moderates and what is commonly termed the Scottish Enlightenment is well established, as names such as Robertson, Ferguson and Hugh Blair bear witness.[49] Witherspoon's satire touches, however exaggeratedly, upon a threatening potential gulf between improved morality and true morality. This would continue to be a keynote in the discourse around improvement throughout the period under study, whether in explicitly spiritual or merely cultural terms. The latter perspective is summarised in a vision of improvement in a novel by Allan Cunningham:

> The trident of Neptune, which the ancient bard employed in obliterating the Grecian entrenchments before Troy, did not accomplish its task more surely than the hand of improvement: it has levelled old towers, smoothed down old manners, and pruned and trimmed into lip-courtesy and external politeness, the rough, blunt, generous spirit of old Scotland.[50]

Witherspoon's basic complaint remains alive almost seventy-five years later in this critique of 'lip-courtesy and external politeness', a hollow reward for the loss of 'old Scotland', the 'pruning' of improvement having been bought at the cost of moral integrity. Similarly, in the *Weekly Visitor* article mentioned above, nostalgia for the gratefully improved 'civilization' of 'forty or fifty years prior' informs a grievance that true 'politeness' has now 'degenerated from the warm effusion of kindness, to cold unmeaning formality', with improvement finitely desirable as well as malleable and relativistic in form.[51]

Still, keeping religion in view, the notion that improvement was a secular or secularising moral construct requires qualification. Thomas Ahnert offers a fuller sense of the religiously devout component of moral improvement that would continue to be a feature of the literary works analysed here, beyond a vague belief in the righteousness of

civilisation. Ahnert's revisionist approach to Enlightenment moral philosophy mitigates the influence of secular rationalism and natural religion, to suggest instead (with the notable exception of Hume) a more
firmly religious intellectual economy. He confirms a tendency towards
greater emphasis on salvation by works rather than faith alone across
the eighteenth century, but frames this as a question of doctrine. Ahnert
detects a process of 'culture', 'an incremental improvement of human
nature by which individuals were turned into properly virtuous agents'.
Building on their classical learning, the Moderates invoked this idea to
oppose the 'religious enthusiasm' they found in 'evangelical, revivalist
circles', with its emphasis on sudden, dramatic 'regeneration and justification'.[52] This enlightened moral 'culture' or cultivation might sound
a lot like Deism. To the contrary, Ahnert argues that 'members of the
Scottish clerical Enlightenment believed that even secular morality
was, in an important sense, incomplete without some form of divinely
revealed faith'.[53] In the dialectics of improvement, the polite and the
spiritual were often opposed, but this should not occlude the degree
to which moral improvement could be a profoundly religious concern,
in this case a form of moderation between 'orthodox doctrinal rigour
and revivalist enthusiasm'.[54] It is worth underscoring the Reformation
itself as a landmark for the historiography of this negotiable ideal;
certainly a basic Christian duty of self-improvement participated in the
extensive culture of improvement, in and beyond literary forms such
as sermons, tracts and confession narratives; while the missionary
work of the Society for Promoting Christian Knowledge in the Scottish
Highlands and Islands, for example, provided an institutional thrust
of improvement that combined spiritual and material goals. This is
not then to dismiss, but rather to counterbalance, the gist of Witherspoon's critique that improvement was a process of polite sacrilege.

Scholarship on improvement has an effect of disciplinary brico-
lage. Michael Morris, for example, explores tensions around the
scope and urgency of improvement in debates over the abolition of
slavery in the West Indies.[55] Matthew Wickman turns to geometry to
argue that improvement – a construct after all deeply concerned with
time – could be embedded in shape and thus materialise in narrative
space.[56] Bob Harris and Charles McKean present a material history
of urban improvements in Scottish burghs between 1740 and 1820,
'sites for the creation of a new, orderly, progressive and efficient urban
order and civil society', where a whole range of activities – from

paving stones to hospitals to policing – signalled 'distinctive attitudes towards the betterment of society' that 'clustered around' improvement.[57] We have hardly even touched the subcategory of political improvement, writ large in Thomas Paine's yoking of democratic revolution to stadial history: 'Time, and change of circumstances and opinions, have the same progressive effect in rendering modes of Government obsolete, as they have upon customs and manners', famously mediated in Scotland by the activities of Thomas Muir and the Scottish Society of the Friends of the People.[58] Yet improvement could be many things to many people, present even in the Burkean conservatism that had appalled Paine in its vision of the 'perpetual decay, fall, renovation, and progression' enacted through tradition's 'stupendous wisdom'.[59]

Improvement was also of significant application to educational discourses, in which the correct types of literary consumption were 'improving'. In the Scottish context, a tradition of moralistic educational writing spearheaded by James Fordyce (whose *Sermons to Young Women* was published in 1766) formed a characteristic branch of the field. This didactic tendency would be reconstituted in the early nineteenth-century novel in works such as Elizabeth Hamilton's *The Cottagers of Glenburnie* (1808), where the improving field is modified by Mary Wollstonecraft's insistence that women also have 'an understanding to improve'.[60] Equally, the categories of scientific and technological improvement, however interrelated with commerce, deserve to be disentangled from an umbrella definition of improvement and instead considered as distinct, potent expressions of the concept. Finally, while the present book is concerned with aesthetic engagements with improvement, it also incorporates the aesthetic dimension *of* improvement, manifest for example in landscape gardening on aristocratic estates in the period, and in the cult of the picturesque. Again, to 'improve' could mean to render more tasteful, in line with improvement's role as a taxonomy of politeness, though the picturesque in particular often exploited the dialogic tendency of the culture to update the rough and the unimproved.[61] Collectively, all this illustrates the way improvement could be – like any other belief system – at once archetypal and plastic, its inner logic of gradual, dialectical progress capable of remarkable adaptation.

National Improvement

'There is a spirit in Scotland, at the present moment, that presages a brighter prospect, and which may repay to the sister kingdom [. . .] the generous fire which was kindled by her laws and examples.'[62] Such was the assessment offered by William Thomson in his *Tour in England and Scotland in 1785*, the Union of 1707 having propagated a 'spirit' of improving emulation in Scotland. This commonplace judgement is indicative of the national complication to improvement in long eighteenth-century Scotland, where this vision of progress was thoroughly imbued with patriotic meaning. In Robertson's 1759 *History of Scotland*, for example, stadial history secured an Anglocentric version of improvement, in which England exerted a civilising force on her backward neighbour. This is implicit in Robertson's statement that, 'In the third period, the History of Scotland, chiefly by means of records preserved in England, becomes more authentic', the term 'authentic' slipping from a designation of factual accuracy to suggest a more general validation by mature, modern England.[63] Murray Pittock has commented on the way that such logic entails an 'infantilization of the national past'; while Kidd describes the 'unusable' nature of aspects of Scottish history for Enlightenment literati who were invested in an identity of 'North Britishness' as a means to participate in English liberties.[64] The political outcome of that position is clear. If aspects of Scotland (historical and contemporary) are infantile, then their incorporation ('improvement') into British modernity is merely the extension of a general developmental process.

This basic dynamic explains the identification of improvement with Scotland in the guise of 'North Britain' that has long been a feature of work on the subject. Berry indeed suggests that 'a central preoccupation' with Britain – 'how its story was the growth of modern independence and liberty' – may have 'heightened the Scots' concern with improvement'.[65] Improvement as a spatial phenomenon was involved in an interaction of local, national and global contexts, and Scotland's experience drew particular stimulus from the Scottish/British cultural ligature. This is not simply because improvement was so often trumpeted as a North Briton's patriotic duty, but also because the association of the unimproved with aspects of historical Scottishness (for example, both the Gaelic and Scots languages) sharpened qualms about the desirability of progress, with nostalgia only one option in an argument against the direction of history. If maligned as 'local', Scottishness might be better equipped to express virtues of folk-cultural authenticity; if rejected as pastness, it could become a counterpoint to modernity. Such tensions are manifest with varying potency in the literature identified in this book, from the simple and the pastoral to the intransigently primitive. National identity remained one critical axis along which improvement could be engaged, and its hierarchies destabilised or overturned. Following Raymond Williams, we might fruitfully interpret this as an interplay between a 'dominant' Britishness and a 'residual' Scottishness. Still, Williams's third 'element' 'in the cultural process' – the 'emergent' – signals the limitations of such a view.[66] Robert Burns's iteration of Ayrshire Scottishness in terms of the pastoral, for example, was altogether too innovative to be characterised simply as 'residual'.

The dialectics of improvement were involved in a symbiotic, mutually complicating relationship with Scotland's national cultures. To be clear, Scottish patriotism need not have been at odds with North Britishness in the late eighteenth and early nineteenth centuries. Kidd observes that a 'normally dormant' form of 'traditional Scottish chauvinism' could be 'provoked by perceived exclusions of North Britons from the liberties of Englishmen'.[67] North Britishness was often a form of Scottish opportunism, rather than an abrogation of residual forms of identification. Equally, while an alignment of improvement with polite North Britishness continued to represent a dominant tendency in Scottish literature between 1786 and 1831, improvement could also have a more 'independent' Scottish character (though political independence was not a live issue during this period). To take an example I have discussed elsewhere, Burns's remodelling of Scottish folksong in a newly improved, polite tradition at least problematises the conclusion that improvement *was* inevitably North British;[68] and much the same could be said of the legacy of Allan Ramsay in the early part of the eighteenth century.[69] In their work on Scottish towns, Harris and McKean comment that improvement was both 'cosmopolitan *and* patriotic', the latter component reflective of 'a country searching for a new role and identity as part of the new Kingdom of Great Britain'. They find print active as both a 'symbol and prime agent of change' within a 'cumulative force of convergence' post-Union that would be challenged by 'a re-emphasis on Scottish national distinctiveness in the early nineteenth century'.[70] Certainly the literary was operative within a porous circulation of ideas that, if it helped to associate Britain with improvement, also destabilised the pattern and its implicit hierarchies.

Writing about the work of David Hume, Andrew Lincoln has observed an 'apparent indifference to constitutional arrangements' that enables Hume 'to present liberty as the product of social and economic progress rather than of political establishments'. This gesture makes commerce the appropriate object of 'loyalty and respect for rules', while the political realm merits only sceptical acquiescence.[71] The same insight might be applied to improvement, which potentially renders national politics merely as local colour to a process of modernisation driven by market forces acting on a global scale. Indeed, Harris and McKean caution that improving emulation may often reveal 'social' rather than 'national' forces.[72] Yet we should not underestimate the shaping influence of political context. Katie Trumpener identifies improvement's dialectic with a relationship between imperialism and nationalism, the former a progressive, improving formation, the latter a defensive reaction invested in safeguarding tradition.[73] Again that thesis requires substantial qualification to reflect the uneven, plural quality of improvement's logic in the period, but it does recognise one way in which it could operate, as a force of collective modernisation potentially at odds with expressions of locality, or at least active in reshaping the constellations of the local. The national question resurfaces in the case studies that follow: Chapter 4, in particular, finds in John Galt's fiction a full-scale retelling of national history. Deeply but imperfectly integrated within a hegemonic, improving Britishness, Scotland offers up a variety of productive complications of improvement's working in the period mapped by the present study.

Dialectics of Improvement

The plurality of improvement presents a challenge and an opportunity to this book, which aims to capture that plurality without becoming diffuse. With this in mind, and guided by my case studies, what follows holds to the central understanding of the term tied to commercial modernisation, while identifying points of tension, overlap and dissonance. This compound narrative structuring the development of

modernity informed new directions in Scottish writing on three different levels: content, form and context. Improvement provided subject
matter for and influenced the shape of these texts. It also suffused
the historical circumstances surrounding their production, not least
in the steady professionalisation of authorship, which is a feature
of commercial modernisation extending to the literary marketplace
itself. What follows is not a dedicated economic analysis of Romantic
literature, versions of which can be found elsewhere in recent work.[74]
Rather, it confronts a wide-ranging debate around improvement and
how it played out in literature. Again, my argument extends the sense
of the 'Romantic' as a counterpoint to hegemonic modernisation to
stress a whole cultural dialogue in which literature was immersed,
a literary tradition that contained and juxtaposed both (or rather,
many) sides of the story.[75]

This approach naturally suggests a dialectical view. The oppositions around improvement may sometimes have been more intractable than the dialectical form suggests. Nevertheless, since my title
recalls Horkheimer and Adorno's epochal *Dialectic of Enlightenment*
(1947), I share with them a recognition that improvement remains
in close proximity to – and in dialogue with – the cultural forms
it purports to supersede. Equally, given the emphasis in the present
book on the form and utility of literature, the dialectical perspective
allows my argument to build upon an element of the existing analysis of Scottish culture, in which the aesthetic is a key historical category.[76] The dialectical operation of improvement is active in Peter
Womack's 1989 *Improvement and Romance*, which posits 'romance'
as 'a kind of reservation in which the values which Improvement
provokes and suppresses can be *contained* – that is, preserved, but
also imprisoned'. In Womack's argument, that interchange structures
the history of the Highlands, the region having been conditioned to
become 'the privileged home of subjectivity', an aestheticised frontier to socio-economic modernity.[77] The process of improvement,
this suggests, generates a compensatory space of romance, in which
the unimproved becomes a useful, nostalgic spectacle. Cairns Craig
works along similar lines in *Out of History* (1996), in which he
argues that an Anglo-British hegemony consigned the Scottish past
to an 'arena of local narrative no longer teleologically connected
to its future'. Still, the Scotland that had been suppressed in this
way, Craig explains, was 'waiting to erupt back into the present and

disrupt the progressive narrative of the historical', in an expression of latent Gothic power.[78] If the unimproved becomes art, in other words, then it inherits the political and discursive volatility of the aesthetic – a tension that has been characteristic of modern criticism of Walter Scott from Georg Lukács onwards.[79]

More recent adaptations of this view can be found in Pittock's observation that in Enlightenment historiography, the Scottish past 'could be a childhood tale, a story, a romance, but not modernity nor reality', the aesthetic condition again providing an exterior or excess to improved, British modernity.[80] Penny Fielding's work argues that the forces of North British improvement in the period – signified by the act of geographical measurement – became entangled in a symbiotic relationship with the 'incommensurable'. As she has it,

> The investment in spatial modernity that produced the *Statistical Account*, or a stadial history that could be scientifically predicted through geography, does not exclude forms of Romantic or amorphous space. Indeed [. . .] it is the very impulse to know the world geographically that produces imaginary spaces that cannot be accounted for.[81]

Here the ligature of improvement demonstrates a dialectical or dialogic involvedness – just as Hegel himself stressed a unity of opposites – mapped on to Scottish culture in a contest over the possession of space.[82] The 'incommensurable' is a theoretical phenomenon not limited to the aesthetic but certainly well adapted to it. Elsewhere, Wickman discovers 'phantoms of experience' emerging in the Scottish Highlands as a logical outcome of modernity; and Gidal finds 'romance and modernity' to be 'mutually interrogating'.[83] In all, if there is a danger for this material to perpetuate an older critical attachment to a fatally divided Scottish tradition – David Craig, for example, wrote in 1961 of an 'alienation from things native' – dialectical tension has proved fertile theoretical ground, emphasising rich complexity over incompletion.[84]

A relationship between North British improvement and unimproved Scottish romance arises at various points in the subsequent case studies, which approach a basic question of how culture interacts with history. Still, in addition to what has been said above about the incomplete association of Britishness and improvement, there are a number of other complications and cautions here. If aspects

of Scottish culture sometimes inhabited the condition of romance –
whether, in Pittock's terms, as 'threat' or 'regret' – this should not
lead us to underestimate the ideal form of *all* national-cultural con-
structs.[85] Even an improved British modernity bound to rationalisa-
tion and Enlightenment was – like improvement itself – a narrative,
an enacted fiction.[86] The intricate category of romance also does not
account for the range of possible representations of the unimproved
in Scotland, not least the sociological delineation of the past offered
by John Galt. In fact, the improvement–romance pattern is actively
ridiculed by Galt's novelistic history, with its attention to the politics
of storytelling. It is worth noting that, unlike a significant portion of
work in this area, including books by Womack and Wickman, I do
not devote my attention purely to the Highlands, suggesting instead
that improvement's dialectic was as active in the Lowland contexts
of, for example, Burns, as it was in the instrumental dramas and dramatic theory produced by Joanna Baillie from her home in Hampstead Heath. National culture itself is also only a part of my interest,
which draws attention more generally to the literary possibilities of
improvement's complex vision of progress, eddying through texts and
genres as a principal source of meaning, generating a range of aesthetic possibilities.[87]

Nevertheless, in this book I develop a slightly different way of
theorising the national–cultural dynamic that underpins this work
on the improvement–romance binary. The dialectics of improvement
were involved in two distinct notions of culture in Scotland during
the long eighteenth century. The first, which was a matter of polite
cultivation, can be loosely associated with 'Enlightenment', and was
often expressed in a North British aspiration to engender the norms
of modernity. The second signified 'culture' in the anthropological,
Herderian sense, and produced a vocabulary of national aesthetics
that I find being deployed by Robert Burns before it would be fully
possessed by Walter Scott. Both possibilities remain in play as part
of a wider literary debate around improvement in these case studies
between 1786 and 1831, including in an overlay of competing models of time. In the literary sphere, improvement became bound up in
the elastic politics of the aesthetic, active and passive, immanent and
transcendent, shifting in and out of history – with the result that in
Scotland as elsewhere the literary was a critical and critically versa-
tile site for its contemplation.

Scottish Romanticism

The case studies that follow provide this book with some purchase on the subject of Scottish Romanticism. The notion that Scotland might have hosted a culture that could be usefully described in this way is still relatively novel, an outcrop of the 'four nations' tendency in the field that has been interrogating assumptions about Britain over the last few decades. A dedicated *Edinburgh Companion to Scottish Romanticism* appeared in 2011, surveying a broad range of texts including travel writing and periodicals alongside more traditional Romantic matter such as lyric poetry and the novel. In its introduction, Murray Pittock outlines a literature in 'dialogue with the arguments of the Scottish Enlightenment' – a breakthrough articulated in work such as the 2004 collection, *Scotland and the Borders of Romanticism*, the editors of which argued that, 'In Scotland, "Classical" and "Romantic" cultural forms occupy the same historical moment and institutional base.'[88] In the present book, improvement offers a conceptual thrust to the argument that Romanticism and Enlightenment are imbricated in the Scottish context and beyond. Indeed, a model of interdependence and friction perhaps inadequately describes the latitude of improving debate *within* Romantic literature. This, I hope, provides a further recentring of the subject as an engagement with local and global narratives of modernisation dominating what geologists now call the Anthropocene. There has been a tendency among some commentators to frame Scottish Romanticism as an ambivalent, elusive phenomenon – Wickman, for example, discusses 'a romanticism of the always already and the never quite yet'.[89] Yet, however self-conscious it was in 2004, the title *Scotland and the Borders of Romanticism* is no longer necessary.

In his 2008 *Scottish and Irish Romanticism*, Pittock tackles the issue of definition by identifying a strain of nationalistic writing stretching from Allan Ramsay to the early nineteenth century, writing that articulated a 'taxonomy of glory' to legitimise a distinctively Scottish voice.[90] I make no such political distinction here, reading instead a multiplicity of perspectives. Still, this does raise the question of what the qualifier 'Scottish' is doing – is Scottish Romanticism from, in, about, connected to Scotland, or a mix of all these? As is touched upon in the coda to this book, when in the late 1820s Thomas Carlyle came to summarise what we might recognise as a kind of Romantic tradition via Robert Burns, he held to an aesthetic form of patriotism (at once British and Scottish) as constitutive, in contradistinction to a cosmopolitan Enlightenment cast as cold and alien. There is certainly an argument that the 'Romantic' has always been inextricably tied to the emergence of nationalism, within antiquarian attempts to mobilise the past. Yet any such essentialism will render only a fraction of the cultural ecosystem. Improvement provides one way of working through this situation, drawing attention to literary moments that are part of a national milieu, but – like improvement – also plural in spatial and thematic terms.

My concern here is with four distinctive contexts, yet there is more to be gained from a consideration of Scottish Romanticism as a varied, modal set of literary works coordinated around the idea of improvement. Romanticism has traditionally been considered a responsive movement, working against popular-cultural trends such as the picturesque and the Gothic (however contingently), just as it has generated a language of political and historical protest. This is implicit in the title of Marilyn Butler's classic study, *Romantics, Rebels, and Reactionaries*. Improvement offers a way to constitute the imaginative reflection associated with Romanticism in a full economic, political and social ecosystem – including, but not limited to, questions of nation. My approach here also contributes to an older debate in Romantic studies – between a self-professedly apolitical Romanticism and a politicised, historically engaged model – stressing a variety of attitudes to improvement that includes one of aesthetic retreat.[91] Clearly, attending to the dialectics of improvement might rather suggest a post- or late Enlightenment frame. A recent essay collection has exploited that approach to much advantage, theorising the workings of the literary imagination in a range of 'Enlightenment' literatures.[92] Certainly institutional and intellectual cultures characteristic of a late Enlightenment were essential to the texts under analysis. Yet the Romantic provides a more effective rubric here not only in terms of genre (poetry, short fiction, drama and the novel) and innovative handlings of the aesthetic, but also in implying a more openly unresolved, dialectically complex attitude towards the Age of Improvement.

The tricky thing with Romanticism is that it is simultaneously a historical and an aesthetic formation. Pittock advises that new applications of the term to the Scottish context 'must encounter and incorporate the stress on the subjective and aesthetic dimensions'.[93] If improvement offers a useful way of doing just that, the question of periodisation remains. In Pittock's work as elsewhere, a plausible case has been made for a long eighteenth-century model, taking account of the Union of 1707 as an origin for cultural factors that would contribute greatly to the direction of Scottish literature. Alternatively, we might fix upon what Ian Duncan calls the 'momentous achievement' of *Blackwood's Magazine* in the early nineteenth century in fostering 'a counter-Enlightenment aesthetic ideology of cultural nationalism'.[94] This updates an earlier identification of *Blackwood's* with 'Romanticism as (at last) Counter-Enlightenment' in Scotland, a belated rupture that my case studies do not find ever to have been secure.[95] A perspective beholden to improvement could also look to the 1760s, when the economic transformation of the Scottish Lowlands entered a critical phase. And the prospect of an endpoint is, if anything, even more ambiguous, since if the eighteenth century has a claim to be an Age of Improvement, then so do the nineteenth and twentieth. In fact, there is little prospect of the hegemony of improvement fading any time soon.

What I offer here takes place within relatively traditional Romantic confines date-wise, the selection of texts making 1786 and 1831 contingent bookends. While this is a period when improvement was generating new and compelling literary responses, many of my core themes are much more broadly applicable, given the porous nature of any account of modernity and its arrival. In generic terms, the book acknowledges the debt of its primary sources to a conception of 'letters' that had been only imperfectly resolved into Victorian distinctions between, for example, the novel and 'non-fiction'. A longer study would look to take account of other kinds of writing, to probe further at the boundaries of the imaginative. Equally, there are many prominent writings in the debate around Scottish Romanticism that are capable of sustaining this book's approach which do not appear here – conspicuous among them James Macpherson's Ossian prose-poetry in the 1760s – in a field that is far from exhausted.[96] The chapters that follow combine thematic and authorial case studies in order to build a picture of how the literary was in conversation with improvement in Scotland. Joanna Baillie remains on the fringes of this canon in existing work, relatively speaking, and if this book encourages more attention to her writing then it will have served a useful purpose.[97]

＊ ＊ ＊

Dialectics of improvement were active in precipitating some of the key aesthetic innovations in Scottish Romanticism across the turn of the nineteenth century. Featuring an extended reading of what would become his most celebrated work in the nineteenth century, 'The Cotter's Saturday Night', Chapter 1 reconsiders Robert Burns's proximity to improvement. It finds new parallels between Burns's handling of the religious and socio-economic dimensions of improvement, the poet mapping a model of spiritual renewal rooted in New Licht Presbyterianism on to the crisis of *laissez-faire* modernisation. That vision of improvement is signalled in the work by a complex overlaying of linear and cyclical models of time, a dialectical vision of history in which – finally – poetry ascends to a powerful role as a medium of secular belonging. 'The Cotter' thus instantiates a complex cultural politics, rather than being a conservative outlier in Burns's oeuvre, as has often been supposed. It is contextualised here within the poet's wider negotiation of improvement in his 1786 Kilmarnock volume, where a valorisation of 'simplicity' leverages both *völkisch* and Christian moral authority. This carefully managed 'simple' aesthetics is applicable at once to poet, region and nation, a remedial component to the process of history as improvement. In this way, the poet emerges as a transitional figure between the improving civic activity of the Scottish Enlightenment ('cultivating') and an aesthetic vocabulary of nationhood driven by the consumption of canonical literature ('culture'), which would be developed later by Walter Scott.

The question of time is taken up again in Chapter 2, which reads James Hogg and Walter Scott within a new, revisionist history of short fiction that is particularly interested in the genre of the 'tale'. Focusing on the half-decade between 1827 and 1831, this chapter highlights a little-noticed selection of Hogg's mature contributions to *Blackwood's Magazine* alongside Scott's *Chronicles of the Canongate* (first series). These years were marked by literary experimentation, when a confident improving persuasion in Scottish culture – then embodied in its most clearly 'post-Enlightenment' form by the Whig *Edinburgh Review* – was threatening to unravel. The formal logic of these short fictions, defined by a curiously focused spontaneity, exacerbates a pluralistic handling of the collision between improvement and tradition. Different models of time (progress, renewal, disruption) and belief (suspension, scepticism, credulity) serve to interrogate improvement in a wide range of contexts around commercial modernisation – as Hogg puts it, 'religion, law, politics, agriculture, and sheep farming'.[98] The chapter unpacks two specific literary innovations in this context. The first looks to acts of transmission in the literary marketplace which by turns sustain, contain and defer the dialectics of improvement. The second sees the emergence of a fully fledged aesthetic vocabulary of culture in Scott's writings that consummates the cultural trajectory heralded by Burns. Both innovations are significantly inflected by the emergent genre of short fiction, the rhetorical instability of which I end by considering as a question of time.

The utility of the aesthetic again comes to the fore in Chapter 3, which offers a new reading of Joanna Baillie's path-breaking drama and dramatic theory, suggesting that it is working through the dialectical logic of improvement. Improvement's plural form is well represented here, in Baillie's attempt to counter what she finds to be pernicious aspects of commercial modernisation and politeness with an alternative vision of moral improvement. She presents the drama as uniquely placed to engender moral growth because of its capacity to invoke 'sympathetick curiosity' in reader or audience. This volatile force is explored in *Count Basil* (1798), read as a model example of historical dialectic; in *The Family Legend* (1810), one of the period's important approaches to the 'primitive' past; and in *The Alienated Manor* (finally published in 1836), a satire of improvement's pitfalls. With roots in the Enlightenment science of man, Baillie's writings sustain a powerful sense of the individual's contribution to networks of social power and the involvement of this contribution in grand narratives of improvement. I situate her commitment to didacticism within the counter-revolutionary atmosphere of the 1790s. Yet, while Baillie seeks to repurpose the enlarged patent theatres into instruments of moral improvement, the pessimism of her social diagnosis threatens to infect her didactic project. The author's residence in Hampstead and engagement with the London stage additionally allows my discussion to introduce a diasporic element, putting pressure on the category of Scottish literature.

Chapter 4 unearths a sweeping account of the Age of Improvement in John Galt's brand of non-fictional fiction ('theoretical history'). It finds Galt exploring the capacity of a modernising society to cope with localised, historically rooted and distinctive cultural forms, in texts that offer a chaotic picture of improvement's collateral effects. His treatment of the piecemeal and portmanteau qualities of improvement draws, I suggest, on the *Statistical Account* in both formal and thematic terms. The economic bounty of improvement comes decisively to the fore here via an emphasis on the experience of the west of Scotland in *Annals of the Parish* (1821) and *The Entail* (1823). Within these fictions, local and national cultures can function as cohesive agents that remedy the destabilising effects of rapid change, yet they can also be perverted into a dark influence working to misdirect the effect of global market forces. The legal fiction of the entail itself in Galt's 1823 masterpiece embodies much of this ambivalence, as an attempt to grip on to continuity that ends up corrupting 'the natural way'.[99] Galt presents history as a contest over the volatile substance of 'story', which his novels rhetorically disavow. His analysis of the law of unintended consequences is permeated by a dry sense of humour. Yet by *The Entail*, Scottish history has become a catalogue of tragic failures (including Scott's historical fiction), as the changes wrought by improvement fracture the nation into incompatible alternatives.

In the coda I turn to a trilogy of essays by Thomas Carlyle written in the final years of the 1820s. 'Signs of the Times' (1829), notably, was published in the last issue of the *Edinburgh Review* edited by Francis Jeffrey, and provides a subversive counterpoint to and unravelling of the journal's Whig ideology. Taking up a critique of the Scottish Enlightenment that had been made by John Gibson Lockhart in *Peter's Letters to his Kinsfolk* and in *Blackwood's*, Carlyle attempts to recover a sense of ideal truth from what he viewed as a culture of dry rationalism.[100] Improvement, in this account, had suffocated Scotland. Carlyle's analysis of what he calls the 'mechanical' and the 'dynamical' in opposition to one another (rather than dialectical tension) effectively performs an elision of Enlightenment and Romanticism. This provides a counterpoint for the book's very different reading of literary texts that are adapting cultures of improvement within a set of changing historical circumstances.

It is not my intention to prescribe only one way of understanding a heterogeneous body of literature or a whole historical epoch. Yet it is clear that there was a keen interest in improvement in late eighteenth- and early nineteenth-century Scotland. Writing 'On different Species of National Improvement' for the *Scots Magazine* in 1808, one commentator conjectured that over the previous few decades 'perhaps the greatest change which has ever, in so short a time, taken place in any part of the earth, has been produced in general over Scotland'.[101] The dialectical operation of improvement offers a useful approach to the literary output of this period, when Scottish culture was contesting its own production of the values and practices we call modernity. It is difficult to agree with an 1824 article in *Blackwood's* which laments that, 'Few subjects have received less careful and minute examination, and, consequently are less thoroughly understood and appreciated, than the vast and rapid progress of this nation in everything connected with the improvement of its inhabitants'.[102] In fact, this was a predominant theme of a varied literary tradition stretching back far into the previous century. Still, while improvement represents a critical stratum of meaning in Scottish literature between 1786 and 1831, it remains interesting in large part because it was controversial. 'I am still fixed in the opinion, that man is perfectible', wrote a correspondent, signed 'Urbanus', to the *Edinburgh Magazine* in 1801, seeking to rebut the philosophy of a 'necessary retrograde tendency towards vice and decay'.[103] As Urbanus's protest makes clear, nothing less was at stake in the debates around improvement than the history, character and future of society. It was a conversation that underpinned the enduring literary achievements of Scottish Romanticism.

Notes

1. A. S., 'On Improvements in Scotland', *Edinburgh Magazine*, pp. 426–30.
2. See 'In our endeavours towards the reformation of our manners [. . .]', p. 75. It is headed by an editorial note that explains, 'We take the following Essay, almost at random, from a small collection which has come into our hands' (p. 74).
3. The original article in no. XVII of the *Political Herald, and Review* is a letter to the editor signed 'A. S.' dated to Greenwich on 1 November 1786. Sibbald's *Edinburgh Magazine* reprinting has also omitted the opening paragraph, which makes clear that the piece results from a

tour 'in the northern parts of this united kingdom' (p. 346), an editorial decision helping to reframe the piece as objective and/or domestic reportage. In its following number, the *Political Herald* carried a riposte to 'A. S.', further evidence of the controversy of improvement. This article takes the former's Whiggish optimism to account, complaining that the improvements in Scotland are driven by exploitative 'English merchants and manufacturers, not with any intention to improve the country, but to augment their capital', asserting bleakly: 'that there is any thing of freedom except the *idea* is positively denied' (see 'To the Editor of the Political Herald; Reply to A. S. on Improvements in Scotland', p. 417).

4. McGill, *American Literature and the Culture of Reprinting*, p. 107.
5. 'Improvements', p. 578.
6. A. S., 'On Improvements in Scotland', p. 426. The phrase is owed to Asa Briggs's 1959 *The Age of Improvement, 1783–1867*.
7. Sibbald, '*Poems, chiefly in the Scottish Dialect*', p. 284; and Mackenzie, 'Unsigned Essay in *The Lounger*, 9 December 1786'.
8. See Devine, *Transformation of Rural Scotland*; and Devine, *Scotland's Empire*, pp. 69–93.
9. Introduction to Phillipson and Mitchison (eds), *Scotland in the Age of Improvement*, pp. 1–4 (p. 1).
10. Carlyle, 'Signs of the Times', p. 459.
11. Makdisi, *Romantic Imperialism*, pp. 6–7.
12. Galt, *Autobiography*, vol. 2, p. 227.
13. Slack, *The Invention of Improvement*, pp. 1, 4, 5.
14. See Smith, *Lectures on Jurisprudence*, pp. 14–16.
15. Williams, *Keywords*, pp. 160–1.
16. Womack, *Improvement and Romance*, p. 3.
17. Smith, *Theory of Moral Sentiments*, pp. 11–12.
18. Berry, *Idea of Commercial Society*, pp. 66, 17.
19. Robertson, *History of Scotland*, p. 5. The year of Robertson's *History* provides ample evidence of the centrality of improvement to Enlightenment thought in Scotland and further afield, 1759 seeing such totemic works as Smith's *Theory of Moral Sentiments*, Voltaire's *Candide* and Samuel Johnson's *Rasselas*, not to mention the draining of Edinburgh's Nor' Loch in the service of improving goals. See Regan (ed.), *Reading 1759*.
20. Tarlow, *Archaeology of Improvement*, p. 12.
21. See Ferguson, *History of Civil Society*, in particular pp. 231–47.
22. Spadafora, *The Idea of Progress*, p. 14. Published in 1990, Spadafora's work on a general 'idea of progress' (p. 7) of which there were 'a multitude of possible expressions' (p. 321) in the eighteenth century does

not give improvement sufficient weight. That said, he does register a 'spirit of improvement' specifically as 'an expectation of continued positive innovation, a belief in the value of hard work, and in progress' (p. 408).

23. See Smith, *Wealth of Nations*, vol. 2, pp. 781–8; and Berry, *Idea of Commercial Society*, p. 165.
24. See, for example, Hume, 'Of Public Credit'; and Cobbett, 'Gold!'
25. Williams is something of an exception: though short of the pluralistic vision of improvement in this book, he develops a keen sense of the 'complications' of improvement, in a 'long process of choice between economic advantage and other ideas of value' that he makes a core theme of eighteenth-century literature and indeed Romanticism (*The Country and the City*, pp. 59, 61, 115–17).
26. See Smout, *Nature Contested*.
27. Jonsson, *Enlightenment's Frontier*, pp. 167–8; Fielding, 'Earth and Stone'; and Dick, 'Scott and the Financial Crash of 1825'.
28. See also John Regan on the way that poetry specifically had become designated as a key record of historical progress earlier in the eighteenth century (in *Poetry and the Idea of Progress*).
29. Sinclair, 'Advertisement', in Sinclair, Withrington and Grant (eds), *Statistical Account of Scotland, I: General*, pp. 7–10 (p. 7).
30. Sinclair, 'Introduction', in *Statistical Account of Scotland, I: General*, pp. 1–3 (p. 1).
31. Sinclair, 'Analysis of the Statistical Account of a Parochial District', in *Statistical Account of Scotland, I: General*, pp. 4–6.
32. Thomas Henderson, 'Parish of Dry'sdale', in Sinclair and Cowan (eds), *Statistical Account of Scotland, IV: Dumfriesshire*, pp. 98–113 (p. 112).
33. Thomas Martin, 'Parish of Langholm', in *Statistical Account of Scotland, IV: Dumfriesshire*, pp. 350–84 (pp. 365–6).
34. See Drayton, *Nature's Government*; and Barnard, *Improving Ireland?*, p. 40.
35. Berry, *Idea of Commercial Society*, pp. 23, 1, 42.
36. Jonsson, *Enlightenment's Frontier*, p. 12.
37. Ibid. pp. 124–5.
38. Ibid. p. 93.
39. See also Devine, *Clearance and Improvement*, which collates essays on the subject.
40. Devine, *Transformation of Rural Scotland*, pp. vi, 65.
41. Leask, *Robert Burns and Pastoral*, pp. 4, 86.
42. Smout, *Nature Contested*, p. 7.
43. Gidal, *Ossianic Unconformities*, pp. 21, 6, 11, 14.

44. See Dwyer, *Virtuous Discourse*, in particular pp. 1–7.
45. Phillipson, 'The Scottish Enlightenment', p. 27.
46. Ibid. p. 32. Phillipson's argument has been adapted more recently by Alex Benchimol in 'Periodicals and Public Culture', p. 87.
47. Sorensen, *Grammar of Empire*, p. 141.
48. Kidd, 'Enlightenment and Ecclesiastical Satire', p. 107.
49. See Berry, *Idea of Commercial Society*, p. 10, on the Moderates' approach to the key issue of patronage as an expression of improvement.
50. Cunningham, *Paul Jones*, vol. 1, p. 6.
51. 'In our endeavours towards the reformation of our manners [. . .]', p. 75.
52. Ahnert, *Moral Culture*, pp. 10–11.
53. Ibid. p. 13.
54. Ibid. p. 12.
55. See Morris, *Scotland and the Caribbean*, for example pp. 141–2.
56. See Wickman, *Literature After Euclid*, in particular pp. 59–62.
57. Harris and McKean, *The Scottish Town*, p. 492.
58. Paine, *Rights of Man*, p. 196. See Carruthers and Martin (eds), *Thomas Muir of Huntershill*.
59. Burke, *Reflections*, p. 30.
60. Wollstonecraft, *Vindication of the Rights of Woman*, p. 139. Fordyce specifically came in for criticism in the *Vindication*. Both Fordyce's work and Wollstonecraft's attack are explicated by Dwyer in *Virtuous Discourse*, pp. 117–40.
61. See Andrews, *The Search for the Picturesque*; and Bermingham, *Landscape and Ideology*, for useful overviews.
62. Newte [Thomson], *Tour in England and Scotland in 1785*, p. 365. Thomson, a Perthshire minister, published his tour in the character of Captain Thomas Newte.
63. Robertson, *History of Scotland*, p. 5.
64. Pittock, *Scottish and Irish*, p. 65; Kidd, *Subverting*, p. 129.
65. Berry, *Idea of Commercial Society*, p. 201.
66. See Williams, *Marxism and Literature*, pp. 121–7.
67. See Kidd, 'North Britishness', p. 361.
68. See McKeever, 'Simplicity, Rightly Understood'.
69. On improving activity and assertive national distinctiveness in Ramsay, see Jung, 'A Scotch Poetical Library', p. 187; and Pittock, *Scottish and Irish*, p. 48.
70. Harris and McKean, *The Scottish Town*, pp. 5, 9.
71. Lincoln, *Scott and Modernity*, p. 6.
72. Harris and McKean, *The Scottish Town*, p. 9.
73. Trumpener, *Bardic Nationalism*, p. 72.

74. See Dick, *Romanticism and the Gold Standard*; Haywood (ed.), *Romanticism, Forgery and the Credit Crunch*; Çelikkol, *Romances of Free Trade*; and Rowlinson, *Real Money and Romanticism*.

75. Compare, for example, Winter, *Secure from Rash Assault*.

76. The dialectical approach has also often been found pertinent to critical writing on Romanticism: Dan Miller, for example, details a long history of such work on William Blake, including the poet's philosophical proximity to Hegel. See 'Contrary Revelation', p. 503.

77. Womack, *Improvement and Romance*, pp. 3, 169.

78. Craig, *Out of History*, pp. 39, 71.

79. Lukács, *The Historical Novel*.

80. Pittock, *Scottish and Irish*, p. 65.

81. Fielding, *Scotland and the Fictions of Geography*, p. 184.

82. That unity is, arguably, the main objective of Hegel's *Science of Logic*.

83. Wickman, *Ruins of Experience*, p. 5; and Gidal, *Ossianic Unconformities*, p. 15.

84. Craig, *Scottish Literature and the Scottish People*, p. 14.

85. Pittock, *Scottish and Irish*, p. 215. See also Gerard Carruthers and Alan Rawes on the 'British use and abuse of the Celtic' in their introduction to *English Romanticism and the Celtic World*, pp. 1–19 (p. 1).

86. On the fraught relations between the categories of 'romance' and 'history', see Duncan, *Modern Romance*.

87. The introduction to Benchimol and McKeever (eds), *Cultures of Improvement*, pp. 1–16, places a greater emphasis on national identity than this book does.

88. See Pittock, 'Introduction: What is Scottish Romanticism?', in Pittock (ed.), *The Edinburgh Companion to Scottish Romanticism*, pp. 1–9 (p. 8); and the introduction to Davis, Duncan and Sorensen (eds), *Scotland and the Borders of Romanticism*, pp. 1–19 (p. 3).

89. Wickman, *Literature After Euclid*, p. 122.

90. Pittock, *Scottish and Irish*, p. 27.

91. See McGann, *The Romantic Ideology*; and Chandler, *England in 1819*.

92. See McLean, Young and Simpson (eds), *The Scottish Enlightenment and Literary Culture*.

93. Pittock, *Scottish and Irish*, p. 3.

94. Duncan, *Scott's Shadow*, p. 27.

95. Davis, Duncan and Sorensen, introduction to *Scotland and the Borders of Romanticism*, p. 13.

96. See here Moore, *Enlightenment and Romance in the Poems of Ossian*.

97. Baillie was the subject of a 'Google Doodle' for 11 September 2018.

98. Hogg, 'Robin Roole', in *Contributions to Blackwood's*, ed. Richardson, vol. 2, pp. 216–29 (p. 218).

99. Galt, *The Entail*, p. 57.
100. See, for example, the treatment of 'the Edinburgh Reviewers' in *Peter's Letters to his Kinsfolk*, vol. 2, pp. 128–9.
101. 'Severus', 'On different Species of National Improvement, particularly in Scotland', p. 598.
102. Stevenson, 'On the Reciprocal Influence of the Periodical Publications', p. 518.
103. 'Urbanus', 'On the Progressional Improvement of Mankind', pp. 439, 440.

Chapter 1

Robert Burns and 'Circling Time'

The first volume of the new Oxford University Press edition of the works of Burns opens with a piece of writing not by Robert but by his father, William. Nigel Leask begins his collection of the *Commonplace Books, Tour Journals, and Miscellaneous Prose* with the 'Manual of Religious Belief', written circa 1777 by William Burnes with the assistance of his sons' tutor, John Murdoch.[1] It is a decision that signals a growing recognition of the 'Manual' as a starting point for Robert's literary growth, clarifying the environments inhabited by a writer who has often been imperfectly contextualised. Long before Robert's first commonplace book would, in Leask's words, 'record [his] dawning creativity and poetic self-fashioning', the 'Manual' offers a glimpse of his immersion in the intellectual culture of late eighteenth-century Ayrshire, where the agricultural transformations helping to drive Scotland's Age of Improvement were in full effect.[2] Certainly Murdoch's presence within the Burnes/Burns family is indicative not only of the pious literacy traditionally associated with Scots Presbyterianism, but also of aspirational horizons, though it would be overzealous to locate William among 'a latent "bourgeois" element' identified by Devine in the population of tenant farmers.[3] Recounting his life from the vantage of 1787, Robert stressed a moment of upward social mobility – his father, previously a gardener, taking on a small farm – as a generational shift, the sons no longer consigned to be 'little underlings about a farm-house'. At the same time, this 'history of MYSELF' compassed grammar, folk superstition, literature, history and 'Polemical divinity', the last of which the poet highlighted as his pathway to notoriety, having 'puzzle[d] Calvinism' as a youth.[4]

Thomas Ahnert is among those to have underscored the theological orientation to the experience of Enlightenment in Scotland.[5] In recent research on the flourishing of booksellers, subscription and to a lesser extent circulating libraries, it is worth emphasising the preponderance of religious and devotional texts in the reading diet in parts of provincial Scotland.[6] That dynamic was certainly present in an Ayrshire society that Burns remembered as 'half-mad' with religious disputation.[7] The 'Manual of Religious Belief', then, a handbook of spiritual self-improvement for a member of Ayrshire's lower middling sort, is emblematic of this life-world. Structured as a dialogue between father and son, the document seems to embody its own influence on the poet. 'Dear Father', it opens, registering a slippage between earthly and heavenly patriarchs that would remain of relevance to Robert's poetry, just as his socially attuned poetics retained a religious dimension.[8] Indeed, when Burns's first edition was published a decade later, one of its central productions and the subject of this chapter – 'The Cotter's Saturday Night' – was a development of the theme, in a complex imagining of life at the knife-edge of improvement.

The current status of the 'Manual' in the field owes something to Liam McIlvanney's 2002 monograph, *Burns the Radical*, which sought to emphasise the poet's involvement in a complex ideological milieu, with Calvinism and civic humanism among traditions forming cords in an intellectual rope. More generally, Leask's editorial move reflects a trend to refocus the scholarly debate on Burns, and on Scottish Romanticism more broadly, towards the issue of religion, which has often been underemphasised. McIlvanney endorses the 'Manual' as the textual origin for Burns's essentially progressive instincts and an expression of the theologically liberal, 'New Licht' wing of Scottish Presbyterianism (as opposed to the more orthodox 'Auld Licht'). Drawing on work by Walter McGinty, he observes that the 'Manual' 'emphasises practical morality over doctrinal orthodoxy', watering down Calvinist predestination with an Arminian leaning towards free will in line with the preaching of Ayrshire New Licht men such as William Dalrymple.[9] Thomas Crawford, who published on the 'Manual' in the 1960s, noted the 'strong liberal tinge' of the document.[10] Leask too draws parallels between its heterodox theology and some aspects of Burns's religiosity. It is worth noting William's emphases in the 'Manual' on humans as God's 'rational offspring' and 'rational creatures', and Leask points to equally Arminian statements by the poet in a letter to Agnes McLehose. He even flags up the controversial lines in Burns's poem 'The Vision' – 'the *light* that led astray, | Was *light* from Heaven' – as having roots in the 'Manual', which discusses 'religion giving pleasure to animal life'.[11]

At the heart of this document, certainly, is an understanding, parental deity – 'failing or shortcoming' being integral to the human condition – alongside a significant emphasis on salvation by works in addition to faith, through what William calls 'our honest endeavours'.[12] Susan Manning has enumerated difficulties in addressing Robert's personal faith, finding the poet altogether more comfortable in the register of critique than confession.[13] Still, his suspicion of Calvinist orthodoxy is a well-worn subject and there are obvious parallels between his experience of the theologically driven Ayrshire Enlightenment (specifically the New Licht tendencies behind the 'Manual') and the vitriol of his Kirk satires.[14] It is certainly missing the point to suggest that Burns – whom Manning describes with only partial irony as 'a better Calvinist than the Kirk' – speaks from an irreligious perspective in those satirical poems, which McIlvanney describes as 'anticlerical' rather than 'anti-Calvinist'.[15] Developing this area, I want to suggest that to the degree that Burns's work, and 'The Cotter's Saturday Night' specifically, is an expression of New Licht Presbyterianism or its close associate, Moderatism, it brings out an important aspect of those positions, reaching back in order to project forwards: non-linear improvement, in other words. Of the Moderates, Colin Kidd notes an emphasis on an 'ongoing critical reassessment of one's religious heritage in the light of Scripture and reason', 'the invocation of Reformation principles' serving to bolster the unfolding 'Protestant Enlightenment'.[16] Faith in this view is a process of cyclical renewal, a characteristic it shares with another totem: culture.

This chapter develops a way of thinking about 'The Cotter's Saturday Night' and about Burns's cultural politics by tracing an aesthetic negotiation of Presbyterian tradition. The poet's attitude towards Ayrshire's Calvinist inheritance in the poem maps on to his larger concern with improvement, the dominant, quasi-secular discourse (or rather set of discourses) in eighteenth-century Scotland, fostered in no small way by the Moderate party in the Kirk. Despite Burns's enthusiasm for ideas of improvement in both cultural and agricultural terms, there are obvious notes of ambivalence in his poetry and other writings. These centre on a threat posed to local, residual cultures – conceived as wellsprings of morality – by the march of progress. In 'The Cotter's Saturday Night', this chapter argues, this historical tension enfolds the question of traditional piety, which receives a similarly qualified approval as other forms of rustic virtue. Widely considered Burns's masterpiece until it became unfashionable during the twentieth century, the poem can appear a conservative outlier within his oeuvre, a memorial of peasant dignity that delivered Victorian Britain its ideal Robert Burns.[17] Yet I contend that it is more effectively understood as subversively progressive, deploying Burns's rustic poetics to negotiate an afterlife for tradition in or alongside modernity, in a manner that anticipates aesthetic strategies commonly associated with Walter Scott a generation later. In religious terms, the work's zealous defence of an Old Testament ideal might suggest a very different perspective towards orthodoxy from the Kirk satires. Still, what Burns offers is largely in keeping with New Licht theology, mobilising what McIlvanney calls 'impeccable Reformed principles' to reconstruct 'a "pure" religion purged of priestly superstitions' as a model for spiritual growth.[18] This act of theological renewal is paralleled and finally subsumed by the poem's secular historical calculation, which looks to amend the present by a return to tradition, via the sophisticated pastoralism Burns calls 'simplicity'. To do so it uses two models of time, contrasting the circularity of tradition with the linearity of progress. As Burns reimagines his origins in the idealised space of the cotter's household, the question of social change in 1780s Scotland becomes very much a matter of faith.

Genesis: 'The Simple Bard'

To many early critics of Burns, including his first editor James Currie, 'The Cotter's Saturday Night' was his crowning achievement. This was not simply a literary judgement; rather, the poem became the foundational relic upon which a cult of personality could be based, the spotless ur-text for a model of Scottish culture in which literature was the echo of – if not (yet) outright substitute for – religious belief. By 1832 the Dumfries newspaper editor John McDiarmid's assessment that 'The Cotter' had 'elevated the tone of moral feeling' was a well-worn commonplace, the poem an appropriate gospel for 'him whose fame is as wide as the world itself': Burns.[19] Currie himself considered the poem sufficiently 'exquisite' to include verses sent to Burns by Thomas Telford (the famous civil engineer) as an appendix to the first volume of his 1800 edition. The 'object' of

Telford's tribute, which Currie unconvincingly finds to be 'of superior merit', is 'to recommend to [Burns] other subjects of a serious nature, similar to that of the *Cotter's Saturday Night*'.[20] The piece interprets the 'sacred views' of dignified poverty in 'The Cotter' as a gateway back to Telford's own childhood and 'happy village joys', to a simpler existence where the 'green hills touch the skies'. Burns's cottagers have thus become guarantors of a pious (Lowland) Scottishness, equally as applicable to Telford's Eskdale as to Alloway, in a timeless 'native music'.[21]

Perhaps even more tellingly, as early as 1789, three years after the poem's first publication, William Gilpin featured 'The Cotter' in the Scottish Highlands edition of his *Observations, Relative to Picturesque Beauty*. There the piece is both an 'illustration' of 'remarks on the present character of the Scotch highlander' and 'a contrast to the bloody scenes' of clan violence. 'The Cotter' is, as we will see, a type of historical fiction, but it is not at all apparent that Gilpin is working by the logic of stadial history to render the Lowland past the Highland present. Rather, eliding the distance between Ayrshire and the West Highlands, he finds in the work an expedient archetype of peasant virtue. 'Equal to any praise', the poem appeals to Gilpin less as a piece of documentary evidence than as moral succour to the savage aspects of Highland history, a prayer that asserts the 'virtuous' component of the Highland character above its 'proneness' 'to acts of revenge'.[22] In a footnote, Gilpin comments of the central episode that 'This pleasing picture of a family supper, I am told, is drawn from the life', the latter phrase pregnant with meaning.[23] For some of Burns's critics, the poem that Byron termed 'a descriptive Sketch' became indistinguishable from the empirical reality of the Scottish poor.[24] Yet in the context of Gilpin's work on picturesque aesthetics – with its unavoidable subtext of reconstructing 'nature' – '*drawn* from the life' tends to flag up the literary quality of the poem. It is noteworthy that, when reproducing the piece, Gilpin omits both the first stanza, where the address to Robert Aiken reveals Burns's adoption of 'simple Scottish lays' as a highly self-conscious act, as well as the final three, which move into a patriotic register and thus underscore the utilitarian, ideological quality of the performance.[25] In clipping 'The Cotter' at both ends so that it carries more effectively as a piece of naive rustic verse, Gilpin simplifies what is a consummate exercise in pastoral mediation, collaborating however deliberately in the theatre of Robert Burns, bard, by encouraging the poem to masquerade as ethnographic source material. During a perceptive discussion of the role of 'The Cotter' in reframing Scottish identity, with 'literature as a substitute religion', Andrew Nash describes how the work 'became seen as a reality that had been captured and put in a frame': 'an act of social history'.[26] Yet, as we will see, it was not social history so much as *poetry* that supplied both the essential medium and meaning of the poem's intervention.

Despite its limitations, Telford's verse epistle manages to echo some of the more pressing tensions in the original poem, in particular the coexistence of its innocent rural ideal with the imperial reality of late eighteenth-century Scotland. Telford writes of 'Thy country's sons, who far are spread', finding these inheritors of Burns's moral idyll negotiating its 'harmless, simple ways' in the context of 'latest days' which must 'aye improve'.[27] Such collisions speak to the heart of Burns's poetry and song, within the dialectical character of improvement during the later eighteenth century. Leask's *Burns and Pastoral* has detailed how improving agriculture informed Burns's aesthetic, and his poetry is a lightning rod more generally for the plural condition of improvement, with print culture among its core material expressions. The poet was immersed in the spread of popular Enlightenment and religious debates, his career triangulating the evolving urban landscapes of Kilmarnock, Edinburgh and Dumfries, just as it reflects a changing agrarian environment. Commercial modernisation and cultural politeness are both urgent forces through which Burns generates cultural capital. He works in general by straddling the polite and the rustic, a strategy that includes moving between the literary marketplace and an ideal of socio-economic independence signalled by the category of the bard. And 'The Cotter's Saturday Night', I want to suggest, represents the dialectical plurality of improvement in a specific way. The poem gestures towards a reconciliation of improvement's commercial and moral arterials, by envisioning a mixed modernity that enfolds traditional culture as a kind of moral lodestone. Equally, however, the poem does harbour a more pessimistic outlook, as an elegy for a traditional way of life that can only be resurrected in the imagination.

This complex performance emerges out of a central treatment of improvement and the unimproved in Burns's oeuvre. When introducing 'The Cotter' in his 1789 *Observations*, Gilpin noted that the poem was 'by Robert Burns, a bard as he calls himself, from the plough: but the images being caught from nature, are such as must give pleasure to every feeling heart'.[28] Clearly then Gilpin was familiar with the narrative underpinning Burns's poetry and paratexts, amplified by early commentators such as Henry Mackenzie in the motif of the 'Heav'n-taught ploughman'.[29] The poet's self-presentation was a form of autofiction in which the rhetorical instability of what Gilpin called 'images being caught from nature' secured the premise upon which the Burns phenomenon would be built. To properly understand how 'The Cotter' participated in this process, and the deliberate quality of its effect on Scottish culture, it is necessary to return briefly to Burns's first declarations of intent. In penning his own 'Anonymous' epigraph, the poet had asserted tight control of his persona in the 1786 Kilmarnock *Poems* – a piece of individual entrepreneurship lacking either a leading patron or a publisher[30] – purporting to speak not so much on behalf of but *as* the Ayrshire and Scottish landscape, as the elect instrument of 'Nature's pow'rs'. His claim on the character of 'The Simple Bard, unbroke by rules of Art', then, suggested not only that a more sophisticated poet would be 'broken-in' but actually 'broken', falling short of the triumphal motif of 'simplicity'.[31] The elusive category of the 'simple' would come to embody much of Burns's cultural energy. His later song collaboration with George Thomson, for example, occasions a debate over the appropriate pitching of simplicity between what both agreed were the distasteful poles of vulgarity and polite artifice.[32]

The Kilmarnock epigraph is very much in this vein: an exercise in calibrating authenticity. Burns lacked the knowledge of classical languages which remained a key status symbol in the period. Yet, couched in what Leask calls 'the fashionable idiom of sensibility', his claim of unsophistication was transparently performative.[33] It is difficult precisely to recreate attitudes to authenticity in the period, but Burns was indebted to a folk tradition in which authorial identity was a negotiable contingency, and habitually either over- or downplayed his hand in the production of songs specifically.[34] The figure of 'The Simple Bard' was a discursive combination of art and reality, or in the terms of the day, culture and nature. In an important contemporary discussion of authenticity in the context of the picturesque, Gilpin gives the examples of a bull attractively coloured by mud around its shoulders, or 'the cheek of a lady, when skilfully painted', to argue that our instincts revolt at the discovery of 'any thing artificial, which we supposed was natural'. Art 'may appear more beautiful' only 'while we are ignorant of' it, due to our instinctive approbation of 'nature *undisguised*': the unimproved.[35] We might find Gilpin a touch disingenuous here, especially since the picturesque gaze is itself always a form of imaginative cultivation. Still, though Burns was featured as one of Gilpin's picturesque objects with an air of compelling naivety, this caution about artifice is not properly applicable to the case of 'The Simple Bard'. That is because Burns does not purport to offer an image of 'nature *undisguised*' in his theatrical self-production, unless the theatre of personality is itself a natural phenomenon.

The Kilmarnock preface sustains much the same tone, recording its distance from the 'elegancies and idlenesses of upper life', from where a 'Poet' might 'look [. . .] down for a rural theme, with an eye to Theocrites or Virgil', in a passage that gives pastoral elitism spatial expression, suggesting the convention of travelling 'down' from the metropolis. I have written elsewhere about Burns's use of the tale form in the very short prose fictions that preceded 'Tam o' Shanter' and that category might be of application here.[36] As Chapter 2 in the present book explores, the tale reached its full potential as a conduit between traditional culture and literary modernity in the early nineteenth century in and around the pages of *Blackwood's Magazine*. Burns occupies a related cultural space in mediating a rustic ideal for his early subscribers, in the curious position of an actual tenant farmer adapting the conventions of the pastoral. Reframing the Kilmarnock preface under the aegis of the tale helps to tease out the element of narrativity, across four paragraphs that establish character ('an obscure, nameless Bard'), setting ('amid the toils and fatigues of a laborious life') and fatal flaw ('So dear is fame'). The piece heaps on the tension ('with fear and trembling') while delineating a struggle against considerable odds ('fair, candid, and impartial criticism'), with the conclusion of the story left unwritten, or rather deferred to the reader's judgement of the volume. Such storytelling energy, combined with the allusion – by disavowal – to classical example, are important components of the text, though registering the artifice at work should not mean dismissing Burns's self-identification with his 'rustic compeers': this is embroidery rather than untruth.[37] Thomas

Crawford seems close to the mark in describing the preface as a 'sober statement of Burns's artistic intent', calculated but not therefore 'insincere', in as much as it develops a literary performance.[38]

This material inhabits the dialectical anatomy of improvement in an interplay of the polite and the rustic, with social class implicated in the gradations of progress. Versions of the same exercise recur in the historical interventions of works such as 'The Cotter's Saturday Night', one of a series of key poems that develop the framework Burns establishes in his paratexts. The paradigmatic figure of 'the Bard' may be heroically 'unfitted for the world', as Burns would subsequently insist in 'On Fergusson', yet especially given his ironic 'relish of its Pleasures', this offers an elite perspective.[39] In 'The Author's Earnest Cry and Prayer' [K81], for example, the rustic persona facilitates a polemical attack on behalf of the nation of Scotland, its mask of knowing unsophistication securing a degree of political *carte blanche* to challenge Westminster over new taxes on Scottish distilling. There as elsewhere, 'simplicity' is an irresistible motif leveraging *völkisch* and spiritual forms of moral authority for an era of rapid improvement. The gesture legitimises a play of the local against the universal, Burns able to superimpose his 'Simple Bard' on to Ayrshire and Scotland at will, with a command of place that has been granted new visibility by the recent upsurge in spatial approaches to Scottish literature.[40] Corey Andrews usefully emphasises the term 'genius' in relation to Burns, which encompasses not simply prodigious talent but also the concept of the *genius loci* that is so relevant to the poet.[41] Equally, Penny Fielding comments that 'Burns is universal *because* he is local, each singular locality being alike in its very singularity', albeit that dynamic runs parallel to the fundamentally cognate quality of the local, with rustic simplicity a universally relatable identifier.[42] Certainly if the line, 'The *Cottage* leaves the *Palace* far behind' (l. 168), is the keynote of both 'The Cotter' and of *Poems, Chiefly*, Burns develops in the edifice of the cottage an interplay of the specific and the general, theory and example.

There is insufficient space here to delve into the linguistic politics of the associative web that unites Robert Burns–simplicity–Scotland, except to observe that in a poem such as the first 'Epistle to J. Lapraik', a physically robust Scots poetry that can 'touch the heart' invokes a sense of environmental determinism, given contemporary notions of the physical effects of 'Northern' language with its increased level of guttural and rasping consonance.[43] Such material had the potential to shade into imperial chauvinism, as in 'To a Haggis', where the 'warm-reeking' national dish conquers a list of continental delicacies: 'French *ragout*', '*olio*' and '*fricasse*'.[44] At the same time, it was a means of turning the weapons of anglicisation upon itself, owning the perception of Scotland's backwardness as a moral virtue. Yet a dominant feature of Burns's cultural politics, as 'The Cotter's Saturday Night' perfectly captures, is the occupation of middle grounds – again, as 'simplicity'. Robert Crawford picks up on the term 'Scotch bard', which Burns offers to share with Lapraik, as a nexus for the poet's capacity as a 'cultural broker', including between 'Scots folk-culture [. . .] and the officially dominant Anglicized culture'.[45] Like 'The Simple Bard', it inhabits the axes of improving discourse, including but not limited to the national question in a country fast becoming a global superpower, yet in which key aspects of the collective identity were bound up in the mixed blessing of unimprovement.

It is imperative to keep in view the fact that the Kilmarnock volume appeared between the American and French Revolutions and with the poor harvests of 1783–84 fresh in the memory.[46] Responding to this turbulent environment, the apparently reticent construct of 'The Simple Bard' is a source of moral succour, dialectically making sense of the changing world of the late eighteenth century. This capacity is different from what Pierre Bourdieu calls 'the economic world reversed', in which 'artistic production' becomes 'a "creation" devoid of any determination or any social function'; rather, the pastoral provides a notionally counter-hegemonic imaginary in which Burns finds a language to reflect on improvement.[47] Burns took advantage of an eighteenth-century appetite for (as Samuel Johnson had put it in 1759) the 'strength and invention' supposedly characteristic of 'early writers', to which he was the modern bardic equivalent.[48] Still, the 'simple' always remained in close proximity to the modern and the polite, and this was not simply a matter of cultural but also of economic capital.

'I was bred to the Plough, and am independent', Burns wrote in the dedication to the expanded 1787 edition of *Poems, Chiefly*, this condition ensuring both artistic and economic dignity.[49] When living in Dumfries in the 1790s, he would famously refuse payment for his songs, to the exasperation of Currie, who believed that the poet 'carried his disregard of money to a blameable excess'.[50] There are reasons to complicate this narrative, although the fact remains of his (furiously indignant) refusal to accept George Thomson's offers of remuneration.[51] And yet the breakout Kilmarnock volume delivered Burns a considerable financial return. Rick Sher has explored the economics of the poet's early publishing experiences, proclaiming Burns 'the eighteenth-century author whose literary career was most clearly and completely made by subscription publishing'. Sher estimates that Burns cleared around fifty pounds for the Kilmarnock *Poems* through 'distribution subscription', in which 'friends and well-wishers bought up large quantities for local sale by word of mouth', before Freemasonry networks helped him on to the impressive financial success of the 1787 Edinburgh edition (perhaps in the region of £700 profit).[52] When considering the poet's attitude to remuneration, the distance between a subscription edition and songwriting commissions, the latter of which might carry a whiff of hackwork, cannot be ignored. Regardless, Burns's stated discomfort with the commercial dimension of publishing – 'the Author has not the most distant *Mercenary* view', he wrote in the proposals for the Kilmarnock subscription – maintains a (fragile) distance from the culture of money that runs parallel to his careful negotiation of politeness, dual markers of modernisation during Scotland's Age of Improvement.[53]

In 'The Inventory', which was written shortly after 'The Cotter's Saturday Night' in early 1786, the economic environment is recast in a poetics part-celebratory, part-satirical. Here the tenant farmer Robert Burns is fully realised – the legacy of his father's upward mobility meaning that he now employs 'three mischievous boys' of his own.[54] Enumerating the contents of Mossgiel farm, the poem attempts to calculate what remains outside the reach of state taxation, priceless and sacred. It is an instance of the anti-capitalist (though the term is anachronistic) tinge that surfaces now and again in the poetry of this improving farmer and later exciseman, moments when the pastoral outright repudiates the georgic's faith in commercial productivity. There are no taxes on mistresses and children, the poem declares thankfully, though Burns has already 'paid enough' for the latter at least, this private tax perhaps moral as much as monetary.[55] Still, if the spectre of marriage confirms that even human relationships are a matter for the exchequer, the bard can at least choose to live in a frugal manner that is the budgetary and existential equivalent of poetic simplicity, a way of prospering by humble means. Finding a metaphor for sex in horse-riding, the poem abjures both activities – 'My travel a' on foot I'll shank it' – declaring for a pedestrian life outside the grip of both kirk and collector, in a mock-heroic vision of bachelor freedom.[56]

The sweep of 'The Inventory' through 'gudes an' gear' suggests a degree of nausea at the material accumulations of life, returning again to the independent bard who can attenuate a grubby world of commercial transactions, just as his aesthetic freedom allows him to manage the taxonomy of polite culture.[57] Indeed, poetry in the end proves indistinguishable from virtue here, as Burns substitutes literary 'effects' for the vulgar kind – although the implicit precondition for this rapture is, of course, the economic and educational opportunities available to an Ayrshire youth. Significantly, midway through the poem, as Burns records his three labouring boys, we find ourselves in another version of the family worship scene that dominates 'The Cotter's Saturday Night'. Here, Robert Burns has replaced his father in occupying the position of patriarch and is testing the boys on their knowledge of the Shorter Catechism ('An' ay on Sundays duly nightly, | I on the questions *targe* them tightly').[58] In tandem with the poet's rollicking masculinity, this moment signals the underpinning of moral virtue in a work about the material necessities of life and what they do not include. 'The Inventory' is largely a comedic poem and its marshalling of the transcendent in a commercial world resists the degree of polemical urgency found in 'The Cotter'. And yet in seeking out forms of salutary human excess and finding in Ayrshire's rural society the requisite moral currency to soften the calculations of modernity, both works perform a similar task. Just as in 'The Cotter', the values of a humble existence, including a private Christianity, are the means of remedying the trajectory of history, foot in front of foot: 'I've sturdy bearers, Gude be thankit.—'[59] That is, at least once they have been transposed into poetry.

With its evocation of native Ayrshire piety, 'The Cotter's Saturday Night' was likely to be a crowd pleaser at the heart of the Kilmarnock *Poems*. Analysing data on first editions of what he calls 'Scottish Enlightenment books', Sher describes Burns's first collection as exceptional in 'bearing an imprint from a Scottish town with fewer than 10,000 inhabitants', even if the Edinburgh edition really made the poet's name.[60] Still, 1780s Kilmarnock was typical of sizeable Lowland burghs in hosting an emergent print culture, dominated locally, as Harris and McKean have shown, by a strong brand of evangelical Presbyterianism.[61] Patrick Scott observes that Burns's printer John Wilson's previous work had been 'mainly dumpy duodecimos and small octavos of Auld Licht theology'.[62] 'One of the principal manufacturing towns in Ayrshire', as the Revd Mr James Mackinlay's return to the old *Statistical Account* explains, with carpet and shoemaking industries each worth in excess of £21,000 annually, Kilmarnock was among a coterie of Scottish burghs at the forefront of the period's economic boom, where Burns's poetic examination of improvement clearly met an existing appetite, and where the vision of traditional spirituality interlaced into a modernising British world in 'The Cotter' must have seemed apt.[63] Thomas Crawford comments on Burns's 'strange mixture of uncontrolled passion and shrewd practical common-sense' and this was equally as true of the Kilmarnock volume as it was of his subsequent foray into the 'frowning world' of polite Edinburgh.[64]

To return properly to 'The Cotter', then, among Burns's most important interventions into the environment of the late eighteenth-century Lowlands, we find a poem drawing on the cultural logic established above. The canonisation of the work has been better understood as an effect of nineteenth-century critical prejudice than it has as a result of its own active force. Deploying the symbolism of 'The Simple Bard', which inhabits medial spaces in the complex iterations of the culture of improvement, 'The Cotter' offers up a vision of tradition-within-progress in the figure of a line overlapping a circle, anticipating the way in which it would come to be understood, and indeed a much larger aesthetic effect achieved by Burns's oeuvre.

The Cotter Idyll and Social Change

'*The Cotter's Saturday Night* is tender and moral, it is solemn and devotional, and rises at length into a strain of grandeur and sublimity, which modern poetry has not surpassed', proclaimed James Currie in 1800, insisting at once upon the value and fundamental sincerity of the poem, which was written in Burns's productive period of 1785–86.[65] In a letter to George Thomson of May 1794, Burns himself described 'The Cotter' as 'my favorite Poem'.[66] The context for that statement is instructive. The painter David Allan had begun an illustration of the text, transplanting Burns's likeness on to the face of the eldest son in the family worship scene and thus amplifying the autobiographical potential of the work. Allan's illustration reveals a layering of sedimentation in the construction of Burns's mythos, and indeed the Burns–Allan connection is more broadly revealing for that process. Looking back to 3 March 1794, we find Burns writing to his friend Alexander Cunningham, describing the details of a seal which he aimed to commission, an extremely self-conscious object to the point of parody, featuring 'a holly-bush', 'a Shepherd's pipe & crook' and the two mottoes, 'Wood-notes wild' and 'Better a wee bush than nae bield'. The poet was having fun subverting the conventions of heraldry. In a phrase that might stand for his whole career, he comments, 'I do not know that my name is matriculated, as the Heralds call it, at all; but I have invented one for myself'. In the course of this pastoral self-fashioning, Burns rejects what he calls 'the nonsense of Painters of Arcadia' in favour of the more authentic stylings of Allan, who is described as 'the *only* Artist who has hit *genuine* Pastoral costume'. Burns is explicitly seeking to curate himself after the polite model of Allan Ramsay, with David Allan's work for the 'quarto Edition of the Gentle Shepherd' providing the desired visual template.[67] This is one of the sequences in the poet's correspondence where the mechanics of his pastoralism are most tellingly on show. He would later describe Allan as 'a kind of brother-brush', commenting, 'I look on Mr Allen & Mr Burns to be the only genuine & real Painters of Scotish Costume in the world'.[68] In these passages Burns exhibits his taste for pastoral representation, based on a careful, potent curation of the real. And if the consecration power of the 'genuine & real' – however subtly interpreted – was critical to Burns's reception during his lifetime and thereafter, then 'The Cotter's Saturday Night' was very much the prime evidential basis for it.[69] With this poem at the heart of his oeuvre, Burns is in the purest sense a pastoral poet, engaged in a polite reimagining or mediation of humble life.[70] Humble life, in this context, takes on a particular shading in the celebration of traditional Presbyterianism.

As noted above, 'The Cotter' is inscribed to Robert Aiken, nephew of William Dalrymple, the New Licht preacher who is a significant presence for William Burnes's 'Manual of Religious Belief'. While this family connection might prepare us for one of Burns's critiques of hypocritical Auld Licht orthodoxy, what actually follows is better explained by the poem's epigraph. Burns borrows a quatrain from Thomas Gray's 1751 *Elegy written in a Country Churchyard* to set the stage for 'The short and *simple* annals of the Poor' [my emphasis], which are crafted in line with Burns's larger cultivation of simplicity.[71] It is worth noting the basic premise of the piece, which explores the leisure time of the 'toil-worn Cotter' (l.14) and his hard-working family, the scene around the 'clean hearth-stane' (l. 24) presented as a respite from the georgic, economic world. The mood is one of domestic bliss, broken only by the poet's anxiety in stanza ten at the possibility of the daughter Jenny being undone by the 'perjur'd arts!' (l. 86) of seduction. There as elsewhere in the poem, we might be tempted to infer a hint of irony in Burns's outbursts: lines such as 'And O! be sure to fear the LORD alway!' (l. 50) could be read as comically overegged, but the pastoralism insists on just enough sincerity to prevent this becoming clear. Certainly a duality of vision is central to 'The Cotter', since the poem seeks to reconcile tradition and improvement, the rustic and the polite, old piety and antiquarian curiosity. Irony is not perhaps the most apposite means of describing this wider condition, since a coexistence of the incompatible emerges as a basic function of history.

At the heart of the work is the episode in which the father figure leads the family worship. The common identification of the father with William Burnes – and thus the entire piece with Robert's childhood – goes back at least as far as Currie's 1800 edition, with additional authority from the poet's brother Gilbert.[72] As often with Burns, this autobiographical element has been distracting as much as revealing for critics, and indeed Leask makes the observation that, despite whatever overlap there might be between William Burnes and the cotter, who is described in the poem as a 'priest-like Father', the Old Testament theology celebrated here is a strange fit with William's more liberal tendencies.[73] I will return to that point shortly. In general, however, the idealised quality of the poem does seem to involve a reflection on memory, including the distortions – useful or otherwise – that it brings. On visiting the poet's house on the Mill-hole Brae (later renamed Burns Street) in Dumfries in August 1803, Dorothy Wordsworth found his widow Jean absent but was let in by 'the servant-maid', and reported seeing 'over the desk a print from "The Cotter's Saturday Night"'.[74] Burns's own collaboration in the 'cotter-isation' of his persona is sufficiently clear from the episode around Allan's illustration. The poem is another rung in a process of self-fashioning announced by the Kilmarnock epigraph, recrossing the boundary between art and history, and a remodelling of his father would not be a far cry from Burns's established method.

The post-dinner worship begins at line 100 with,

> The chearfu' Supper done, wi' serious face,
>   They, round the ingle, form a circle wide;
> The Sire turns o'er, with patriarchal grace,
>   The big *ha'-Bible*, ance his *Father's* pride:
> His bonnet rev'rently is laid aside,
>   His *lyart haffets* wearing thin and bare;
> Those strains that once did sweet in ZION glide,
>   He wales a portion with judicious care;
> '*And let us worship God!*' he says with solemn air. (ll. 100–8)

Soaked in an affectionate glow, their bellies cheerful, the family forms into 'a circle wide'. It is the same formation that Gilbert described when discussing the social ritual of a 'rocking' in the Burns household, in which everyone delivered a song – sitting in a circle being a shared feature of these memorials of Ayrshire sociability.[75] The reference to 'ZION' and indeed 'patriarchal grace' outlines the Old Testament parts of the worship, reinforced with subsequent mentions of '*Abram*', '*Moses*', '*Amalek*', '*Job*' and '*Isiah*' [*sic*] (ll. 119–25). Again, this material might seem at odds with the religiosity of the Kirk satires. Yet it is critical to emphasise, as a number of commentators have, that this episode is at its heart an idealised vision of 'true religion', based on the family worship traditions of Scottish Presbyterianism.[76] Manning argues that Burns looks to Auld Licht rhetorical excess as an antidote to a torpid, polite Moderatism, and the patriarchal worship represented here is certainly a source of poetic vim.[77] However, the memorial of pious simplicity in 'The Cotter' does not contradict the basic tendency of the New Licht. In fact, it develops an apt reforming energy based in (to quote McIlvanney) 'the competence of the layman; the primacy of scripture; the right of private judgement', offering a view of spirituality that is diametrically opposed to the hypocritical and dogmatic Auld Licht ridiculed in texts such as 'Holy Willie's Prayer'. The 'principles of independence' on show in the cotter household draw on Ayrshire's deep Covenanting history and speak to a New Licht invested in renovating Presbyterian tradition, in a gesture that is dialectically similar to Burns's 'simple' poetics.[78]

'The Cotter' presents very much a space of private worship, free from the compromises of institutional religion. Appropriately, then, at the heart of the image is the 'big *ha'-Bible*', a hereditary heirloom that is the textual underpinning to this social ideal. The keynote of humble dignity is centred on the father, whose '*lyart haffets*' (grizzled temples) are 'thin and bare' – reflecting his circumstances if not, perhaps, his quality of life. In the following stanza, the characteristically Burnsian nationalisation of pastoral virtue is made clear, when he describes the musical aspect of the scene:

> The sweetest far of SCOTIA's holy lays:
>   Compar'd with these, *Italian trills* are tame;
> The tickl'd ears no heart-felt raptures raise;
>   Nae unison hae they, with our CREATOR's praise. (ll. 114–17)

The poem is building up a familiar associative web, tying together Scottishness, humble virtue and robust masculinity. In this context, traditional piety is very much part of the picture, one ingredient in a general aspect of simplicity. Later on, the poem reflects, 'Compar'd with this, how poor Religion's pride, | In all the pomp of *method*, and of *art*' (ll. 145–6). This is much the same sentiment found in the first 'Epistle to J. Lapraik', where Burns writes, 'What's a' your jargon o' your Schools, | Your Latin names for horns an' stools; | If honest Nature made you *fools*' (ll. 61–3). 'The Cotter', then, provides a religious inflection of Burns's pastoral inversions, which ostensibly revise the dominant logic of modernisation to favour the unimproved. Religion is at the centre of that traditional base here. The portrayal of the cotter's faith in this way is not absolute, of course, but is a question of relative degrees of improvement in the social architecture of the 1780s. Burns, as always, is dealing in 'simplicity' rather than the primitive.

The poem does something quite specific with the temporal framing of the scene. The picture of organic traditional integrity is not quite framed as timeless, but rather as inhabiting a circular model of time. Burns writes,

> [. . .] thus they all shall meet in future days:
> There, ever bask in *uncreated rays*,
> No more to sigh, or shed the bitter tear,
> *Together* hymning their CREATOR's praise
> In *such society*, yet still more dear;
> While circling Time moves round in an eternal sphere. (ll. 139–44)

The image is literally of heaven, where 'circling Time' safeguards eternal bliss for the elect, but just as the pious worship imbues the family with divine qualities – the father is described as 'The *Saint*, the *Father*, and the *Husband*' (l. 137) – so this cyclical temporality comes to infuse the social myth we are presented with. In an image that Currie found 'the most deeply affecting of any which the rural muse has ever presented', the cotter's familial circle incarnates a time-worn, perennial ritual of devotion in 'forming a wider circle round their hearth'.[79] The idyll, then, does not present a freeze-frame, but rather an image of 'circling', a cyclical renewal of tradition within 'an eternal sphere'.

In the final section, things take a new turn. The closing three stanzas form a kind of coda to the piece, extrapolating from the image of domestic bliss into a national-political register in a process of geographical enlargement that is characteristic of Burns's poetry. 'From Scenes like these, old SCOTIA's grandeur springs' (l. 163), writes Burns, making the transition absolutely clear. He continues his polemical defence of simplicity, notably in line 168's aphorism, 'The *Cottage* leaves the *Palace* far behind'. However, the sentiment is now put explicitly in the service of Scotland's political character, the 'grandeur' 'That makes her lov'd at home, rever'd abroad' (l. 164). This patriotic turn comes complete with a reference to William Wallace as the iconic opponent of tyranny (ll. 182–3). In a key couplet for the ideological deployment of the cottage idyll, Burns writes, 'A *virtuous Populace* may rise the while, | And stand a wall of fire, around their much-lov'd ISLE' (ll. 179–80). Suddenly 'circling Time' has become a 'wall of fire' which, for all the reference to Wallace, is apparently protecting the island heartland of the British Empire. Read this way, the moment certainly loads pressure on the idea of Burns's Scottish nationalist tendencies. That said, echoes of the medieval notion of the 'island' nation of Scotland may be relevant here.[80] The statement is in a way more interesting if the national vessel for modernity is Scotland, since that rubs against the grain of the familiar implication of Britishness and Scottishness in improvement's historical logic. Yet either way, time-lost rural Ayrshire has given way to the space of the imperial present, with cotter religion enlisted as moral security, the poem shifting on its axis to expose its modern agenda.

The gesture takes on an important aspect in the socio-economic climate of the late eighteenth century, which was placing huge pressure on the social model Burns celebrates. In what remains the standard text on the uneven processes of agricultural improvement that were rapidly changing the rural Lowlands, Devine describes the cotter system as fast becoming a historical memory by the time Burns was writing, outpaced by developments in labour and land management. The term 'Lowland Clearances' has been gaining ground in recent years.[81] While mass eviction and displacement seem to have been largely limited to upland areas in the Lowlands (where a switch from arable to pastoral farming could slash local labour demands), Devine identifies the cotter experience as the most dramatic component of this history:

> While the consolidation of direct tenancies and the erosion of multiple tenure took place over long periods of time, the removal of the cottars was concentrated in the last few decades of the eighteenth and the early years of the nineteenth century. In its scale, speed and effect it was more reminiscent of the patterns of clearance in the Highlands than any other aspect of lowland social change in the period.[82]

Compensatory manufacturing and proto-industrial opportunities helped to prevent a decimation of the local population in relatively prosperous regions such as Ayrshire, so that 'the cottar population was not so much expelled from rural society as relocated within it'.[83] And yet it is clearly vital that Burns produces his paean to the cotter lifestyle in the midst of its disappearance. (As noted, Burns was not himself a cotter but a tenant farmer, and when Peter Zenzinger criticises him for adopting the 'leisured classes' view of rural happiness' he is underestimating that distinction.)[84] This historical crisis orients the work, which becomes at once a form of historical fiction, a memorial, a protest against 'the bitter tear' (l. 141) of history and an attempt at cultural salvage. If the emergent category of the casualised 'day labourer' was the cotter reborn for a *laissez-faire* world in which 'commercial connections had replaced customary relationships', Burns's poem registers concern at a concomitant loss of tradition.[85] Leask confirms that 'Burns's cotter is evidently a practitioner of the old "runrig" cultivation [. . .] rather than [. . .] the consolidated field system of the "improved" farm',[86] and the poem is designed to sublimate this vocation as part of its image of spiritual purity. In this light, and drawing on the edifice of 'The Simple Bard', it is tempting to find the poet's opening declaration to be 'No mercenary Bard' (l. 2) entangled with images such as 'The frugal *Wifie*' (l. 90) in a larger mobilisation of 'cotter' virtue against the march of capital.

What I want to suggest the poem signals with 'circling Time', then, is a recovery of traditional virtue in the landscape of modern Britain, suturing the antagonism between modernising goals and residual social structures. With Presbyterian tradition at its centre, rural Scottish life offers up an organic wholeness capable of sustaining, in moral terms, the relentless teleology of improvement – guarding against the festering influence of '*Luxury*'s contagion' (l. 177). The formal impression of the closing stanzas seems to introduce a new linearity, the 'coda' branching off from the rest of the work into patriotic rapture, as if modernity is a historical tangent. This latter material contributes its own sense of timelessness, the ahistorical quality that all nationalisms require, emphasised in reference to a 'bright succession' (l. 189) that will 'never, never SCOTIA's realm desert' (l. 187). And indeed the model of improvement being imagined here significantly combines both the traditional circle *and* the modern line. Appropriately in light of this hybrid temporality, the rigid lines of text disclose various kinds of formal circling: in the repeated 'O's (ll. 172, 176, 181, 187), parentheses (ll. 185–6) and tumbling rhymes.[87] If the motif of enclosure is normally associated with agricultural improvement, it is reimagined here for the residual society under threat, which guards the national exterior at the same time as forming its core. Yet such eternal virtue is now the sympathetic counterpart to the modern imperial order – we might even be tempted to read what Burns calls the '*patriotic tide*' as a reference to British naval power (l. 181). The allusion to '*crowns* and *coronets*' (l. 178) sustains the insistent circling, beside the key image of the '*virtuous*

Populace' as 'a wall of fire', in which the cyclical time-space of tradition is a symbiotic counterpart to the relentless, forward movement of history.[88] The overarching form of the poem reflects this structure, in the integration of traditional Ayrshire with the polite pastoral, with the Bible the textual axis around which this imaginary geometry moves: guardian of humble virtue, driver of intellectual sophistication, primary source of Burns's pastoral (re)vision. In this way, 'The Cotter's Saturday Night' imagines traditional morality salvaging the path of improvement, safeguarding eternity within the temporality of modernity.

Reading the coda, Currie concludes that 'The noble sentiments of patriotism with which it concludes, correspond with the rest of the poem'.[89] Congruent or not, the ethno-nationalism of the closing passage certainly modifies the effect. Traditional piety becomes the guarantor of the 'much-lov'd ISLE', while Abraham's God becomes 'The Patriot's GOD' (l. 185), in a gesture that wrings all the patriotic capacity from this iteration of Burns's leitmotif of simplicity, with the eschatological language of the 'wall of fire' trumpeting the process of transcendence at work. In the most general terms, this circular power now sustaining modern history achieves something like, but perhaps even more powerful than, the iterative character of memory – signalling the dialectical involvement of art, and culture more broadly, within the onward flow of history. Indeed, this circling effect is presented as explicitly literary in form, a gift of 'the *Patriot-bard*' (l. 188). Having sublimated its Ayrshire cottage into the *locus classicus* of humble virtue, the poem invites a much larger theoretical calculation about the value of culture itself as the counterweight to economic modernity – poet, poem and cottage expressions of a social force offering discursive leverage upon the transformations of history. Thus the poem does not simply model the intervention of 'circling time' but enacts it, with poetry itself stepping into the breach as a medium of historical salvation ('simplicity'), form and function working in unity. Theoretically, print culture itself might be conceived as a means of reinscribing the present; certainly all textual religions offer a version of this act of reform. It is in this sense that 'The Cotter' anticipates its own installation – and indeed that of the figure of Robert Burns – as the secular religion of an industrialised, modern Scotland, a totem of virtue integral to a positive sense of Scottish identity that could help to make sense of the nineteenth century, amply registered in the spread of Burns clubs worldwide.

Burns, then, familiar as he was with the social consequences of the period's agricultural transformations, turns to poetry for a response. The resulting dynamic can be understood as provisionally squaring improvement and tradition or, perhaps more interestingly, as an attempt to reconcile alternative models of improvement. Burns's poetry gestures to the potential antagonism between commercial modernisation and virtue either religious or secular (a distinction that means little in the idyllic space of the cottage). Yet in its drive towards a vision of historical balance, 'The Cotter' wants to imagine that moral and spiritual growth can reinscribe the trajectory of commercial improvements, including in the agricultural realm, in a vision of mixed modernity. Indeed, if the poem's religious politics are read as an expression of New Licht Presbyterianism, it becomes legible as an attempt to mediate between spiritual and commercial varieties of improvement active in the Ayrshire Enlightenment, rendering poetry the literary medium for its redemptive moral culture. In doing so, it revises the discourse of Christian-capitalist civilisation that was solidifying during the eighteenth century. As we saw in the introduction, fears that socio-economic modernisation was incompatible with moral improvement were a stock feature of the improving field. But the poem's vision of a future imbued with the lessons of the cottage might be viewed as a pastoral reimagining of the elite discourse of improvement offered by the Moderates, the latter being implicit in William Robertson's assessment of 'Truth begin[ning] to dawn' across an upward, justified trajectory of Scottish history leading to the Age of Improvement.[90] Ahnert has helped to revise the association between Moderatism and secularisation and, while John Witherspoon's stinging attack at mid-century on a Moderate party that, in Colin Kidd's words, 'preferred politeness to displays of piety' clearly registered a tendency, the spiritual component of their support for improvement is clear.[91] By insisting on a concession to 'circling Time', the poetic intervention of 'The Cotter's Saturday Night' has something in common with improvement as conceived by a writer such as Robertson, where the discourse could be commercial and spiritual at once, functioning as a Whiggish middle way between unfettered economic exploitation and static traditionalism, as indeed between enlightened scepticism and fundamentalism – as active 'moderatism', in other words.

The pastoral always involves polite mediation, and the retrospective aspect of 'The Cotter' heightens a sense of the unimproved being recovered on new terms. In fact, it executes 'a familiar pattern of actual loss and imaginative recovery' that Ann Bermingham associates with eighteenth-century rustic landscape painting, landscape gardening and the picturesque, which signal the 'coincidence of a social transformation of the countryside with the rise of a cultural-aesthetic ideal of the countryside'.[92] But it is quite distinct from the Tory nostalgia some commentators would subsequently read into it. In religious terms, 'The Cotter' is not so much (in Corey Andrews's words) 'relatively orthodox' as it is subversively progressive in its address to Christianity.[93] Speaking generally, what Burns offers here is a piece of progressive calculus more than it is reactionary sentiment. And yet the rhetorical urgency of 'circling Time' in the context of the vehement worship scene does threaten a less appeasable version of cottage innocence, with the potency of the moral nucleus straining against the terms of its recovery. Even in this deeply sentimental work, the old world might resist the calculation of the pastoral to take up a stronger language of protest against class oppression and improvement, just as the figure of Burns himself retains a defiant rustic edge. The balance of emphasis here probably lies with ensuring a stake for residual, rural cultures within commercial modernity, even if the cotters achieve their ultimate transcendence in death. Still, if the poem moves to represent a fading life-world in a polite medium that is compatible with that modernity, the possibility that this is a futile or even damaging endeavour, and that all Burns can offer is a hollow elegy, remains. The final question, in other words, is a formal one: Burns's address to the cottage is contingent upon the efficacy of poetry.

Towards the Aesthetic Nation

Near the start of Sydney Owenson's 1806 novel *The Wild Irish Girl*, the English aristocratic Horatio M—— is making his way on foot across the Irish landscape when he encounters 'something like a human habitation': a '*hut*, or *cabin*, as it is called'. Owenson takes the opportunity for a long ethnological footnote on these 'wretched hovels', reflecting on a curious coincidence of dignity and poverty: 'even in these miserable huts you will seldom find the spirit of urbanity absent – the genius

of hospitality never'.[94] We are told later of the 'dreadful fevers' the
Irish peasantry contract as a result of 'the exposed state of their damp
and roofless hovels', yet Owenson insists on the miraculous virtue that
persists in deprivation. In the character of Lady Glorvina, the novel's
embodiment of the Irish nation, are mixed 'the language of a court'
and 'the artless inhabitant of a cottage'.[95] On actually entering one
of these cottages, Horatio finds himself promptly 'admitted into the
social circle' and given 'the best seat at the fire', his new perspective
from within the circle of traditional virtue allowing him to account
more fully for the value of the unimproved – or rather for the unevenness of improvement's hand, since moral excellence and economic
backwardness are combined in the peasantry.[96]

It would be difficult to overstate the importance of this revelation as a topos in eighteenth- and early nineteenth-century literature. 'Man finds his lodgment alike in the cave, the cottage, and the
palace', Adam Ferguson explained in his 1767 *Essay on the History
of Civil Society*, an equation that recurs across this period, as does
the stronger construction of Burns – 'The *Cottage* leaves the *Palace*
far behind'.[97] 'The country cottage', as Malcolm Andrews puts it,
forms 'England's [he means Britain's] most enduring and appealing
architectural expression of the Horatian ideal', representing for the
eighteenth century 'a happy blend of pastoral and Horatian aspirations'.[98] As critical to picturesque taste as to pastoral poetry, counter-
ing both metropolitan and continental sophistication, the 'national
emblem' of the cottage was well established as a sentimental ideal by
1786, having been celebrated in myriad examples from the 'peaceful
cottage' of Pope's *Windsor-Forest* (a work quoted by Burns at line
138 of 'The Cotter') to the 'mossy' and 'chearful' cottages threaded
into Thomson's *Seasons*.[99] Simplicity in material form, the cottage
and its moral enigma remained a stock feature of travel accounts
throughout the period. Take Richard Ayton, for example, writing on
the small village of Powhellin near Annan on the Solway Firth in the
1815 second volume of his and William Daniell's *A voyage round
Great Britain*. 'Mud-huts have the cardinal merit of being perfectly
weather-proof', Ayton reflects, finding the inhabitants at once 'sunk
into a state of profoundest piggishness in all their forms of living, yet
highly civilized, intelligent, and moral'.[100]

Without meaning to suggest equivalency between references to cottage virtue across decades, genres and national borders – John Keats,
for one thing, insisted that 'A Scotch cottage [. . .] is a pallace to an

Irish one' – the point is that Burns's idealisation of the cottage reflected a long-standing preoccupation.[101] Certainly in the years following the poet's death, his own handling of the subject rapidly accrued meaning, including around the thorny biographical questions that characterised early responses. Seeking to overturn an image of dissipation in the poet's later life in Alexander Peterkin's 1815 *Review of the Life of Robert Burns*, James Gray returned to 'The Cotter' as moral security for the poet's character.[102] Similarly, for John Wilson, influentially reappraising Burns in 1840, the work was 'charged with those sacred influences that connect the human heart with heaven', though he found the attack on 'a lordling's pomp' (l. 169) disquieting.[103] When reflecting on this 'Poor unfortunate fellow', Keats instinctively reached for the cottage motif; and indeed Keats's companion on his 1818 pedestrian tour, Charles Brown, found himself quoting 'The Cotter' at the moment of entering Ayrshire, demonstrating the thorough imprinting of the landscape with the poem, just as the birthplace myth it inspired would insinuate itself into Scottish culture.[104]

This is not the place to enter into a fuller reception history.[105] Instead, I want to develop a way of thinking about the cultural politics of Burns's poetry, especially though not exclusively within a national context. In an earlier essay, I argued that the central scene of 'Tam o' Shanter', as Tam peers into the demonic ceilidh, discloses a consciously aestheticised tableau of Scottishness, with Kirk-Alloway's window-frame serving the function that – in a now-classic argument – Cairns Craig attributed to the painting of Edward Waverley and Fergus Mac-Ivor towards the end of Scott's 1814 novel, by which 'life in history has been turned into art'.[106] In its reinscription of rural life, 'The Cotter' performs an equivalent gesture and, like 'Tam o' Shanter', is a good reason for considering Burns as a transitional figure between typically eighteenth- and nineteenth-century ideas of culture.[107]

As we know, Burns was deeply indebted to the culture of improving sociability that has so often been remarked as a feature of eighteenth-century Scotland, and which was far from limited to the cross-pollination of clubs and societies that constituted polite Edinburgh. Scion of an Ayrshire Enlightenment – with its potent religious inflection – libraries, convivial clubs and masonic lodges formed critical elements of the poet's world, part of a cultural groundswell in the Lowlands.[108] For all Burns's complicated relationship to cultural as well as commercial forms of improvement, his experience bears out Mark Towsey's view that libraries, for example, vitally impacted the life of Scottish 'country lairds and tenant farmers, as well as urban professionals, merchants, manufacturers and tradesmen'; while, as Leask suggests, this enabling milieu somewhat undermines the poet's own 'sentimentalized image of worldly incapacity'.[109] Similar trends were underway across western Europe and there is a risk of special pleading here: while engaged in building the evidence base, Towsey resists trumpeting the popular reach of Enlightenment in Scotland, as others have done.[110] (This is a separate issue from popular literacy, the comparatively high rates of which in Scotland are well established.)[111] The patriotic imperatives which animated much of this activity are however clear, suggesting that the experience of Enlightenment across classes in Scotland needs to be considered as in part an expression of cultural nationalism, with the stress on the modifier 'cultural', and with North British cachet within the context of the Union the dominant political aspiration. Relevant stresses on patriotic civic activity are not difficult to locate, from Adam Ferguson's 'bustle of civil pursuits', by which 'means the idle, as well as the busy, contribute to forward the progress of arts', to the preface to the 1755 first *Edinburgh Review*, which elaborates an overarching vision of 'literary improvements', presenting the scholarly review as 'a means of inciting' the population 'to do honour to their country', in order that '*North Britain*' may emulate 'the more mature strength of her kindred country'.[112] At a more local level, the language used by Burns to describe his collaboration with Robert Riddell in the Monkland Friendly Society in Dunscore parish, Nithsdale, makes the patriotic flavour of such associations clear. Burns hails 'the improvement of that part of his own species, whom chance has thrown into the humble walks of the peasant' as a service 'both to them as individuals, and to society at large'.[113]

On the other side of the turn of the nineteenth century, Ian Duncan has detected the emergence of a new cultural discourse based in an aesthetic vocabulary of nationhood:

> This shift involved the displacement – bitterly contentious – of an oligarchic and republican ideal of citizenship based on civic virtue, developed by the moral philosophy of the Scottish Enlightenment and sustained by the Edinburgh reviewers, to an aesthetically based cultural nationalism promoted by the *Blackwood's* literati.[114]

Inspired by the work of Friedrich Schiller, the *Blackwood's* circle – so this argument goes – popularised a newly aesthetic understanding of the nation, which was to be mediated through the work (production, possession and appreciation) of canonical literature. As part of this, the literary offered a medium for the preservation of aspects of Scottish culture (such as Jacobitism, orality or the supernatural) which seemed incompatible with the trajectory of modernity, through a process like that described by Peter Womack, who argues of the Highlands specifically that 'romance' became 'a kind of reservation' for 'the values which Improvement provokes and suppresses'.[115] This is an interesting version of the more general idea of '*culture* as an abstraction and an absolute' that Williams described as emerging in response to the industrial revolution in his 1958 *Culture and Society*, and which was deeply involved in political questions around class, democracy and, of course, art.[116] Transposed in this way, then, 'Scotland' – though the effect might be applicable to any other entity whatsoever – acquired the political instability of the aesthetic itself, as potentially either redundant excess or discursive pathogen, or both simultaneously. This might have the effect of enabling the final ideological triumph of a British hegemony in Scotland, by retooling distinctive, residual cultures into an inoffensive form. Still, all representation has a latent power, and the aesthetic could offer a language of political contestation.

In Duncan's telling, the pageantry surrounding George IV's visit to Scotland in August 1822 was the consummation of this new cultural register, with Edinburgh 'a new kind of national capital – one constituted not upon politics or finance but upon cultural production and aesthetic forms'.[117] The efficacy of Burns, iconic national bard and totem of 'simplicity', as source material for this emergent paradigm should be clear, but I want to suggest that he anticipates the Blackwoodian gesture in both the overarching category of 'The Simple Bard' and in the textual intervention of 'The Cotter'. To say so is not, however, to imply that Burns – or Scott – invented a radically new cultural practice. Indeed, Duncan's analysis of a 'shift' might be better modified to describe a sharpening into the nineteenth century of extant practices of 'aesthetically based cultural nationalism', with consumer culture (including literary tourism) among constituent factors in a consolidated, popular faith in the nation-as-text. Sticking to relatively recent history, the 1760s Ossian controversy provides ample evidence of the aesthetic as a potent arbiter of national consciousness.[118]

'The Cotter's Saturday Night', then, a poem with the 'big *ha'-Bible*' at its core, contemplates poetry as a means of secular belonging, laying claim to the rhetorical power of simple truth. In doing so, it advertises as inspiration a Protestant ethos that resacralises text in its displacement of superstition to Catholicism, just as Christianity itself marshals the Bible as the textual gateway to eternity. There is no stretch required to associate the poem's model of true religion – refusing 'the pomp of *method*, and of *art*' (l. 146) – with Burns's version of poetic merit, 'unbroke by rules of Art'. Midway, the work imagines a watchful deity, 'well pleas'd' with 'the language of the *Soul*' on display in the cotters' Saturday-night tribute, God then rewarding their virtue by the decision to 'in His *Book of Life* the Inmates poor enroll' (ll. 152–3). Again the poem figures the *textual* as the depository of human righteousness in a period of historical uncertainty, the cotter class salvaged in the medium of literature – a very different kind of salvation by 'works'. Memorialised in this way, the poem's subjects become a spiritual reservoir for the reading public, who can commune with Ayrshire humility newly consolidated as text, just as in the opening dedication Burns invites Robert Aiken to imagine 'What A**** in a *Cottage* would have been' (l. 8). Thus in the final lines of rapture, Burns pleads to God to replenish both the '*Patriot*' and 'the *Patriot-bard*' as Scotland's '*Ornament* and *Guard*' against the vicissitudes of history, poetry taking its place as a critical language of national life (ll. 188–9). Therefore, where Leask finds that 'the poem's conclusion strongly disavows the fact' that the cotters are now 'purely a literary or moral idea', quite the opposite is true.[119]

In an overlay of the line and the circle as models of time, with history redeemed by culture, 'The Cotter' invites the Scottish nation to inhabit a cottage ideal while in the arms of an emergent industrial order, just as a bard was an anachronism in the 1780s. While Owenson's *Wild Irish Girl* provided emergent discourses of Irish nationalism with a set of tropes, 'The Cotter' was a significant means of understanding Scottishness in the nineteenth century – the 'stateless nation' perhaps conveniently predisposed to enter the condition of poetry – and this is to some degree what the poem anticipates.[120] 'The Cotter' is a work that self-consciously sports with its own iconicity: the tableau of after-dinner worship 'round the ingle' (l. 101), for example, is as staged a prospect as we find in Burns. John D. Baird usefully comments on the novelistic quality of the work, but there is more telling ekphrasis with Allan's engraving, which seems implicitly called for by the original.[121] Predictably, then, Nash finds the terms 'picture' and 'photograph' used in subsequent descriptions of the poem.[122] This overtly emblematic and reverential work discusses after all not 'a' cotter's Saturday night but '*The* Cotter's Saturday Night'. Thus John Wilson's vision of a Scotland in which a thought of 'The Cotter' or 'Scots, wha hae' [K425] enables a 'poor man' to 'walk an equal in the broad eye of day as it shines over our Scottish hills', in a nation thoroughly impregnated with 'the immortal genius of Burns', and in which the 'The Cotter's Saturday Night' has become 'a religious establishment, it is to be hoped, for ever', was a caricatured but not unpredictable reading of the original.[123] Burns's sublimation as a national icon was developing a logic encouraged by the poet himself, in which the aesthetic was decisively a medium of consecration.

'The Cotter' is in many ways a strange item within Burns's oeuvre, not among his most urgent works at least to current tastes, with an obviously retrospective vision of the rustic not always in evidence elsewhere. Nonetheless, its central dynamic is an outcome of his wider self-appointment as 'The Simple Bard', who offers to speak on behalf of cottage, region and nation, providing an 'unbroke' poetic link between these realms that can embody the shock of history.[124] Still, the question remains of the aesthetic's unstable rhetorical power, of what exactly a poetical reimagining of the cotters means. In his approach to Scottish history, Scott has often been criticised for depoliticising the past – in *Waverley* consigning Jacobitism, for example, to the status of a 'childhood story'.[125] And yet the precursor model of Burns, with his very different politics, might help us to perceive a more formal aspect to the literary casting of history, in which the movement of time repossesses the past as culture. Equally, as Scott's febrile reception history demonstrates, far from being proscribed by the aesthetic as a historical register, the political remains contingent and subject to interpretation.[126] (That is, unless we take the view that 'culture' is always a poor echo, or even betrayal of history.) In the case of the 'The Cotter's Saturday Night', at least, the political efficacy of the cottage idyll is assured us within the poem in the decisive imagery of the 'wall of fire', though the medium of pastoral verse does little to assuage a sense that this recuperation of the cottage might be empty rhetoric, at least for the rural poor in 1786 and thereafter.

John Barrell has examined how the cottage became 'thoroughly politicized in the intense propaganda war between loyalists and radicals' in the 1790s, as a site of conflict between a romance of contented poverty and radical indignation.[127] Leask finally approaches 'The Cotter' in the latter terms, finding that its conclusion 'breathes radical energy into the quiescent genre of cottage pastoral', with the pastoral's conventional 'attack on luxury and aristocratic privilege' granted a sharp edge.[128] Yet 'The Cotter' could serve 'radical' discourses of a very different nature: in, for example, a chauvinistic retelling uncovered by Corey Andrews, or in the ultra-conservative essentialism propagated by John Wilson, for whom the poem contained 'the records of a purer, simpler, more pious race' and a sublime of 'unquestioning, humble, wise, submission'.[129] 'Simplicity', as this suggests, was a very tractable ideal. Without oversimplifying a denominational landscape in which political tendencies were rarely straightforward, it is clear that Burns recuperates a vision of true religion that might contain subversive political energies, with associations including the century's patronage disputes, a residual covenanting legacy and more plainly – with France's *ancien régime* struggling to fend off bankruptcy – the threat of the poor. I certainly agree with those who question the assumed conservatism of the piece, which seems Whiggish in general terms. Still, Burns's image of a linear modernity being reframed by traditional virtue, his generously dialectical modelling of improvement, can support a range of specific political interpretations. That, however, is a subordinate issue here. In fact, the readiness of the piece to serve divergent agendas (a capacity it shares with Burns himself) is indicative not simply of the ideological latitude of the pastoral but also of an underlying preoccupation with the condition of poetry *per se*.

Reimagining a fading rural Ayrshire as the ethical core of the modern nation – whether Scotland or Britain – 'The Cotter' performs a piece of historical sleight-of-hand in which a newly mythic past can eddy into and perhaps amend the present. It might seem a naive gesture, though the aspirational paradox is an integral component of the pastoral, and indeed in the end, the motif of the line within the circle is perhaps as much a diagnosis of the movement of history as it is sentimental escapism. There is always a kind of hedging in Burns's work, which is never entirely convinced by either the rustic or the polite, the traditional or the modern. In this instance, the outcome – 'simplicity' – amounts to a sophisticated vision of mixed modernity, which requires poetry as a guardian of tradition and moral lodestone. 'The Cotter' presents a mixture of sincerity and theatricality that is distinctive of Burns's early performances. And yet that tonal complexity does not, I think, negate its strong claim for the historical agency of the aesthetic, at least not fully. The poem would not presume to replace religion, but its vision of culture is a redemptive one. The cottage idyll, it suggests, offers a means to complicate improvement, to invigorate its moral arterial, to wrestle against the economic monopoly on time itself and move backwards, dialectically and circuitously through its passage – itself something of a radical proposition.

Against the background of wholesale processes of change that had really got going in Scotland in the 1760s, Burns naturally shared his contemporaries' preoccupation with the complex range of attitudes, actions and effects that constituted improvement. Rooted in a changing agricultural landscape and invested with a sophisticated intellectual politics, 'The Cotter's Saturday Night' emerges out of a middling-sort experience that was central to the Ayrshire Enlightenment. In national terms, it develops a view of improvement that addresses the residual legacy of Scottish Presbyterianism that had been secured within the 1707 Union deal. Equally, though as I have suggested the theological component of the work finally concedes primacy to its secular – and aesthetic – calculation, 'The Cotter' is nevertheless a reminder of the Protestant version of Christian 'simplicity' that was a major feature of the culture of improvement in this period. The poem finds in its cottage sublime a means of redeeming the path of history, however contingently. In doing so, it summons a much larger tendency shared by religions and by culture itself, delivering a moral charge repeatedly upon the present through the vehicle of print. It is an important engagement with the dialectics of improvement at the advent of modernity, a mixture of sentiment and historical analysis in which the present fails to entirely trump the past, in which the rural poor become a paragon of virtue, and in which the modern world can rely on the force of 'circling Time'.

Notes

1. Burnes, 'Manual', in *Commonplace Books, Tour Journals, and Miscellaneous Prose*, ed. Leask, pp. 12–16. The MS, 'A manual of religious belief, composed by William Burnes for the instruction of his children', is object no. 36699 at the Robert Burns Birthplace Museum in Alloway.
2. *Commonplace Books, Tour Journals, and Miscellaneous Prose*, ed. Leask, p. 34.
3. Devine, *The Transformation of Rural Scotland*, p. 68.
4. Robert Burns to Dr John Moore, 2 August 1787, in *The Letters of Robert Burns*, ed. Ferguson and Roy, vol. 1, pp. 133–46 (pp. 135–6). This edition is hereafter cited as *Letters*.
5. See Ahnert, *Moral Culture*.
6. See Harris and McKean, *The Scottish Town*, pp. 384–6; and also Towsey, *Reading the Scottish Enlightenment*, pp. 113–14, 135, 149–50.
7. *Letters*, vol. 1, p. 136.
8. Burnes, 'Manual', p. 12.
9. McIlvanney, *Burns the Radical*, pp. 136–7. See McGinty, 'Literary, Philosophical and Theological Influences' and, more recently, *Burns and Religion*.
10. See Crawford, *Poems and Songs*, pp. 39–40 (p. 40). Crawford casts some doubt on the authorship of the 'Manual', which he notes could be 'entirely Murdoch's composition' or a modified version of William's work, though he tends to endorse the accepted view.
11. *Commonplace Books, Tour Journals, and Miscellaneous Prose*, ed. Leask, pp. 10–15. The letter in question is Robert Burns to Agnes McLehose, 8 January 1788, in *Letters*, vol. 1, pp. 201–3. See also Burns, 'The Vision' [K62], in *The Poems and Songs of Robert Burns*, ed. Kinsley, vol. 1, pp. 103–13 (ll. 239–40). Kinsley's edition is used for all citations of Burns's poetry here, with reference to his numbering system as [K].
12. Burnes, 'Manual', p. 14.
13. Manning, 'Burns and God', in particular pp. 118, 123, 129.
14. See Kidd, 'Enlightenment and Ecclesiastical Satire before Burns', for a fresh reading of the place of the Kirk satires within the period.
15. Manning, 'Burns and God', p. 115; McIlvanney, *Burns the Radical*, pp. 161–2.
16. Kidd, 'Subscription, the Scottish Enlightenment', p. 514.
17. Thomas Crawford noted in the 1960s that 'it has long been fashionable to despise' the poem (*Poems and Songs*, p. 174). A visceral example of this is Ferguson's 'The Immortal Memory', which condemns the Burns of this 'mawkish' work as 'a sterile hybrid produced by inseminating an impressionable and imperfectly educated mind with the sentimentalism

of Henry Mackenzie and William Shenstone' (pp. 444, 450). Raymond Bentman reflected in 1972 that 'The Cotter' had become indicative of a 'bad Burns' who was 'primarily English in diction and sentimental in tone' ('Robert Burns's Declining Fame', p. 210).

18. McIlvanney, *Burns the Radical*, pp. 161–2.
19. McDiarmid, *Picture of Dumfries*, pp. 32, 86.
20. *The Works of Robert Burns*, ed. Currie, vol. 1, pp. 369–70.
21. Thomas Telford, 'Pursue, O Burns ! thy happy style', in *The Works of Robert Burns*, ed. Currie, vol. 1, pp. 370–6 (ll. 26, 8, 9, 14).
22. Gilpin, *Observations*, vol. 1, pp. 215, 211–12.
23. Ibid. p. 221.
24. Lord Byron to John Murray, 1821, in *The Complete Miscellaneous Prose*, ed. Nicholson, pp. 120–60 (p. 150). See J. H. Alexander on how 'The Cotter' became John Wilson's 'favoured example' of the 'vital contact between imagination and reality' ('Literary Criticism in the Later "Noctes Ambrosianae"', p. 21).
25. Burns, 'The Cotter's Saturday Night' [K72], l. 5. Further citations of Kinsley's printing of the poem appear in the main text.
26. Nash, 'The Cotter's Kailyard', p. 188.
27. Telford, 'Pursue, O Burns !', ll. 113, 127, 131, 132.
28. Gilpin, *Observations*, vol. 1, p. 215.
29. See Mackenzie, 'Unsigned Essay in *The Lounger*, 9 December 1786'. Marilyn Butler argues that 'Heav'n-taught' was a nod to the 'precept that right reason was universally available', rather than a misreading of Burns's level of education ('Burns and Politics', p. 90).
30. See Scott, 'Describing the Kilmarnock', pp. xxii–iii.
31. Burns, 'Epigraph to the Kilmarnock Edition' (1786), in *The Poems and Songs of Robert Burns*, ed. Kinsley, vol. III, p. 970.
32. See McKeever, 'Simplicity, Rightly Understood'. For more on Burns's songs and their relationship to ideas of improvement, see Newman, 'Localizing and Globalizing'.
33. Leask, *Robert Burns and Pastoral*, p. 4.
34. See McKeever, 'Burns's Tales of Aloway Kirk', pp. 23–4.
35. Gilpin, *Observations*, vol. 2, pp. 90–2. On the relationship of the picturesque and the pastoral in eighteenth-century Britain, see Andrews, *The Search for the Picturesque*, pp. 3–23. Certainly what Andrews calls the 'reactionary, anti-utilitarian element in Picturesque taste' (p. 65) does not capture the unstable politics of Burns's work.
36. McKeever, 'Burns's Tales of Aloway Kirk'.
37. Burns, 'Preface to the Kilmarnock Edition' (1786), in *The Poems and Songs of Robert Burns*, ed. Kinsley, vol. 3, pp. 971–2.
38. Crawford, *Poems and Songs*, pp. 109–10.

39. Burns, 'On Fergusson' [K143], ll. 6–7.
40. See Gidal and Gavin, 'Introduction: Spatial Humanities and Scottish Studies'; and Stafford, *Local Attachments*. For Burns's transition between Ayrshire and national contexts as played out between the Kilmarnock and Edinburgh volumes, see Carruthers's introduction to *The Edinburgh Companion to Robert Burns*, pp. 1–5 (pp. 3–4); and Sher, *The Enlightenment & the Book*, p. 231. See also Leask on the equivalent dynamic in 'The Vision', in *Robert Burns and Pastoral*, pp. 103–8.
41. See Andrews, *The Genius of Scotland*.
42. Fielding, *Scotland and the Fictions of Geography*, p. 44.
43. Burns, 'Epistle to J. Lapraik, An Old Scotch Bard' [K57], l. 77. See Fielding, *Scotland and the Fictions of Geography*, pp. 60–1. Sorensen finds 'Northern' or 'Scotch' applied promiscuously to ballads in the period ('Alternative Antiquarianisms', p. 243).
44. Burns, 'To a Haggis' [K136], ll. 18, 25–7.
45. Crawford, *Devolving*, pp. 88–9.
46. A clustering of environmental effects in Europe in these years has been linked to the Laki eruption in Iceland. See Thordarson and Self, 'Atmospheric and Environmental Effects'.
47. Bourdieu, *Field of Cultural Production*, pp. 164, 36.
48. Johnson, *Rasselas*, p. 27.
49. Burns, 'Dedication: To the Noblemen and Gentlemen of the Caledonian Hunt' (1787), in *The Poems and Songs of Robert Burns*, ed. Kinsley, vol. 3, pp. 977–8 (p. 978).
50. *The Works of Robert Burns*, ed. Currie, vol. 1, p. 229.
51. See Ferguson, 'Cancelled Passages', p. 101, which argues that Burns may have had future plans to publish in his own capacity.
52. Sher, *The Enlightenment & the Book*, pp. 230–4. Patrick Scott notes that Burns 'visited a number of masonic lodges in the area' of Kilmarnock as part of the publicity for his first edition ('Describing the Kilmarnock', p. xxiii). See also Scott's essay regarding the finances of the Kilmarnock edition (pp. xxv–vi).
53. 'Proposals, for Publishing by Subscription, Scotch Poems, by Robert Burns' (1786), in *The Poems and Songs of Robert Burns*, ed. Kinsley, vol. 3, p. 970.
54. Burns, 'The Inventory' [K86], l. 34.
55. Ibid. l. 58.
56. Ibid. l. 67.
57. Ibid. l. 3.
58. Ibid. ll. 40–1.
59. Ibid. l. 68.
60. Sher, *The Enlightenment & the Book*, pp. 267–8.

61. Harris and McKean, *The Scottish Town*, p. 386.

62. Scott, 'Describing the Kilmarnock', p. xxiii.

63. See James Mackinlay, 'Parish of Kilmarnock', in Sinclair and Strawhorn (eds), *Statistical Account of Scotland, VI: Ayrshire*, pp. 286–310 (pp. 289–90). See also Burnett, 'Kilmarnock and the Kilmarnock Edition'.

64. Crawford, *Poems and Songs*, p. 109.

65. *The Works of Robert Burns*, ed. Currie, vol. 1, p. 315.

66. Robert Burns to George Thomson, May 1794, in *Letters*, vol. 2, pp. 294–5 (p. 294).

67. Robert Burns to Alexander Cunningham, 3 March 1794, in *Letters*, vol. 2, pp. 284–6 (pp. 285–6).

68. Robert Burns to George Thomson, 19 November 1794, in *Letters*, vol. 2, pp. 327–31 (p. 331).

69. See Leask, *Robert Burns and Pastoral*, pp. 210–11.

70. On the polite roots of the poem in Augustan verse, see Radcliffe, 'Imitation, Popular Literacy', pp. 251–64.

71. Burns, 'The Cotter', p. 145.

72. *The Works of Robert Burns*, ed. Currie, vol. 1, p. 85; vol. 3, Appendix, p. 8.

73. *Commonplace Books, Tour Journals, and Miscellaneous Prose*, ed. Leask, p. 10.

74. Dorothy Wordsworth, *Recollections of a Tour*, pp. 6–7. For the importance of 'The Cotter' to William Wordsworth's engagement with the legacy of Burns, see Stafford, 'Plain Living and Ungarnish'd Stories', p. 133. See also Leask, 'Burns, Wordsworth and the Politics of Vernacular Poetry'. I have been unable to locate an exact date for the renaming of Mill-hole Brae and it is possible that this was a gradual process. Certainly 'Burn's Street' [*sic*] appears in John Wood's 1819 'Plan of the Towns of Dumfries and Maxwelltown from Actual Survey'.

75. *The Works of Robert Burns*, ed. Currie, vol. 3, Appendix, p. 7.

76. See, for example, Nash, 'The Cotter's Kailyard', p. 192; and Leask, *Robert Burns and Pastoral*, pp. 227–8.

77. Manning, 'Burns and God', p. 126.

78. McIlvanney, *Burns the Radical*, pp. 161–2.

79. *The Works of Robert Burns*, ed. Currie, vol. 1, p. 315.

80. Dauvit Broun explains how this 'was exaggerated wildly in the medieval imagination: Matthew Paris (d.1259), in his celebrated map of Britain, portrays the landmass north of the Forth as an island linked to the rest of Britain by Stirling Bridge alone' ('Britain and the Beginning of Scotland', p. 125).

81. See Aitchison and Cassell, *The Lowland Clearances*.

82. Devine, *The Transformation of Rural Scotland*, p. 140.
83. Ibid. p. 153.
84. Zenzinger, 'Low Life, Primitivism and Honest Poverty', p. 52.
85. Devine, *The Transformation of Rural Scotland*, p. 156.
86. Leask, *Robert Burns and Pastoral*, p. 222.
87. I am grateful for conversations with Matthew Sangster that helped to develop these observations.
88. Compare, here, William C. Strange on fire as a motif in 'The Cotter', which he finds moving from the private to the public in a crescendo of fire imagery, 'demonstrating the social graces of the inner light' ('The Fire Argument', p. 214).
89. *The Works of Robert Burns*, ed. Currie, vol. 1, p. 315.
90. See Robertson, *History of Scotland*, p. 5. Ahnert discusses the importance of Christian revelation to Robertson's vision of the civilising process in *Moral Culture*, pp. 101–2.
91. See, for example, Ahnert, *Moral Culture*, p. 68; and Kidd, 'Enlightenment and Ecclesiastical Satire', p. 107.
92. Bermingham, *Landscape and Ideology*, p. 9.
93. Andrews, *The Genius of Scotland*, p. 78.
94. Owenson, *The Wild Irish Girl*, p. 20.
95. Ibid. pp. 125, 69.
96. Ibid. p. 28.
97. Ferguson, *History of Civil Society*, p. 13.
98. Andrews, *The Search for the Picturesque*, p. 7.
99. See Andrews, 'The English Cottage', p. 56; Pope, *Windsor-Forest*, l. 86; and Thomson, 'Summer', in *The Seasons*, pp. 58–143 (ll. 64, 223).
100. See Macleod (ed.), *Sailing on Horseback*, pp. 79–80.
101. Walker (ed.), *Walking North with Keats*, p. 171.
102. 'Letter from Mr James Gray', in Peterkin, *Review of the Life*, pp. lxxxiii–xci (pp. lxxxiv, lxxxvi).
103. Wilson, 'On the Genius and Character of Burns', pp. xxvii, xxx. See Leask, *Robert Burns and Pastoral*, pp. 233–4, on more developed fears about the poem in Wilson's 'The Radical's Saturday Night'.
104. Walker (ed.), *Walking North with Keats*, pp. 170, 240.
105. See Nash, 'The Cotter's Kailyard'; Whatley, 'Political Legacy of Robert Burns', pp. 646–50; Leask, *Robert Burns and Pastoral*, pp. 231–6; and Radcliffe, 'Imitation, Popular Literacy', pp. 264–75.
106. See McKeever, 'Tam o' Shanter and Aesthetic Cultural Nationalism'; and Craig, *Out of History*, p. 39.
107. Prior constructions of a transitional Burns include Raymond Bentman arguing that the poet 'shows the transition from Augustan to Romantic modes' ('Robert Burns's Declining Fame', p. 223).

108. See Carruthers, *Robert Burns*, p. 7.

109. Towsey, *Reading the Scottish Enlightenment*, p. 294; Leask, *Robert Burns and Pastoral*, p. 84.

110. See Withrington, 'What was Distinctive about the Scottish Enlightenment?', p. 15.

111. See Miller, *The Formation of College English*, p. 147.

112. Ferguson, *History of Civil Society*, p. 175; and 'Preface', *Edinburgh Review*, 1 (1755), pp. iv, ii.

113. See 'Robert Burns's Letter on the Monkland Friendly Society Library', in *Commonplace Books, Tour Journals, and Miscellaneous Prose*, ed. Leask, pp. 164–5 (p. 164).

114. Duncan, *Scott's Shadow*, p. 14.

115. Womack, *Improvement and Romance*, p. 3.

116. Williams, *Culture and Society*, pp. xviii, xvi.

117. Duncan, 'Urban Space and Enlightened Romanticism', p. 73.

118. See Lemke, 'Nostalgic Ossian and the Transcreation of the Scottish Nation'.

119. Leask, *Robert Burns and Pastoral*, p. 225.

120. The term was coined by Nairn in *The Break-Up of Britain*, p. 31.

121. Baird, 'Burns and Cowper', p. 121.

122. Nash, 'The Cotter's Kailyard', p. 188.

123. See Wilson, 'On the Genius and Character of Burns', pp. ix, xxviii.

124. Compare Leith Davis on Burns actually being tasked with 'imagining the nation into being' in response to 'disparities within the nation' ('Re-presenting Scotia', p. 69).

125. Pittock, *Scottish and Irish*, p. 187.

126. Ibid. pp. 189–90.

127. See Barrell, *Spirit of Despotism*, pp. 220–1.

128. Leask, *Robert Burns and Pastoral*, pp. 231, 228, 229. R. D. S. Jack makes a similar point in claiming that the 'sentimental tradition' serves a vigorous 'attack on social divisions' in the poem, with the pastoral a way to 'indirectly indict the ruling classes' ('Robert Burns: Poet of Freedom', pp. 46–7).

129. See Andrews, *The Genius of Scotland*, p. 217; Wilson, 'Some Observations', p. 523; and Wilson, 'The Radical's Saturday Night', p. 258. Christopher Whatley outlines the nineteenth-century contest over the poem, between Tory and radical positions ('Political Legacy of Robert Burns', pp. 646–50).

Chapter 2

Short Fictions of Improvement by James Hogg and Walter Scott

'I am a borderer [. . .] between two generations', announces Chrystal Croftangry in the early stretches of Scott's 1827 *Chronicles of the Canongate*.[1] Living at the 'threshold' of 'the two extremities of the moral world', sandwiched between Edinburgh and the neighbouring wilderness, he has a vantage-point on history as improvement, which is expressed via competing versions of time: 'one exhibiting the full tide of existence, pressing and precipitating itself forward [. . .] the other resembling some time-worn anchorite, [. . .] silent and uninvolved' (pp. 51–2). This dual perspective shapes the text, for example in Croftangry's opinion of modern travel: 'I like mail-coaches, and I hate them.' Though convenient, mail-coaches cultivate 'abominably selfish' passengers and wear away 'originality of character' by 'setting the whole world a-gadding' – they are a form of 'retrograde to barbarism' (pp. 29–30).[2] Traversing Britain's upgraded road network, the mail-coach becomes a measure of history, of time itself. In his classic essay on the subject, E. P. Thompson traces the rise of 'clock time' as an integral feature of modernisation, with time being mapped on to money ever more efficiently.[3] This is a history to which 'habitual customers' of Croftangry's mail-coach seem especially subject. 'Their only point of interest on the road is to save time', he explains, 'and see whether the coach keeps the hour'. They are blinkered by a new temporal economy marked by the rotations of the coach's wheels. In fact, this 'flying chariot' economises both time and space, 'rattling' around the country, allowing 'only twenty minutes' for dinner, with its passengers 'jingling against each other' (pp. 29–30). Still, Croftangry is no primitivist. While he mourns changes to his lost family estate, which are in poor aesthetic taste and unproductively 'naked' (pp. 32–3), he regrets a missed opportunity there for the exercise of 'care and improvement' (p. 27). Improvement, then, is once again a plural field to be traversed with caution, its dialectical complexities eliciting no easy answers or glib value judgements. Such concerns were by 1827 firmly established in Scott's Waverley Novels, yet *Chronicles* accentuates this agenda. In doing so it reflects the formal impetus of short fiction, which by the later years of the 1820s represented a popular though still relatively undefined body of writing, with particular leverage on questions of improvement.

Romantic short fiction has become an area of keen scholarly interest in recent years, buoyed by greater attention to the periodical press, which stood central to the early nineteenth-century literary marketplace and the creative innovations that sustained it.[4] *Blackwood's Edinburgh Magazine* holds a privileged status as the foremost publisher of short fiction in the period, and the literary culture orbiting *Blackwood's* ensures that the early history of short fiction has a meaningful Scottish dimension. Work on *Blackwood's* associates including James Hogg and John Galt has been essential to this new scholarship, which is acting to reshape the canonical history.[5] In brief, where an older critical totem identified the genre with a model of the short story predicated upon aesthetic unity – and thus with texts by Edgar Allan Poe, Nathaniel Hawthorne and, later, Robert Louis Stevenson – the Romantic perspective has introduced a rich prehistory, characterised by (sometimes chaotic) experimentation.[6] This has led to an emphasis on the 'tale' and the 'sketch', both forms that combine pithy finality with irresolution, while at the same time highlighting a proximity to the oral tradition which the tale in particular often attempted to signal. Tim Killick's 2008 monograph, subtitled *The Rise of the Tale*, highlights a long history of short fictions across popular and literary traditions, and while he opts not to deploy the label 'short story' within the Romantic milieu, his work necessitates a more protracted lineage of the form.[7] The 'tale' specifically was an expansive category encompassing an amorphous body of writing, as Anthony Jarrells has shown, but Killick's attention to what he calls 'regional short fiction' is a germane starting point here:

> In the 1810s and 1820s, short fiction became a form of literature in which local traditions could be cherished, but tales and stories also acted as a forum in which ideas of history, progress, nationhood, and cultural authority could be fiercely contested.[8]

Short fictions were especially fitted to approach the culture of improvement, not least because of the tale's (apparent) rootedness in locality and orality. The category of the tale was freighted with notions of folkloric authenticity – free of the 'novel's burden of verisimilitude'[9] – and could appear as a conduit between literary modernity and ideas of 'tradition'. In that role, it was fashioned into a vehicle for essaying improvement in all its collateral intricacies. This aspect of Romantic short fiction was not limited to subversive contestation; rather, the form generated a distinctive encounter with the full dialectical effects of the phenomenon.

By virtue of its relative indeterminacy, Romantic short fiction presented a unique opportunity for debate, including around what Killick calls 'the hegemonic post-Enlightenment philosophy of the novel' (embodied for him in the Waverley Novels, which he finds insist on the 'tragic failure' of tradition).[10] It is unnecessary to caricature the novel here, itself a dynamic genre, yet it is certainly tempting to view the short form as potentially more spontaneous than longer fictions, able to resist elaboration and resolution in a way that might be ideologically freeing. At the same time, however, short fiction's anecdotal and emblematic qualities pull in the direction of unity or at least compression, granting it a strange duality – capable at once of great impulsive deviance and of surgical precision. Hogg is a fine exemplar of this; equally, parts of Scott's *Chronicles* retain a clarity of focus only sporadically achieved by his novels, while exacerbating elements of ambiguity that had long haunted his longer efforts. (It is worth noting that, since both Hogg's and Scott's novels often work like episodic portmanteaus, they themselves appreciably rely on short fictional effects.) If short fiction resists certainties entertained by the novelistic world, it does so by a curt immediacy, bound to the power of the rhetorical question.

That said, we must remain sensitive to the way that in a collection such as Hogg's *Shepherd's Calendar*, for example, meaning accrues between as well as within items, in a semiotic exchange that is equally as applicable to an issue of *Blackwood's*. Certainly *Chronicles* requires careful parsing on this front. Following the maxim for aesthetic unity, 'The Two Drovers' sequence has long been cited as a candidate for the first short story in the English language.[11] *Chronicles* self-describes as 'a publication of a miscellaneous nature', combining 'a sort of greengrocer's stall' with 'ironmongery wares' in a nod to consumer choice

(p. 51). In a telling passage, the narrator is being harassed by the printer's boy, who is 'come to torment me for *copy*', causing Scott to reflect on the distinction between 'the volunteer author' and 'his needy brother' (pp. 122–3). Coming hard on the heels of economic crisis for Scott, this flirtation with short fiction was with a relative hinterland of the trade.[12] The short form was less prestigious in both cultural and financial terms than the novel, and Croftangry explains his decision to bundle the material into a greater whole as a strategic one in this context (p. 52).[13] The substantial integration of its constituent parts certainly renders *Chronicles* more than a miscellany.[14] Yet whether we declare it a collection, a novel or something else altogether, the short fictional form is critical to its achievement.

This chapter, then, traces the motif of improvement through texts by Hogg and Scott, where it functions as a complex field of thought and activity surrounding the advance of commercial modernisation. For his part, Hogg treats improvement in primarily epistemological or spiritual terms as a harbinger of modern scepticism, while Scott's interest in the category of history makes improvement above all a temporal question. I want to unpack two aesthetic innovations in this light, both of which are inflected by the formal characteristics of short fiction and experiment with how the genre might contribute to the improving debate. The first, addressed initially here in a clustering of Hogg's later contributions to *Blackwood's* in 1830 and 1831, applies a discursive solution. Hogg moves towards an emphasis on debate itself, leveraging the iterative quality of short fiction and the mechanisms of the literary marketplace to invite an ongoing discursive commerce. Enacting a capacity for 'repetition and alterity' in the short form, this looks to acts of transmission to by turns sustain, contain and defer the dialectics of improvement.[15] David Stewart comments of Romantic short fiction that it 'had a tendency to shift and mutate in the telling', and Hogg presents this instability as a function of reception as much as creation.[16] Hearing all sides, finally displacing authority to the reader through what was by 1830 long-standing ironic play in *Blackwood's*, Hogg invokes a living public sphere that is invited to deliberate improvement indefinitely, in a process that stubbornly foregrounds a question of aesthetic form.

I find kindred strategies at work in Scott's *Chronicles*, which amplifies the instability of the Waverley Novels, constantly re-unearthing tension points in improvement in a superimposition of linear and cyclical temporalities. The final stretches of the chapter then move to stress Scott's evolution of the aesthetic discourse seen emerging with Burns in Chapter 1. This rendering of history has been read by critics variously as a form of imperial control or dissonant signalling, and short fiction acts to sharpen the controversy. Equally, while I suggest that the politics of *Chronicles* are in the end above all literary, the message once again the medium, this turns on a question of the aesthetic's temporal dimension, since Scott is wrestling with time itself as a critical arbiter of meaning.

The focus here is primarily on the half-decade between 1827 and 1831, which Killick and others position within a moment of generic emergence. By David Stewart's estimation, the 1820s 'saw a sharp rise in the publication of short fiction' that would continue through the 1830s.[17] The form's widespread popularity thus predated its nineteenth-century codification. Describing this environment, Penny Fielding has recently suggested that the Scottish novel underwent a rethink during the 1820s, which was symptomatic of an exhaustion of ideologies of improvement.[18] The rise of short fiction, certainly, was taking place in an era dominated by the end of the Napoleonic Wars, a period characterised by economic ructions. Angela Esterhammer finds a predominance of 'improvisation' and 'speculation' in texts from the middle of the decade;[19] and the contraction of the British fiction industry across 1825–26 seems to have focused intellectual soul-searching already characteristic of an experimental 1820s. Work by Alex Dick on the financial crash of 1825 emphasises the impact of 'the end of the wartime economy and the breakdown of the old monopoly trade networks', providing a major staging post in the evolution of British market capitalism which led Scott at least to a re-evaluation of the commercial nucleus of improvement.[20] Croftangry's reading of the disaster that has overtaken his old estate is apropos: its most recent proprietor had become financially overstretched, occasioning a hollow programme of improvements that are finally synonymous with 'decay' (p. 33). Improvement in its various forms was far from dead in these years. Yet just as Fredrik Jonsson traces disillusionment creeping into projections about the Highlands' improvability as the nineteenth century arrived, there are signs in the literary sphere in the 1820s that a core faith in improvement that had characterised the thrust of Enlightenment in Scotland was eroded.[21] The second *Edinburgh Review* remained the clearest expression of that residual persuasion, but its Whiggish optimism was having to contend with a massing of less sanguine views, as part of a wider sense of revision and possibility.

Hogg found in the short form an instrument for approaching 'both the *lights* and *shadows*' of improvement, a way to reflect on a long history of modernisation in his native Borders and in Scotland at large.[22] In the opening sequence of the supernatural tale 'Mary Burnet' from *The Shepherd's Calendar*, he offers a routinely artful explanation for his sources, culminating in the assertion, 'At all events, I pledge myself to relate nothing that has not been handed down to me by tradition.'[23] Yet Hogg is not content merely to report tradition or even to defend it against the process of improvement. Rather, he seeks to exploit the capacity of the modern literary marketplace to present all sides of the question. Short fictions, in this context, become units of cultural currency in a state of indefinite circulation that might, in turn, envelop the very dialectical urgency of improvement.

Questions of Perspective

The persona of a rustic traditionalist inadequately explains Hogg's relationship with the culture of improvement. In his 1803 'Journey through the Western Highlands and Islands of Scotland', Hogg exercises his trained agrarian eye on the landscape. 'The greatest part of it', he explains,

> is certainly calculated only for the rearing of this usefull animal [sheep]; yet there are still many places not stocked with them, or but very partially so. But as there is now such a number of enlightened farmers in the country and its neighbourhood, experience, the most effectual teacher, will soon convince the natives of their real interest.[24]

Confident in the ability of 'enlightened farmers' to demonstrate over time the 'real interest' of the Highland peoples, Hogg rehearses an archetypal improving vision here. The effect is heightened when we remember the importance of the Blackface and Cheviot breeds of sheep – with roots in Hogg's native region – in the Highland Clearances, then approaching their most brutal phase.[25] Indeed, this places his ensuing comment on the Duke of Gordon's lands into a sinister light: 'His Grace's lands are rather overstocked with poor people.'[26] Hogg's attitude to forced evictions in his youthful Highland journeys remains conflicted.[27] However, born and raised in one of the most agriculturally prosperous areas of Scotland, he is speaking from the outlook of an assertive farming culture, manifesting that culture's role as an architect of and model for improvements elsewhere. We must not lose sight of such perspectives in Hogg's work, which bears out the plurality and unevenness of improvement: sheep farming might be a useful application as far as Hogg was concerned, but that did not make improvement *per se* a benevolent force.

If improvement had major implications for a shepherd, it was also impacting the literary world, where a patronage system was giving way to a purer market economy.[28] The resulting deliberations in Hogg's short fictions tend to centre on his lifelong interest in the supernatural as an emblem of traditional culture, with belief itself positioned as a fundament worked upon by improvement. The supernatural occasionally functions as a language of resistance in Hogg, a sign of a 'past that refuses to be lost'.[29] Yet these works pull towards a more symmetrical relationship in which improvement and tradition are integrated components of a single social world, dialectical in the Hegelian sense of a unity of opposites. Anthony Jarrells describes a fractional critique in Hogg, in which 'Enlightenment history' is not rejected but rather incorporated into a complex sense of modernity that models the 'heterotemporal time of the tale': both provincial and cosmopolitan, traditional and improved.[30] Hogg's short fictions insist upon multiple perspectives on the supernatural, with a melange of credulous and sceptical positions set in motion to throw modernity's conflicts into relief. The supernatural functions in a variety of ways across Hogg's extensive output and what follows surveys a few germane, largely neglected examples. It is worth noting his dismissive use of the mode as a function of Highland culture in 'A Horrible Instance of the Effects of Clanship', where superstition offers an excuse for murder.[31] Also notable is the sceptical tone of pieces such as 'Nancy Chisholm', where intimations of the supernatural are a result of the limitations of the 'medical faculty'.[32] However, the readings here concern Hogg's Lowland territory and develop a sense of relativism, before suggesting that a turn to sociability and to literary form offers an endpoint. Frequently in isolation and certainly when read together, Hogg's tales prioritise a conversation above any one perspective within them.

'Robin Roole' demonstrates Hogg's juxtaposition of improvement and tradition at its most overtly adversarial and establishes the main parameters of the conflict in his work. The professed aim of the piece is reflected in the title of an alternate version, 'On the Separate Existence of the Soul', which was rejected by Blackwood in September 1831.[33] Hogg begins with a survey of historical theories on the subject, before moving on to an illustration of a particular position – this transition from general premise to anecdotal evidence is a characteristic pattern in these pieces. His basic contestation is that we possess an independent metaphysical essence which 'roams at large' during 'deep sleep, in trances, and all standings still of the corporeal functions'. Implicating the logic of 'fine fairy visions' in his reasoning, Hogg is working at an intersection of Christian theology, idealist philosophy and folk belief.[34] A year earlier the poem 'A Real Vision' had appeared in *Blackwood's*, in which Hogg wrote that scepticism might make children '*good*, | (As Bramah makes his pens with a machine,) | But never great'.[35] Complementing 'Robin Roole', this poem fears that scepticism and rationality, which are framed as the epistemological counterparts of modernity, reduce people to a state of hollow materiality. There are certainly reflections of Thomas Carlyle here, whose 'Signs of the Times' had appeared in the *Edinburgh Review* in 1829. Hogg takes Carlyle's vision of moral decline as centred on the primacy of the 'Mechanical' (systematic knowledge) over the 'Dynamical' (ideal truth) and inflects it towards his favoured territory of the supernatural, retaining Christian faith as a bedrock to his argument.[36] Indeed, as many commentators have noted, Christianity and folk belief habitually occupy the same canvas in Hogg, where the potential for heresy seems largely muted by a nod to tradition and an obvious good humour. Killick astutely suggests that it is their shared ability to 'act [. . .] powerfully on the imagination' that underpins this parallel sympathy in Hogg.[37]

The eponymous hero of 'Robin Roole' finds himself locked in intellectual opposition with his aristocratic landlord, 'Mr William Marsden, junior, of Gillianbrae'. Broadly conservative in outlook, Robin is nonetheless open to a gradual renegotiation of tradition, believing in 'the propriety of sticking by old established customs, and of improving these by degrees, leisurely and prudently'. In contrast, his young master is frenziedly immersed in the culture of improvement, his 'dashing education' having produced an unqualified obsession with the mechanisms of capitalism: 'circulating mediums, monopolies, debts, stocks and productions'. With the laird a disciple of political economy – 'he would cite Adam Smith, [David] Ricardo, and even went as high as Dr [Andrew] Coventry' – the tale revises the motif of fanaticism to describe the world of economic rather than religious discourse.[38] Indeed, the belligerent aristocratic orator reads as an almost cartoonish product of the 'mechanical' thought that Carlyle had claimed was dominant in modern institutions, which he described with the sinister appellation of 'hives'.[39]

The laird's impatience with Robin's challenges – he terms him variously 'a mere ninny' and an 'old fool' – combine with his dismissal of Scots 'jargon' to paint a picture of immoral, and indeed atheistic, patrician arrogance.[40] Though Robin is a shepherd rather than a tenant farmer, the episode nonetheless brings to mind Devine's work on class tensions in the agricultural world at this time, including 'tenants [who] were critical of the new methods on the grounds that they reflected the theoretical thinking of gentlemen amateurs rather than the practical approach of experienced farmers', such as Hogg.[41] It is also worth noting T. C. Smout's gloss on the link between aristocratic self-interest and the declarations of patriotism that were used to justify the pursuit of improvement in the late eighteenth century. John Barrell and Nigel Leask have both emphasised limitations to the aristocracy's role in agricultural improvement.[42] Yet 'the twin ideas that national enrichment was synonymous with patriotism, and that national enrichment was best attained by allowing the upper classes a free hand in the pursuit of wealth' are cogent here.[43] Certainly, although 'Robin Roole' is set 'in former days' – the narrator claiming to have recovered part of the story from 'Winkworth's Feudal Evidences' – its concerns are very much those of the relatively recent past, looking back across the golden age of improvement in Scotland that had begun in earnest in the 1760s.

Language, then, marks an irreconcilable boundary between improvement and tradition, opposites legible to one another only as 'jargon', whether in Robin's rural dialect or the laird's political economy, which is a litany of 'cleaning, altering and improving' that values the landscape only by the number of 'bolls per acre'. Robin is humiliated in front of 'the rest of the shepherds', who declare the young laird's agricultural theory 'logically proven', but logic will turn out to be an insufficient means of proof. When the laird comes into possession of his hereditary estate on the death of his father, what follows reads like a bleak condensation of changes wrought on the Scottish countryside in the name of improvement:

> The small farmers were all turned out; down went their houses and up went granaries, barns and thrashing mills in their place. Marshes were to drain, hedges to raise, and manures to frame, and a hundred things were all going on at once. The shepherds were all called from their flocks to join in the labours of the field, a thing that they were never used to, and took very ill.[44]

This snapshot records the fading of the cotter system and the continuing enclosure of the land, alongside large-scale farming techniques that contain early glimmers of industrialisation. Even the shepherds' customary role is overturned as they are pulled into this nightmarish vision, their pastoral guardianship (both literal and symbolic) disregarded in the pursuit of efficiency. Presiding over it all is the 'new master', who is 'exacting the most severe labour' from his subordinates.[45] As the narrative by which the Enlightenment conceptualised the transition towards commercial modernity, there remained a suggestion of teleological certainty to the unfolding of history as improvement. Yet the process had nonetheless to be energetically secured, reflecting a 'belief that progress [lay] in the exploitation of the advantages offered by a potentially rewarding environment'.[46] This emphasis on active intervention has gone completely into overdrive in the figure of the laird, who, seizing the occasion of his inheritance, is attempting to hotwire stadial history.

Though the laird is a gruelling taskmaster, the practical manifestations of his improving mania are actually a secondary consideration. In a demonstration of the breadth of improving discourse, the difference in opinion at the heart of the story sprawls into two antithetical visions of society. As Hogg writes, 'it went so far that they disputed about every thing; religion, law, politics, agriculture, and sheep farming'.[47] If Scott's *Chronicles* construes improvement as a debate over time, the issue is no less fundamental here. Returning to the patriotic question, this dispute is significantly couched in national terms. Robin's pride in being 'a free-born Scotsman' transforms his pious conservatism into an alternative paradigm for the nation, one that re-engages traditional culture in the face of an anglicised and sacrificial improvement.[48] Thus the story gestures to the implication of identity formations in the Scottish narrative of improvement, improvement linked with an anglicised North Britishness. In collaboration with its obvious class politics, the opposition of Robin and the laird – coded linguistically in Scots and standard English – suggests the pattern referred to by Phillipson and Mitchison, in which patriotic improvers were 'periodically unnerved by the nagging suspicion that improvement was being achieved at the cost of national identity'.[49] The imperial hegemony might require improvement to be a journey south, in an erosion of native culture. Much the same concern is applicable to Robin's conservation of rural piety from a class perspective: improvement is a threat to this cultural base on both vertical (class) and horizontal (nation) axes. The laird's insistence on theory over custom is a source of widespread antagonism, but it is the religious implications of his philosophical positivism that really disturb Robin, who accuses him of betraying his status as an 'example' to the lower classes with his 'blasphemous tenets'. As Hogg explains, the laird 'never ceased from casting obloquy on all Robin's exploded notions, as he called them, of religion'.[50] Condescending in his overwhelming adherence to reason, the laird is an embodiment of the dangers of an elite that puts its own contingent assumptions and the profit motive before all else.

Exasperated, Robin prays for a demonstration of divine power and is answered when the souls of the two men are transplanted into each other's bodies, offering proof 'that the body of man is but a frame, and his soul all in all'.[51] This of course negates the laird's entire worldview, not merely his prior insistence that such an occurrence was '*actively impossible*'.[52] Now possessed of the aristocrat's wealth and privilege, Robin is able to undo 'all the extravagant speculations in improvement' and return things to their previous state, with the result being that 'every virtuous person on the estate was cherished and rendered happy'.[53] It is at this point, however, that an interesting dilemma emerges. For although Robin and the laird's souls are now in occupation of different physical vessels, material conditions are seen to be crucial in shaping them, most dramatically in the case of the laird, whose new condition among the peasantry eventually moulds him into 'a humble and repentant sinner'.[54] The transplanting of subjectivities is a vivid means of evoking Adam Smith's social adhesive of 'sympathy', the ability to imagine oneself in another's place, which is employed here in correcting the laird's monological outlook. Yet despite Hogg's protestations about the separation of body and spirit – 'Let no man [. . .] suppose that the soul is an existence subordinate to the corporeal functions' – the inner being is clearly shaped by physical circumstances and the two spheres cannot perhaps be so readily abstracted.[55] If somewhat at odds with the premise of the tale, this element confirms the interpenetration of material and metaphysical realms found so often in Hogg, where the two planes are wildly imbricated, and further necessitates a socio-economic order that is sensitive to the more intangible aspects of existence with which it must be enmeshed.

Through the agency of the supernatural exchange, then, a process that borrows at least as much from the realm of folk belief as it does from Christian faith, the erroneous programme of improvements and the laird's underlying intellectual assumptions are exposed. There is a clear anti-capitalist charge to this fantasy, which also calls to mind the agency of storms in *The Shepherd's Calendar* – dictating 'the progress of improvement in Scots farming' – as the natural order reinscribes human efforts.[56] In this clearest indictment of hasty progress, Hogg demands that sufficient attention be paid to both cultural tradition and the numinous (inseparably bound up in the figure of Robin) or there may be dire consequences. And in fact, tied to the disgruntled insistence on respect that forms the ethical heart of the story, the reinjection of Robin's viewpoint into the commercialising world has a strangely prophetic character, anticipating the resilience of spiritual beliefs in many modern societies. Providing the climax to a tale of clashing views, the supernatural, Smithian exchange is a suggestive call for a plurality of vision, beginning to articulate a polyphonic treatment of improvement and tradition. Indeed, though Robin's position is finally validated, including his credulous view of the supernatural, it is noteworthy that he does not reject discourses of improvement outright, but favours instead a gradualist approach that is amenable to dialogue. Finally, though the tale delivers the supernatural in a relatively matter-of-fact style, its explicit servicing of a moral lesson slightly moots the question of authenticity. That lesson may be *about* the existence of the supernatural, but this utilitarian production of a tale unavoidably foregrounds the storytelling act, implying that other stories might as easily serve other conclusions. In that way, 'Robin Roole' reminds us of the instability of any message ('improving' or otherwise) in Hogg's fiction.

These philosophical tensions are developed in 'The Mysterious Bride' (1830), which introduces an enlarged sense of subjective contingency into Hogg's treatment of the supernatural. If 'Robin Roole' endorses a delicate balance between improvement and tradition, involving the acknowledgement and considered renegotiation of alternative viewpoints, this piece revels in the unstable coexistence of multiple perspectives. The tale opens with one of the most frequently quoted passages in Hogg, which condemns Walter Scott as a 'renegade' who is defaulting towards a culture of scepticism, his treatment of the supernatural watered down like a 'half-and-half' toddy. Hogg dismisses the incredulity that plagues society 'now-a-days', before a statement of personal experience: 'I wish they had been where I have often been', with the present story framed as a 'relation of facts that happened in my own remembrance'. The narrator thus calls upon both personal and collective memory to justify the supernatural tale, developing his identity as, variously, a witness of and spokesman for these events. Of course, this is nothing if not playful and the authenticating gesture is quickly undercut via a dig at Burns, whose 'best songs' were 'sung one hundred and fifty years before he was born'.[57] This may reinforce a greater wisdom implicit in the workings of tradition but clearly satirises the pose of authorial fidelity. The dynamic is typical of Hogg, offering us a variety of corroborating angles and proceeding to unevenly support and challenge them. The reader is thrown into a forum of heated debate, the author ventriloquising arguments until the story begins to embody a larger conversation.

Taking us back to 1777, the tale centres upon a roadway where the Laird of Birkendelly encounters his ghostly, possibly demonic paramour. Hogg informs us of the unusual layout of the route, which is flanked by 'two thorn hedges [. . .] so close, and so high, that a rabbit could not have escaped'.[58] The restricted passageway is a powerful symbol for the kind of intellectual certainty that the story at once conceives and discharges. Carelessly riding of an evening, the laird catches glimpses of a woman, who is intermittently lost among gaps in the perspective before disappearing. The impassable formation of the hedges ensures that she could not have exited into the surrounding fields and submits proof of the supernatural, though these moments of blindness raise a seed of doubt. In a dextrous irony, the unexpected appearance of the woman and her equivocal vanishings render even this most certain of paths a space for bewilderment and ambiguity. The road is linear but contains inconsistencies and blind spots, in a strong metaphor for the culture of improvement. Yet it is at the end of the tale that the figure of the road really comes into its own. An old woman of low social standing named Marion Haw arrives in the community and proceeds to explain the strange events of the laird's gruesome death via a lingering family curse. Her account is 'so plausibly correct, but withal so romantic', that it is deemed '*a made story*' by the locals. Hogg's emphasis on the phrase refashions the suggestion of a 'made-up' falsehood into a matter of epistemology.[59] Marion's tale is indeed 'made', that is to say constructed, as all knowledge must be, and the narrator introduces a subversive relativism to the question of whether her materials are rooted in empirical evidence, folk tradition or the creative workings of imagination (the Scots term for poet, 'makar', may be relevant here), all of which are capable of 'making' reality. In this context, the latter two options interact with an earlier mention of the Latin inscription on the laird's eerie engagement ring, 'Elegit', insinuating a consensual act in the workings of the supernatural.[60] And when read against the figure of the family curse, Hogg's probing stress on subjective belief ends up bound to a delicate question of fate: does one, after all, choose to love?

Claiming to have knowledge of the spot where a young lady was murdered long ago, Marion leads a party to the 'Birky Brow', a rise around which the spectre had appeared. In Marion's day there had been no road there, but as she comments, 'the hail kintra's altered now'. When a corpse is indeed dug up from 'deep, deep below the road', the mystery is apparently explained and the haunting exorcised.[61] A former laird is supposed to have murdered a 'Jane Ogilvie' in order to marry 'the great heiress of Birkendelly'. (In this way, 'The Mysterious Bride' reframes a discussion of death's universal reach – annihilating time, heedless of social class – in the poem immediately preceding it in its first appearance.)[62] Hinting at a sinister history involving a collective cover-up, the episode endorses Sarah Sharp's point that Hogg is not unequivocally celebratory of rural life. As she suggests, his work contains intimations of 'an underlying internal threat' in the memorialising function of folk culture.[63] Yet for our

purposes the symbolism is clear. Buried beneath the modern roadway, the community finds forbidden proof of the supernatural. The
location of the haunting illustrates the ability of cultural tradition to
evolve and adapt over time, the phantom effortlessly transitioning
into the framework of the improved countryside. That malleability is
also present in this 'traditional' story's obvious debt to the contemporary Gothic. And despite the revolutions of history, the supernatural remains urgent. If the sure perspective of the road had already
been shown to give way to doubt and the inexplicable, here below
the surface of this icon of modernisation, rotting bones are exhumed
to unravel stadialism and show that improvement can barely sup-
press, never mind eliminate, the 'facts' of traditional belief. That is,
if one should choose to believe.

'All that I choose to tell you is this'

The questions of perspective that structure 'Robin Roole' and 'The
Mysterious Bride' establish a judicial aspect to Hogg's engagement
with improvement and the supernatural. In a number of instances this
expresses itself in the literal motif of a trial. 'Story of Adam Scott'
(1830) is the tale of a Scottish drover who is attacked by two Englishmen when on his way back across the border laden with the proceeds
of a large sale. After the attempt on him fails, Adam finds himself
wrongfully accused of robbing and assaulting his assailants and must
stand trial in an unsympathetic English court at Carlisle.[64] The story
bears clear parallels to 'The Two Drovers' from Scott's *Chronicles*,
in which the Highland drover Robin Oig is embroiled in a culture
clash and ends up murdering his counterpart Harry Wakefield, who
is described as 'the model of Old England's merry yeomen' (p. 129).
Notably, however, where in Hogg's 'Story of Adam Scott' the Union
of 1707 is still recent history, Claire Lamont estimates that 'The Two
Drovers' takes place around the late 1780s.[65] Scott presents Robin as
a relatively improved Highlander, not entirely devoid of traditional
superstition but sufficiently so to find the farewell ceremony of the
'*deasil*' performed by his aunt an embarrassment. Still, the foresight
of this 'sybil' that Robin's dagger will draw English blood (pp. 127–8)
ends up playing a critical role in the murder – 'the recollection of the
fatal prophecy confirmed the deadly intention' (p. 138) – as Robin's

fatalistic side finds in the prediction encouragement, perhaps even licence, to act. Thus the residual presence of supernatural belief in 'The Two Drovers' can bring Robin only calamity once he sets out on his journey. Scott informs us that the Highland drovers 'avoid as much as possible the highways [. . .] and the turnpikes' (p. 124), but to reach the Yorkshire markets Robin must cross the great improved thoroughfares sooner or later, a journey that perverts the 'Taishataragh (second sight)' (p. 127) into a destructive anachronism.

In 'Story of Adam Scott', the supernatural retains a more benevolent power as a feature of Scottish culture, associated with the rural Borders rather than the Highlands. The innocent protagonist is helpless to defend himself within the English legal system until an elderly relative named Auntie Kitty dreams of the events of his misadventure and causes help to be sent. She enlists the efforts of one Thomas Linton on Adam's behalf, a 'very superstitious' man who declares, 'it was weel enough kend that the Englishers war a' grit leears', on his way to securing Adam's release.[66] English lying, then, is the discursive inverse of Auntie Kitty's dream, a vision to which Linton ascribes unconditional authenticity. The dream crosses the geopolitical distance between Carlisle jail and the fictional village of Kildouglas, arming Adam with a protective shield that no drove road can negate. Close social intimacy expressed in the supernatural thus brings its agency to bear upon both the xenophobia and institutional injustice suffered by Adam.

There is another implicit reversal of Enlightenment historiography here as the supernatural resolves a legal and economic crisis, resisting the hegemony of improvement to remain a meaningful competence in an atmosphere of cross-border suspicion. Pittock identifies Hogg's use of the supernatural with a Scottish 'threat', 'the violation of the expected in British space by remaining traces of the lost national other', and we might cite this as an example.[67] Still, it is interesting that the first printing of the piece in *Blackwood's* follows a lyric by Felicia Hemans about Highland emigration, 'We Return no More!', suggesting rather an elegiac perspective (if the reader proceeds serially).[68] Equally, we need to be careful not to overemphasise the national quality of the supernatural in Hogg, who is generally more interested in the local and the regional, though the places defined by the circulation of folk tradition (ageless, collective) must often be nebulously defined.

At the same time, for all this radical vision of supernatural forces that are horizontally aligned with the rational world, the tale also suggests the potential benefits accruing from the depersonalising effects of modernisation. Locked up in Carlisle at a period when, 'without a special messenger, there was no possibility of communication' to Scotland, the established mechanisms fail Adam as no one is prepared to 'go a message for him'.[69] Adam is saved by extraordinary means, but this insularity nonetheless challenges the assumption that material improvement is necessarily corrupting. The story tests a close-knit, empathic social model against the technological apparatus of the modernised present. The former's promise of community solidarity is able in this instance to extend across borders both figurative and literal, but the latter might yet offer a more reliable social framework.

Auntie Kitty's dream is the occasion for one of Hogg's most emphatic endings. Offering up the lesson of the tale, the narrator transitions from the events of the trial to state, 'Why should any body despise a dream, or any thing whatever in which one seriously believes?' Dreams are a recurring device in these short fictions, an emblem of a lively intercourse between material and metaphysical realms. In 'George Dobson's Expedition to Hell and The Souters of Selkirk', for example, the narrative runs fluidly in and out of apparent dream-states, with reality exposed as a function of perception, while Hogg again declares the 'distinct existence of the soul' in a similar manner to 'Robin Roole'.[70] Dreams end up positioned in a middle ground between normative reality and the realm of the supernatural in Hogg, a strategy captured in his titling of a section of *The Shepherd's Calendar* as 'Dreams and Apparitions': a revealing taxonomic decision that pulls towards a collapsing of the distinction between the two.[71] Indeed, Hogg's point about the separation of soul and body renders dreamers themselves a kind of temporary spectre. More than an expression of the subconscious, the dream is an access point into the ambivalent world of the numinous with which these tales are concerned.

It is the sense of subjectivity in the closing epithet to 'Story of Adam Scott' that particularly demands attention here, as Hogg's conditional handling of the supernatural reaches its apex. This is some distance from the concluding moral of 'Robin Roole'; didactic finality has been replaced by an open question. By enlisting the figure of the dream in his assertion of relativism, Hogg emphasises a fluid negotiation of perspectives, his stories passing through frames of reference as easily as waking up or falling asleep. Again dissolving stark binaries between reality and fantasy, and between the material and the metaphysical, these gestures serve to permit multiple viewpoints. Within this unstable context, if only 'one seriously believes' in something, then that must be taken as compelling evidence. The distinction between dreams and reality is contingent after all upon a set of phenomenological securities which may be unreliable. That said, 'serious belief' is a negotiable term. It might be possible to insist on a debt to Hume's epistemology here. Ian Duncan describes how

> Hume's case, that all representation is a fiction, a *poesis*, since all experience is mediated through the imagination, provides a stronger and more comprehensive theoretical base for fiction than any that had appeared hitherto, delivering it from the sentence of inauthenticity, of categorical opposition to reality.[72]

Hogg's discussion of the competence of belief does bear upon a form of this radical vision, which potentially threatens the hierarchy of reality and fantasy via the common mediating node of the imagination, as the place where all experience is constituted.[73] In Duncan's argument, Hume's intervention provides a vital theoretical underpinning to the enactment of modern, consensual modes of belief in, particularly, Scott's Waverley Novels.[74] However, the idea of an ironic condition of belief (e.g. the suspension of disbelief) does not quite do justice to the permissiveness of Hogg's attitude, or rather it is only part of the picture. 'Serious belief' as an authenticating category is capable of incorporating genuine or unsceptical belief alongside more ironic positions, all of which may constitute a valid engagement with cultural knowledge. In fact, often individually and certainly when taken as a series, Hogg's supernatural short fictions invite an even broader multiplicity of perspectives, in which doubt and outright denial are also present as acceptable, implicit responses to the author's proffering of the supernatural. John Plotz describes the effect as one of 'polydoxy', or 'the intersection of profoundly disjunctive belief systems within a single piece of fiction'.[75] Underpinning this gesture, I would suggest, is a stress on the community that is 'imagined' by this heterogeneity of opinions and sustained by the act of transmission, as well as on the vehicle of that process: short fiction. Hogg's relativism does destabilise normative truths, but this conversational register is finally more important. Hume had famously turned to society to mitigate against an existential crisis of scepticism, and a similar gesture remedies this moment of historical conflict for Hogg, for whom the culture of the tale is paramount.[76]

Sandwiched in the pages of *Blackwood's* between articles on parliamentary and financial reform, 'An Awfu' Leein'-Like Story' (1831) develops this position.[77] This tale centres on a question of inheritance, following the character Mr Sholto as he searches for a will that may restore his fortune, with the supernatural again bound up in economics. When Sholto encounters the grave of his uncle, a series of strange events leave his lower-class companion, Andrew, convinced that the buried man has risen again. As Hogg's stories go, this appears a fairly secure example of a sceptical mode: the reader is invited to see through Andrew's misconceptions towards the real, worldly explanation. However, Hogg's sign-off complicates the issue. The narrator begins by asserting the availability of an explanation that he is reluctant to divulge: 'Now this story is true, but again needs explanation. But is it not a pity to explain away so good and so ridiculous a story, which was most solemnly believed by the principal actor?' It would be a shame to 'explain away' the supernatural, 'solemn' belief constituted as a fragile, delicious contingency. Far short of the insistent relativity above regarding 'serious belief', there is nonetheless a desire here to preserve the enabling milieu of Andrew's conviction, even while it is contextualised as unwitting. The narrator continues,

> All that I choose to tell you is this: The young man who received the L.5000 was a surgeon and apothecary; the betrothed sweetheart, and shortly afterwards the husband, of Miss Sally Aymers, who, it will be remembered, was an offended girl of great shrewdness and activity. This is the main cue to the story; and after this, if any gentleman in Britain or her colonies (I except Ireland) will explain to me perfectly, how every circumstance was effected, I shall be in his debt for the best bowl of whisky-toddy ever was drunk. And if any lady do it, I shall be in hers for a song.[78]

Declining to conclusively settle the matter, Hogg's narrative voice passes the question on to his readership with a set of clues (Irish readers are excluded as part of the unmistakably Blackwoodian

flavour of this performance).[79] Killick notes that the 'various narrative frames' in Hogg's tales act to transfer 'the burden of the decision regarding [their] function and veracity [. . .] on to the reader',
and this moment is a vivid enactment of that handover, delivering
the puzzle to a public forum with an open invitation to socialise
with the author over whisky or a song.[80] The reward is ostensibly
geared towards a perceptive sceptic – albeit the supernatural here
is 'leein'-like' rather than emphatically false – but the act has larger
reverberations. Postulating a heterogeneous readership across these
supernatural fictions, Hogg's stress falls on a kinetic cultural process,
rather than the authentication of any particular worldview, unless
that worldview is one of heterogeneity itself.

The genre of the tale was involved in an attempt to confront (perhaps consume) its idealised oral antecedents. Hogg's breaking of the
fourth wall to present *Blackwood's* as radically dialogic might then
appear to magnify the echoes of orality in print. Yet Stewart enlarges
on the immediate context for this gesture in the periodical culture of
the 1820s, arguing that this competitive and heterogeneous marketplace tended to cultivate a 'spectacularized aesthetic' in which style
itself ('personality') became paramount. More specifically, he traces a
lineage of widely deployed conversational effects, which would reach
an apogee in the 'Noctes Ambrosianae' series in *Blackwood's*. For
Stewart, the virtual bar-room sociability in the 'Noctes' actually serves
to register the impossibility of a personal – never mind corporeal –
relationship to the reader, acknowledging the alienation between
magazines and their mass readerships.[81] Intimacy is performed as an
ironic joke which readers are invited to share. By 1830, indeed, such
'quizzing' material was old hat in *Blackwood's*. Working in this environment, Hogg refuses to shut down any of the possible responses
to the supernatural in 'An Awfu' Leein'-Like Story' and elsewhere,
conceiving as he does so a diverse, imagined community of readers,
with the commercial exchange of the literary marketplace serving
a discursive commerce. Readers collaborate in the construction of
meaning in any text, of course. But open questions in this context
are in the end largely rhetorical questions; the proffered dialogism of
short fiction is itself laden with self-parody. In general, the fact that
Hogg's tales are suffused with playful irony does not negate their discussion of improvement. To the contrary, the performative register
is critical in opening up the ideological distance between scepticism

and belief. Indeed, the literariness of Romantic short fiction does not negate its political capacity, but it does advertise rhetorical effect as a volatile commodity, redirecting the reader to consult the terms of the experience.

Hogg's short fictions project a sliding scale of ideological possibilities sustained at an important juncture in the process of modernisation, mapping as they do a mass readership at the end of the 1820s. They offer a sophisticated arbitration of history that confirms the author's dexterity in ventriloquising multiple positions across the dialectical field of improving discourse. Hogg bears out the fundamental plurality of improvement that has been underemphasised in contemporary critical debate, a plurality that was not limited to a range of views *on* improvement, but compassed different and potentially antagonistic forms *of* improvement, from gradualism to extreme change, from religion to sheep farming. Hogg's own faith in tradition in these later stories does not generally rule out a place for improvement – providing it is not at too heavy a moral or cultural cost – in another reminder of the complexities of the debate itself, which was never easily divisible into progressive and conservative camps. Instead, his fiction postulates the supernatural as an inbuilt excess to modernity, the two locked in a circular, iterative process that continually renegotiates their boundaries. This supports Penny Fielding's view that Hogg's interest in 'the incommensurable' is of a 'post-Enlightenment' character, a symptom of 'measurement and its limits'.[82] From this perspective, Hogg's jocular attack on Scott's work as being like a 'half-and-half' toddy ends up looking disingenuous, his own pluralistic approach to the supernatural upholding an entire range of positions. Drawing links to oral storytelling, Fielding observes that while Hogg invites 'the reader's participation [. . .] he or she is persuaded that any attempt to fix the story as either truth or fiction will prove futile'.[83] But it is not merely the truth-value but also this invitation that is self-consciously abridged. Such recognition was integral to Romantic periodicals and to *Blackwood's* especially, which proceeded upon 'irresolution' as a 'tantalising' commercial and aesthetic ploy.[84] And it is an overriding characteristic of Hogg's short fictions that they make the dialectics of improvement a topical expression of that tendency.

Hogg's tales exploit the dual capacity for thesis and enigma in Romantic short fiction, pinpointing only to subvert meaning. In doing so, they look to ensure that *Blackwood's* sustains or at least performs a discursive, iterative exchange, imagining its pages shared and moulded in the manner of a folktale, limiting the authority of any one viewpoint within an omnivorous public. Given that the act is premised upon the modern market economy, this might be a gloriously ironic means of challenging the hegemony of improvement from within, wielding the transactional medium of print against the dominant philosophy of scepticism. Yet the formal condition of the tale remains conspicuous. These items would have been immediately recognised by a large cross-section of readers at the outset of the 1830s as conventionally knowing performances. To observe this is not to diminish Hogg, who – as in Killick's description of 'Mary Burnet' as 'an anti-folktale' – is forever drawing attention to the alienation of modern print.[85] Mischievous Blackwoodian textuality does not dissolve the political, but it does insistently yoke any such effect to an aesthetic value judgement. The underlying question will always be: what is a short story worth? That is particularly unanswerable in a period when short fictions and the magazines they proliferated in were still working out their intermediate position in the literary field, somewhere in between newsprint and the novel.

Roads of Improvement

Reporting on the parish of Keir in Dumfriesshire in the first *Statistical Account*, the Revd James Wallace stated emphatically that 'The badness of our roads is a great bar to improvements of every kind.'[86] Roads are a key point of enquiry in the *Account*, nestling between 'Inns and ale houses' and 'Harbours' as the thirty-first item in the list of 'Queries' Sinclair 'had the honour of circulating among the Clergy of the Church of Scotland'.[87] Indeed, Harris and McKean describe 'the dramatic nature of road improvements in Scotland from the final third of the eighteenth century, and their crucial contribution to accelerating change in both the rural and manufacturing economies'.[88] Reflecting upon plans for a canal between Perth and Lochern, Sinclair explained that 'it is certainly a matter of great moment to open a communication, by means of goods roads and water carriage, to the inland parts of the county'. These lines of commerce were critical to a landscape 'only in the dawn of improvement'.[89] The construction of military roads in the Highlands established by Field Marshal George Wade in the 1720s and delegated to Major William Caulfield from 1740 certainly played a monumental role in the history of that region. Supporting the movement of goods and people, state power, culture, tourism and scientific endeavour, roads could be literal and figurative conduits of civilisation in the Highlands as elsewhere. Later, in the first decade of the nineteenth century, Henry Dundas would turn to roads and canals as the infrastructural answer to the problem of Highland emigration, attempting to manage the uneven work of commercial improvement by scoring lines of productivity on to the landscape.[90] Yet in his history of the military roads, William Taylor takes a familiar line in describing the opening of the 'closed book' of the Highlands, with consequences of local cultural 'disintegration'.[91]

There is a case to be made for the road as the dominant motif in Scott's *Chronicles*, embodying the flow of history as improvement. And just as the implied, extra dimension to a map of the military roads is time itself, *Chronicles* presents the Age of Improvement as a struggle over the understanding of time.[92] This works at a macroscopic level, in the passing of the old ways; at a more intimate level in individuals' relationships to time; and on a meta or self-referential level, reflecting upon fiction itself, an art form ostensibly bound to the sequential. For all prose's ability to challenge and disrupt time, to perform cycles and returns, one word must come after another. Still, as Stuart Sherman has shown, building on E. P. Thompson among others, an ambivalent formal relationship to linearity is a key source of meaning for the modern consciousness of text.[93] In contemplating the advance of improvement, the anatomy of the short form acts to clarify certain of the more disruptive energies in Scott's fiction.

To return to 'The Two Drovers' sequence: Scott's tale reaches its climax when Robin Oig is sentenced to death for the murder of his English companion Harry Wakefield. A disagreement over pasturage had escalated rapidly, largely as a result of the two men's different notions of what constitutes a fair fight. Robin, the judge explains, is deserving 'rather of our pity than our abhorrence', since 'he failed in his ignorance, and from mistaken notions of honour' (p. 146). Much of the tale turns on this final scene. The key question is the degree to which the fiction confirms the judge's view of the sombre necessity of Robin's punishment as a mechanism of the advance of civilisation (explicitly linking the Highlanders with 'North American Indians'), as mapped on to the north–south axis of the drove roads (p. 145). Having sunk his dagger in Harry's chest 'with such fatal certainty and force, that the hilt made a hollow sound against the breast-bone' (p. 141), Robin himself concedes the justice of his sentence, satisfied to 'give a life for the life I took' (p. 146). Yet W. J. Overton detects an element of bias laced by Scott into the judge's outlook, inviting us to question the outcome, while Seamus Cooney finds the fiction pulling towards cultural relativism, essaying 'two goods in conflict', though this is a subversive effect beyond Scott's control ('the tale triumphing over the teller').[94]

The initial dispute over pasture is an interesting premise. The tale carefully ensures that Robin is the wronged party. He acts generously at least until a sense of wounded honour – having 'secretly worshipped' (p. 139) his descent from Rob Roy, the 'Robin Hood' of 'Lochlomond' (p. 126) – compels him otherwise. Through the agency of an untrustworthy bailiff, Robin and Harry have both agreed to rent the same patch of ground, a transaction in which the land, overdetermined under excessive commercial pressure, dissolves the social bonds of the tale and brings the two adventuring business-men into conflict. Fielding's observations on ideological fracturing in the 1820s Scottish novel, which sees the land refusing its role as 'the substrate for the improvement of the future', are interesting here, though in this case the tension is largely over complexities inherent within improvement.[95] There is a degree of persistent ambiguity over whether this encounter should be understood as a sad inevitability – the land serving its proper function in a process of national *Bildung* that demands the sacrifice of Robin's residual manners – or something else. Are we to find the tragedy ineluctable or merely ideological? Or put differently, how inexorable, how 'objective' is its flow of narrative time? This effect is sharpened by the dual condition of the tale, in which the epigrammatic clarity of the moral (literally here, a verdict) is offset by the plasticity of the tale form as deployed by Scott: hedged by surrounding material, 'illustrative' rather than authoritative, 'a stone to the cairn' of Highland lore circulating in the literary marketplace and self-consciously beholden to the many hands of its 'gentle reader[ship]' (p. 124).

Scott's fiction has often been read as operating through sentimental pragmatism, in texts that flirt with historical controversy but that are resigned finally to what *Waverley* calls the 'real history' of the British present, with commercial improvement its most vital expression, whatever generous compromises moderation and (as Sarah Winter has recently argued) 'equity' may demand.[96] This tends to emphasise a reading of *Waverley* itself in which the novel borders on the condition of propaganda, having been published a year before the Battle of Waterloo, actively shoring up the imperial hegemony by offering a blueprint for unity in nostalgic regret. With the teleology of stadial history stiffening the *Bildungsroman*'s own developmental logic, Jacobitism or any other expression of historical alterity becomes a fatal attempt to deny time itself: 'the cause is lost for ever!'[97] On the other hand, critics have highlighted instabilities in the Waverley Novels, whether this is taken as subversion on Scott's part, a reflection on improvement as a vulnerable account of history, or an effect of the literary.[98] The Waverley Novels seem to have struck many readers in continental Europe as models of dissent, and if neither language nor reader can be counted upon, the very determinacy of history in Scott is also open to debate, primed as it is with chaos and accident.[99] Short fiction, I want to suggest, helps to frame Scott's approach to history and improvement as a question of form.

'The Highland Widow' sequence in *Chronicles* is presented as having been sourced from, 'Neither bard nor seannachie [. . .] nor monk nor hermit, the approved authorities for old traditions'. Rather, it comes via Donald MacLeish, a postilion traversing the improved roadways who served Croftangry's friend, Mrs Bethune Baliol, as a tour guide on her Highland travels (p. 67). This layering of literary distance – the story at best third-hand – establishes an indeterminate ground, and Donald is an intriguing medium for this unearthing of the history surrounding the roads. The postilion is an exemplary model of an individual adapting himself to the dialectics of improvement, since he combines a 'turn for legendary lore' with a 'knowing shrewdness belonging to his actual occupation' (p. 69). Journeying 'along General Wade's military road, which never or rarely condescends to turn aside from the steepest ascent' (p. 72), Donald is a font of local knowledge who compasses both the linear path of modernisation and the cyclical movement of memory, in a positive coexistence of improvement and tradition that is largely denied by the tale he tells. Indeed, he is reluctant to divulge the story of Elspat MacTavish, who is found sitting underneath an oak tree in her usual trancelike state, her presence both literally and symbolically 'aff the road' (p. 73), providing a reminder of the origins of this commercial thoroughfare in the history of war. Elspat, in other words, is the antithesis to Donald's comfortable mixed modernity.

As the tale proper unfolds, Donald/Baliol/Croftangry/Scott paints Elspat at the time of the events in question as having been 'quite unconscious of the great change which had taken place in the country'. Widow of a fearsome cateran or cattle raider, Elspat had become so isolated as to be living outside time; or rather, to be continuing in another modality of time, as a remnant from before 'the substitution of civil order for military violence' (p. 78). Infatuated with the old ways, she was able to see her son only in terms of his father, an expectation of generational contiguity that the experience of improvement had rendered absurd. 'The children of the mountains will be such as their fathers, until the mountains themselves shall be levelled with the strath' (p. 97), she insisted, not understanding – or refusing to understand – that improvement was reshaping the natural world just as profoundly as the human. Thus, to Elspat, the rule of law in modern commercial society remained merely 'words that frighten children', the 'tame and dishonoured life' it signified being the equivalent of a 'death-sleep of the soul' (pp. 82–3). Resolutely primitive, her 'selfish affection for her son [. . .] resembled the instinctive fondness of the animal race', the narrative voice explains, with Elspat stuck firmly in a world of 'legendary history' (p. 93) populated by the exploits of her husband and orchestrated by what E. P. Thompson calls 'older collective rhythms', which predate the advent of 'Recorded time' and the realm of the military roads.[100] Elspat spends much of the tale watching the road waiting for her son, unable to decipher what the roadway signifies, seeing in place of the march of commerce only a daydream of 'dark soldiers dressed in their native tartan' (p. 85). Even her reckoning of Christianity remains tied to a 'powerful race' of Catholic priests behaving like warlords, albeit her analysis of the transactional character of the religion – working by 'confession, alms, and penance' (p. 119) – also pricks at the conscience of a Protestant Britain in which exchange is now more important than honour.

When Elspat's condition propels her son into tragedy, Scott brings the question of time to a head. Hamish is comparatively pragmatic and has enlisted in one of the new Highland regiments, accepting that 'yesterday was yesterday' (p. 90).[101] Indeed, even the spirit of his desperado father MacTavish Mhor appears in the tale only to caution Hamish against Elspat's primitive fundamentalism (pp. 95–6). Elspat then attempts to prevent her son returning to his regiment in time by drugging him, in order to retain him in the condition of the unimproved figured as a hovel of 'wants and wretchedness' (p. 98). Believing that Hamish will not submit to the shameful punishment of whipping, she assumes that he will return not simply to the olden times but to 'olden time' (pp. 102–3), which she maintains in parallel to commercial modernity, rather than it being a supplanted phase on a stadial or linear trajectory of history. Deceived into missing his deadline, Hamish is thus lured into a different kind of 'death-sleep'. After he awakes and begins to panic, a passing minister is 'startled' to be approached by an armed Highlander and asked the time, but the family's liminal condition, divided across eras, has now resolved itself into tragedy. Hamish is late, appropriately having missed the Sabbath, which forms no part of Elspat's calendar, in which days are marked by the cycles of the sun as it returns to 'climb Ben Cruachan' (p. 100), a form of time that in the new era of improvement is equivalent to timelessness. Hamish, frozen to the spot, resolves to wait for his punishment. With the enormity of her crime beginning to dawn, Elspat goes 'wandering in the wilderness', 'seeking rather than shunning the most dangerous paths' (p. 104), so complete is now her separation from the civilised space of the great military roads. In this she highlights what Fielding calls the 'doubled spatiality' of those very roads, enlightened spaces that also bear witness to 'discontinuities and heretogeneities' in the national consciousness; or what Ruth Livesey describes as the 'halts, stops' and 'accidents' of a nation manifested by stage-coach journeys.[102] Hamish's enlistment in the British army remains legible to Elspat only as a betrayal, not simply of her but of an entire mode of life, which is signified by oral storytelling: 'I attended to the voice of *my* mother' (p. 90), she says. In this way, Hamish transgresses against the very medium of the tale, the son becoming a harbinger of literary modernity and the circulation of print. Thus, when the men arrive to take Hamish into custody as a deserter, Elspat's whispering in her son's ear to compel him to the act of murder – 'beware the scourge' (p. 109) – is a voice in his head from a different paradigm. Her influence on this fatal moment sees a flattening of past, present and future into 'the same moment of time' (p. 110), a phenomenon that threatens to entirely overwhelm the implicit history of improvement, cultural trauma arriving as an anomaly in the flow of time.[103]

If Elspat is a sign of orality, of the category of the tale within Scott's hybrid non-novel, then her victory is of a desolate kind. She succeeds in enforcing enough of the time-world of the tale upon Hamish for him to experience a cyclical return of his father's death, albeit this takes place within the improved realm of the regimental execution rather than the hillside skirmish. Elspat embodies the threat of an irreconcilable gulf at the threshold of modernity – the dialectics of improvement merely a byword for cultural obliteration – which points up the alienation of print and orality, forms able to brush against one another, even communicate imperfectly, but which remain fundamentally different. In the end, the authority of 'the worthy clergyman of Glenorquhy' reaches across the tale, a man whose 'reason acquiesced in the justice of [Hamish's] sentence', though he still 'mourned over the individual victim' (p. 116). And yet, if such bittersweet finality is rarely watertight in the Waverley Novels, the explicit recourse to the short form in *Chronicles* only amplifies the case. Cairns Craig notes of the series that, 'In every novel, and *between* the novels [. . .] the forward movement of progressive history is continually undone'.[104] *Chronicles* places this iterative undoing into overdrive, until the minister's estimation, or the act of judgement in 'The Two Drovers', become points in a cyclical journey, dubiously able to supplant what comes before and after. They are only acts of speech, after all, in fictions that accentuate the contingency of telling. It is notable that Scott resists settling the issue of Elspat's final disappearance. The text lends credence to the minister's view that the 'unhappy woman's instinct had taught her, as it directs various domestic animals, to withdraw herself', but allows the supernatural sufficient oxygen to remain in play. More abstractly, the generic baggage of prose fiction might confirm the inevitability of improvement here, as surely as the story of Elspat can only live in the progress of words – mass-produced, printed words – with each line of text a roadway of modernisation. But then, to the degree that the tale invokes the cyclic, the incommensurable and the timeless, it resists that effect, its sentences threatening eternal return. Like pastoral poetry, Romantic short fiction as a genre carries with it a superimposed temporality – linear and cyclical at once, (un)-improved – that enacts historical dialectic at its most tempestuous here. Where in Chapter 1 such a condition was potentially a means of historical mediation, 'The Highland Widow' makes the coexistence of the line and the circle an insoluble mess.

For Killick, *Chronicles* is another example of Scott's 'linear discourse' at work, the 'narrative preamble and multiple authorial personae, ensuring that the "traditions", when they finally emerge, are muffled by a weight of ponderous antiquarian logic'.[105] Yet this security of purpose is difficult to believe of a text that opens by highlighting the law of unintended consequences – 'human purposes, in the most trifling as well as the most important affairs, are liable to be controlled by the course of events' (p. 11) – as the structuring principle not only of improvement but also of literature. Indeed, it seems equally possible to interpret *Chronicles*'s literariness – characterised by what Frank Jordan calls 'proliferating ironies' – as insisting on a plurality of voices with little centralising perspective, if not engaging a sincere attachment to the unimproved, then at least insisting that the debate be had, again and again.[106] Perhaps this only means repeatedly hammering home the 'course of events', Elspat's animalistic madness to be condemned whenever the commodity of Scott's text is taken from the shelf, but the process is restive. This reflects not only the development of Scott's work in the 1820s, or his personal circumstances following 1825, but also the generic influence of Romantic short fiction. Orbiting around a Blackwoodian culture in which little could be said definitively and even that might not be taken seriously, the short form heaps pressure on what teleological and ideological certainty finds its way into Scott's novels. The chaos of history may disclose a deeper determinacy, but the context of short fiction with its emphasis on rhetorical questions leaves neither 'the course of events' nor their meaning secure.

Donald MacLeish's perambulations of the improved roadways disclose an experience of history in which 'destructive and disruptive arguments about the interpretation of tradition have themselves become a solidified, solidifying tradition'.[107] We are back, then, in the condition of Hogg's 'bowl of whisky-toddy', debating and deferring instances of the situated, plural discourse of improvement, with the literary marketplace serving a discursive commerce, Elspat and all she represents living on (however mutilated) in the medium of short fiction. That medium ensures that the story remains unsettled, not least because it underlines the act of telling in a slightly different way from the novel proper. Lower status and more openly commercial, short fiction augments the sense of storytelling as a practicality, a job, at the same time as the imprint of the tale marks the threshold of voice and text. The result is a form that amplifies the rhetorical ambivalence of 1820s historical fiction. In her reading of *Chronicles*, Alison Lumsden finds the 'disjunctions and dislocations' salvaged, if at all, only through the questionable agency of storytelling; while for Fielding, 'The Highland Widow' offers 'a bleak vision of circumstances in which storytelling is no longer possible'.[108] The tale does indeed goes to some lengths to problematise the condition of narrative, with improvement one of its principal topoi, but the contest is in the end less about the availability of story than its value. Croftangry pronounces himself 'in favour of the present age in many respects, but not in so far as it affords means for exercising the imagination, or exciting the interest which attaches to other times' (p. 53), and what exactly this ends up meaning is paramount.

The Picture of Menie Grey

Midway through *Chronicles*, during a segue towards the novella-length narrative 'The Surgeon's Daughter', we encounter another of the text's periodical self-evaluations. Croftangry's friend Fairscribe complains of the work-in-progress that 'you have brought in Highlanders into every story, as if you were going back again, *velis et remis*, into the old days of Jacobitism'. Constantly re-unearthing the disputed past, challenging the establishment of 'Kirk and State [. . .] as they were settled at the glorious Revolution', Croftangry's short fictions strike Fairscribe as a perverse 'tartan fever' that revels in violence (p. 154). 'There is too much fighting in history', he observes. 'It nourishes false notions of our being' (p. 152). In response, Croftangry explains that the present order is 'too well settled [. . .] to be affected by old remembrances, on which we look back as on the portraits of our ancestors, without recollecting, while we gaze on them, any of the feuds by which the originals were animated' (p. 154). Historical fiction, in other words, is memory attenuated into entertainment.

Fairscribe's criticisms turn out to be hollow, or at least narrow, in as much as he directs Croftangry to Indian subject matter, where he 'will find as much shooting and stabbing' (p. 155) without the same controversy. The imperial periphery, in other words, is sufficiently distant to neutralise anxieties around the spectacle of history as improvement. The exotic other is less inclined to switch from object to subject than its domestic counterpart. More specifically, Fairscribe points out a painting of his relation Menie Grey as source material, suffused with 'old stories' whom 'none living can be hurt by', both time and space collaborating to depoliticise narrative. Yet, for all Fairscribe's caveats, this 'hint that the original had been the heroine of a tale' (p. 156) brings the canvas vividly to life, the portrait moving in that sense between semantic paralysis and contagion.

Croftangry variously terms his project 'light literature' (p. 148) and 'the romance of real life' (p. 154), the former narrowing the category of entertainment, the latter gesturing at something more complex. Discussions of Scott's rendering of the past have long centred on the portrait of Edward Waverley and Fergus Mac-Ivor in his 1814 novelistic debut, a souvenir of war that radically modifies its subject. Hanging beneath the piece, even Edward's weapons, in action only a few pages earlier, are finally consigned to the status of artefacts, to be 'generally admired', as the history they signify shifts from the ontology of the verb to that of the noun.[109] This then is a possible outcome of the dialectical agency of improvement: progress encounters the primitive and reconstitutes it as romance, little more than picturesque dressing. Of course, it depends on a particular understanding of the aesthetic, regarding which Scott's fiction is unresolved. Lincoln observes that the historical romance 'offers to remedy (as reading experience) the loss it exposes as history', but what that parenthesis implies is negotiable.[110] Scott's work is shot through with dismissals of itself as frivolous nonsense – the introduction to *Chronicles* promises a 'mass of empty fiction' (p. 8) – but this conflicts against the suggested power of romance. This latter position incorporates Scott's justification of literature as a sociological tool, an argument that draws on conjectural historiography and is secured by his belief that 'The passions [. . .] are generally the same in all ranks and conditions, all countries and ages'.[111] More forcefully, Jane Millgate insists on a 'deeper immersion' in romance, which 'is not in competition with historical truth' but 'is the medium through which that truth is expressed'.[112] This prepares the ground for Duncan's assertion that Scott's fiction embraces the 'socially accepted illusion, that accommodates modern consciousness', sceptically accepting a world constituted in narrative.[113] There is a danger of both relativism and presentism there (Shakespeare offered similar insights), but the suspension of disbelief as a mechanism of social order does flag up a constructive role of the imagination we all recognise: not quite the triumph of romance over history, perhaps, but their collaboration.

By 1827 *Chronicles* is poking fun at 'modern romancers and novelists' who have exhausted the 'primitive habits and manners' of the Highlands, so that 'kilted Highlanders are found as frequently [. . .] on the shelves of a circulating library, as at a Caledonian ball'. The process of aestheticisation is complete, has in fact passed from tragedy into farce – certainly 'the market is forestalled' (pp. 123–4). *Chronicles* must be understood in this light. Take Elspat, for example, sitting silently beneath a huge oak tree to mourn the passing of an ancient culture. Mrs Baliol beholds her as an affecting, cryptic emblem of the past: Baliol describes 'gazing on this victim of guilt and calamity till I was ashamed' (p. 76). Fielding finds a darkly parodic imposition of 'literary taste' here, with Baliol reconstituting the widow in the language of John Home's *Douglas*.[114] If art offers itself as a means of salvaging something from the destructions of improvement, there is a latent possibility that the act of looking is a further lever of alienation, especially when suffused with the 'spectacularized aesthetic' characteristic of an 1820s periodical marketplace from which these fictions cannot be disembedded.[115] Eventually, the elderly Baliol herself comes to share something of Elspat's condition, in a text that threatens to make the aesthetic the only ontological condition available. She explains that she has always been either 'something too young' or 'a little too old', while the author Croftangry reconstructs her as 'some fairy, who cheated us by retaining the appearance of a mortal' (p. 64). Timeless, a store of tradition, Baliol is accessed in the terms of art, the text foregrounding her mystique as an explicitly literary effect, which provides the subject of flirtatious, winking repartee.

Later, with Croftangry concerned about his lack of knowledge of India before embarking on 'The Surgeon's Daughter', Fairscribe assures him 'you will tell us about them all the better that you know nothing of what you are saying' (p. 155). *Chronicles* is sending up its own narrative condition. All of this play takes on a particular shading in the context of shorter fiction, the gallery of a Highland widow, two drovers, Baliol, Croftangry, a surgeon's daughter and so on, all bound up in the form's interchange of epigrammatic clarity and spontaneity, iteratively enforced and undone, the instability of the Waverley Novels in microcosm. And though the 'green-grocer's stall' of *Chronicles* is sold as a novel, its explanation that this is in response to the unattractive economics of short fiction is consequential. Scott, as usual, is pointing to the craftsman's necessities, underscoring the texture of the artefact and the commodity throughout. In general terms, it is perhaps a function of the modern literary marketplace to put the formal currency of any statement self-consciously on trial. Pungently artificial, the 1820s tale certainly embraces the complexities of (re)producing tradition – as in Margaret Laidlaw's reported complaint that Scott had been killing the oral tradition with his folkloric research, revised by Edwin Muir as 'nail[ing] the singing tragedies down | In dumb letters under a name' – to achieve a refined, ironic self-consciousness.[116]

Chronicles ends by comparing fiction to a Paisley shawl (pp. 287–8) – substantially counterfeit, in other words – but like Fairscribe's quip about the advantages of ignorance, this also gestures at a more serious point about the gravity of the imagination. In the painting of Menie Grey, which had not 'attracted more than a passing look' from Croftangry until the insinuation of a tale, at which point it 'seemed to speak' (p. 156), Scott asks us to revisit the competence of the sign, which is understood significantly as a function of time. The portrait of Menie Grey is an inverse of the painting in *Waverley*: it is raw historical source material, rather than (or as well as) history made into art. Menie's image is a snapshot, static and removed from history, as dead as its original, but the receptive viewer activates it into historical motion, enables it to speak anew in the present. This potent sense of its temporality makes it a compelling metaphor for Scott's fiction and short fiction especially, the overt literariness of which does not default to 'uselessness'.

Menie's portrait inhabits a liminal condition, provisionally outside the flow of history, but capable of being threaded once again into our chronology. That, I think, is the way Scott asks us to conceive of the *Chronicles*: like a painting in dialogue with history.[117] Scott, indeed, peppers his writing with references to fine art that invite us to make this parallel. When describing the figure of Janet MacEvoy in *Chronicles*, for example, he quips that '[David] Wilkie, or [David] Allan, would have made a capital sketch of her' (p. 54). Again, the self-conscious insistence upon the condition of the artefact in Scott seems to take sustenance from the short-form units in *Chronicles* as elsewhere in the Waverley Novels, with these discrete, faux-antiquarian commodities particularly legible in that way. Scott's writing frequently directs this awareness towards an emblematic conception of the tale form. And in the historical portrait of Menie Grey as elsewhere, this gesture develops the link between rhetorical agency and temporality in his work. Visual artwork plausibly shares with short fiction a level of dexterity in frustrating the sequential and the linear: Scott encourages us to think about these forms as slices of culture that dip in and out of time itself.

In 1788 Joseph-Louis Lagrange published his *Mécanique analytique*, in which he develops an idea of time as a fourth dimension in addition to three-dimensional space. Time, crucially, is the implicit fourth dimension of the portrait of Menie Grey, which is waiting to be brought alive again – to be made present – on each viewing. That same condition is true of short fiction for Scott, as part of an interaction in his writing between the linear quality of text and the heterodox temporality of an image. Lincoln usefully observes that 'Scott distinguishes between "the picturesque in action and in scenery"'.[118] *Chronicles* constantly transitions between the registers of action and scenery, between movement and nominal stasis, just as it develops a tension between linear and cyclical forms of time that is inherent in the tale form, and indeed just as the text concerns itself above all with a dialogue between improvement and culture. Yet it is not simply that the text describes different ideas of time: it also presents short fiction as inhabiting them. Clearly the time-value of the aesthetic was current in the 1820s, in literary forms including the historical novel and the periodical magazine, a period when boom/bust capitalism was revealing commercial modernity itself as disconcertingly cyclical. Scott's adaptation of the tale in *Chronicles*, as emblematised in the portrait of Menie Grey, has a profound sense of temporal complexity. These tales are individual units of cultural currency circulating in the public sphere, each capable of representing the past and informing the present, developing and challenging the grand narrative of improvement, gesturing in multiple ways through time.

Scott thus couches the unstable rhetorical effect of short fiction – and historical fiction more broadly – as a question of time, *how* it speaks dependent on *when* it speaks. And in the end, for all his allusions to 'splendid uselessness',[119] the 'romance of real life' implies the imaginative shaping of reality *now* as much as it does realistic

escapism to *then*. Fairscribe's fears about the latent violence of historical fiction recognise the power (in temporal terms, the 'currency') of
the imaginative and the ideal, a conceptual space that literature after
all shares with politics, economics and history. Indeed, even if we insist
that fiction speaks only from a position of atemporal abstraction, Terry
Eagleton reminds us of the ideological potential, the 'natural' effect,
of that which has been 'uncouple[d] from history'.[120] In *Chronicles*
certainly, the tale's temporal ambivalence, repeatedly in and out of
history, linear and cyclical at once, is a sign of its rhetorical complexity. The text may never take itself entirely seriously, but it provides an
opportunity for creative movement within and against the revolutions
of Thompson's 'clock time', or improvement. The obsolete portrait of
Menie Grey has been moulded by time but the relationship is mutual:
the stories it tells are a wellspring of memory, the means to shape the
future by revisiting the past, or at the very least an intriguing commodity that complicates the present.

For Emily Rohrbach, the early nineteenth century sees an erosion of confidence in the predictability of the future, a point which
we might adapt to observe that in the short fictions of an uncertain 1820s, the long-standing dialectical plurality of improvement
is inflamed.[121] In Scott and Hogg's short fictional approaches to the
Scottish experience here – the former a partitioned non-novel, the
latter items in the *Blackwood's* textual economy – the complexity of
improvement emerges with a variety of emphases, but the literary
imagination is exploring its role in the negotiations that structure
history, its capacity to reinscribe the present. Menie Grey is distinguished by her purity and 'utmost simplicity' (p. 256) in a globalised
world of 'Ambition and Avarice' (p. 198). This marginal position
might stand for the degree to which Romantic short fiction plays
upon its own 'uselessness'. Still, like the *Chronicles* itself, the picture
of Menie Grey possesses a volatile temporal dimension that marks
a more complex set of rhetorical possibilities. It is part of the fascination of the tale form in this period that it draws such attention
to its own uncertainty and to the condition of literary narrative *per
se*. In that respect, Hogg and Scott both ask us to reflect on what a
rethinking of improvement in prose fiction might achieve ideologically. The material exigencies of history persist, of course. But then
improvement itself had always been a narrative, a framing and a
shaping of events much more than simple description.

Notes

1. Scott, *Chronicles*, p. 50. Further citations of this edition are given in parentheses in the main text.
2. On Scott and mail-coaches, see Livesey, *Stage Coach Nation*, pp. 28–55.
3. Thompson, 'Time, Work-Discipline, and Industrial Capitalism', p. 59.
4. See, for example, Stewart, *Romantic Magazines*; and Wheatley, *Romantic Feuds*.
5. See Plotz, 'Hogg and the Short Story'; and Jarrells, 'Provincializing Enlightenment'. Regarding Galt, Hewitt (ed.), *Galt: Observations and Conjectures*, is a case in point, featuring four essays on short fiction.
6. See Pritchett (ed.), *Oxford Book of Short Stories*, pp. xi–xii.
7. Killick, *British Short Fiction*, pp. 11–12.
8. Jarrells, 'Provincializing Enlightenment', p. 263; Killick, *British Short Fiction*, pp. 123, 155.
9. Killick, *British Short Fiction*, p. 154.
10. Ibid. pp. 124–5.
11. Both Walter Allen and V. S. Pritchett made this claim in 1981, with Pritchett sharing the title between 'The Two Drovers' and 'The Highland Widow'. See Allen, *The Short Story in English*, p. 9; and Pritchett (ed.), *Oxford Book of Short Stories*, p. xi.
12. For a concise summary of these events, see Lamont's notes to *Chronicles*, pp. 290–1.
13. For more on Scott as a writer of short fiction, see Scott, *The Shorter Fiction*, ed. Tulloch and King; and Lumsden, 'Scott and *Blackwood's*'.
14. See Lumsden, *Walter Scott and the Limits of Language*, p. 190.
15. See Fielding, *Writing and Orality*, pp. 101–2.
16. Stewart, 'Romantic Short Fiction', p. 83.
17. Ibid. p. 74.
18. Fielding, 'Earth and Stone', p. 166.
19. Esterhammer, '1824'.
20. Dick, 'Scott and the Financial Crash of 1825', para. 6. See also May, 'Horrors of My Tale', pp. 101–1; and McCracken-Flesher, '*Pro Matria Mori*', in particular p. 70.
21. Jonsson, *Enlightenment's Frontier*.
22. Hogg uses the expression in *The Three Perils of Woman*, p. 25. He is alluding to John Wilson's *Lights and Shadows of Scottish Life*.
23. Hogg, 'Mary Burnet', in *The Shepherd's Calendar*, pp. 200–22 (p. 200).
24. Hogg, *Highland Journeys*, p. 82.
25. On the influx of southern sheep breeds to the Highlands, see Richards, *Debating the Highland Clearances*, pp. 49–50.
26. Hogg, *Highland Journeys*, p. 82.

27. Ibid. pp. 36, 110.
28. See Alker and Nelson (eds), *James Hogg and the Literary Marketplace*.
29. Pittock, *Scottish and Irish*, p. 212.
30. Jarrells, 'Provincializing Enlightenment', pp. 269–70.
31. Hogg, 'A Horrible Instance of the Effects of Clanship', in *Contributions to Blackwood's*, ed. Richardson, vol. 2, pp. 132–44.
32. Hogg, 'Nancy Chisholm', in *Contributions to Blackwood's*, ed. Richardson, vol. 2, pp. 1–13 (p. 9).
33. Hogg, 'Robin Roole', in *Contributions to Blackwood's*, ed. Richardson, vol. 2, pp. 216–29. For the publication history, see Richardson's introduction, pp. xi–lvii (pp. xxiv–xxv).
34. Hogg, 'Robin Roole', pp. 216–17. Similar ideas are explored in Hogg's *The Pilgrims of the Sun*.
35. Hogg, 'A Real Vision', in *Contributions to Blackwood's*, ed. Richardson, vol. 2, pp. 121–5 (ll. 16–18).
36. See Carlyle, 'Signs of the Times', pp. 439–59.
37. Killick, *British Short Fiction*, p. 142.
38. Hogg, 'Robin Roole', p. 217.
39. Carlyle, 'Signs of the Times', p. 444.
40. Hogg, 'Robin Roole', pp. 217, 219, 224.
41. Devine, *The Transformation of Rural Scotland*, p. 66.
42. Barrell, *The Idea of Landscape*, pp. 65–6; Leask, *Robert Burns and Pastoral*, p. 32.
43. Smout, 'Problems of Nationalism', p. 19.
44. Hogg, 'Robin Roole', p. 218.
45. Ibid.
46. See the introduction to Phillipson and Mitchison (eds), *Scotland in the Age of Improvement*, pp. 1–4 (p. 4).
47. Hogg, 'Robin Roole', p. 218.
48. Ibid. p. 219.
49. Phillipson and Mitchison, 'Introduction', p. 4.
50. Hogg, 'Robin Roole', p. 219.
51. Ibid. p. 223.
52. Ibid. p. 219.
53. Ibid. p. 226.
54. Ibid. p. 228.
55. Hogg, 'Robin Roole', p. 229.
56. Hogg, 'Storms', in *The Shepherd's Calendar*, pp. 1–21 (p. 1).
57. Hogg, 'The Mysterious Bride', in *Contributions to Blackwood's*, ed. Richardson, vol. 2, pp. 155–67 (p. 155).
58. Ibid.
59. Ibid. pp. 166–7.

60. Ibid. p. 165.
61. Ibid. p. 167.
62. Ibid. See 'An Autumn Walk' by 'Delta' [David Macbeth Moir], in the December 1830 issue of *Blackwood's*.
63. Sharp, 'Hogg's Murder of Ravens', p. 31.
64. Hogg, 'Story of Adam Scott', in *Contributions to Blackwood's*, ed. Richardson, vol. 2, pp. 112–21.
65. See Lamont, notes to *Chronicles*, p. 429.
66. Hogg, 'Story of Adam Scott', pp. 119–20.
67. Pittock, *Scottish and Irish*, p. 215.
68. See Hemans, 'We Return no More!' in the July 1830 issue.
69. Hogg, 'Story of Adam Scott', p. 118. The piece following Hogg's is by William Mudford and critiques the practice of voting by proxy enjoyed by the British peerage, an innovation utterly baffling to 'the people of the island of Tongabatoo'. See 'The Silent Member, No. IV: Voting by Proxy'.
70. Hogg, 'George Dobson's Expedition to Hell and The Souters of Selkirk', in *The Shepherd's Calendar*, pp. 118–41 (p. 119).
71. See Hogg, *The Shepherd's Calendar*, p. 118.
72. Duncan, *Scott's Shadow*, p. 133.
73. See, for example, Hume, *Treatise of Human Nature*, pp. 82–3.
74. Duncan, *Scott's Shadow*, p. xii.
75. Plotz, 'Hogg and the Short Story', p. 115. See also Jason Marc Harris on Hogg's 'holistic structure of human imagination' (*Folklore and the Fantastic*, p. 125), and Meiko O'Halloran on a 'kaleidoscopic' quality (*Hogg and British Romanticism*, p. 6).
76. See the final stretches of Book 1 of Hume's *Treatise of Human Nature*, where the author, driven by the study of philosophy to 'fancy [him]self some strange uncouth monster' (p. 172), writes: 'I dine, I play a game of back-gammon, I converse, and am merry with my friends' (p. 175).
77. The articles in question are William Blackwood's own 'On Parliamentary Reform and the French Revolution, No. IX: Consequences of Reform' and 'Sir H. Parnell on Financial Reform' by 'A Bystander'.
78. Hogg, 'An Awfu' Leein'-Like Story', in *Contributions to Blackwood's*, ed. Richardson, vol. 2, pp. 202–16 (p. 216).
79. On *Blackwood's* and Ireland, see Roberts, 'The Only Irish Magazine'.
80. Killick, *British Short Fiction*, p. 138.
81. Stewart, *Romantic Magazines*, pp. 84, 131–50.
82. Fielding, *Scotland and the Fictions of Geography*, p. 184.
83. Fielding, *Writing and Orality*, p. 128.
84. Stewart, *Romantic Magazines*, pp. 204, 134.
85. Killick, *British Short Fiction*, p. 147.

86. See James Wallace, 'Parish of Keir', in Sinclair and Cowan (eds), *Statistical Account of Scotland, IV: Dumfriesshire*, pp. 257–64 (p. 261).

87. Sinclair, 'Introduction' and 'Analysis of the Statistical Account of a Parochial District', in Sinclair, Withrington and Grant (eds), *Statistical Account of Scotland, I: General*, pp. 1–3 (p. 1), pp. 4–6 (p. 5).

88. Harris and McKean, *The Scottish Town*, p. 110.

89. Sinclair, 'Remarks concerning the formation of a Navigable Canal, betwixt Perth and Lochern', in *Statistical Account of Scotland, I: General*, pp. 350–2 (pp. 350–1).

90. Jonsson, *Enlightenment's Frontier*, p. 234.

91. Taylor, *Military Roads*, p. 128.

92. Ibid. p. 9, for just such a map.

93. See Sherman, *Telling Time*, for example pp. x–xi.

94. Overton, 'Scott, the Short Story and History', p. 220; Cooney, 'Scott and Cultural Relativism', pp. 7, 9.

95. Fielding, 'Earth and Stone', p. 166.

96. Scott, *Waverley*, p. 283. See Winter, 'Scottish Enlightenment Concepts of Equity', pp. 258–60.

97. Scott, *Redgauntlet*, p. 396. David Daiches describes 'the inevitability of a drab but necessary progress' ('Scott's Achievement', p. 36); Tom Nairn reflects that 'the purpose of [Scott's] unmatched evocation of a national past is never to revive it' (*Break-Up of Britain*, p. 115); and for Pittock, Scott's 'past may be magnificent, but it is over' ('Introduction: Scott and the European Nationalities Question', in Pittock (ed.), *The Reception of Sir Walter Scott in Europe*, pp. 1–10 (p. 2)).

98. For example, Julian Meldon D'Arcy (overzealously) portrays the Waverley Novels as carriers of 'dissonant' nationalist meaning (*Subversive Scott*, pp. 73, 29); Duncan finds in *Rob Roy* (1817) the revelation that 'savagery and commerce sustain rather than cancel one another' (*Scott's Shadow*, p. 110); and Alison Lumsden explores 'the complexities and suggestive potentialities of communication' (*Walter Scott and the Limits of Language*, p. 3).

99. Pittock, *Scottish and Irish*, pp. 189–90. Evan Gottlieb spoke at the University of Glasgow in May 2018 on the subject of 'Scott's Plots and Meillassoux's Contingencies: Unbinding the Waverley Novels from Historical Necessity'.

100. Thompson, 'Time, Work-Discipline, and Industrial Capitalism', p. 67.

101. See MacKillop, *More Fruitful than the Soil*, for the evolution of Highland military culture during the period.

102. Fielding, *Scotland and the Fictions of Geography*, p. 86; and Livesey, *Stage Coach Nation*, p. 30.

103. See May, 'Horrors of My Tale', for more on trauma in Scott.

104. Craig, *Out of History*, p. 70.

105. Killick, *British Short Fiction*, p. 125.

106. Jordan, 'Chrystal Croftangry', p. 192.

107. Trumpener, *Bardic Nationalism*, pp. 123–4.

108. Lumsden, *Walter Scott and the Limits of Language*, pp. 180, 193; and Fielding, *Writing and Orality*, p. 110.

109. Scott, *Waverley*, p. 338.

110. Lincoln, *Scott and Modernity*, p. 23.

111. Scott, *Ivanhoe*, p. 19.

112. Millgate, *Making of the Novelist*, pp. 35, 40.

113. Duncan, *Scott's Shadow*, p. 260. See also Lee, *Nationalism and Irony*, p. 24.

114. Fielding, *Writing and Orality*, p. 114.

115. Stewart, *Romantic Magazines*, p. 84.

116. Hogg, *Familiar Anecdotes*, pp. 124–5; Muir, 'Complaint of the Dying Peasantry', in *Selected Poems*, p. 76 (ll. 9–12).

117. Compare, here, Wickman on Scott's fiction inhabiting geometrical metaphors, shapes which comprehend time as a key term (*Literature After Euclid*, pp. 59–62).

118. Lincoln, *Scott and Modernity*, p. 24.

119. Scott, *Guy Mannering*, p. 302. The phrase recalls Kant's 1781 definition of 'beauty' as 'purposiveness [. . .] without representation of an end' (*Critique of the Power of Judgment*, p. 120).

120. Eagleton, *Ideology: An Introduction*, p. 59.

121. See Rohrbach, *Modernity's Mist*, in particular pp. 28–57.

Chapter 3

'The Great Moral Object' in Joanna Baillie's Drama

In February 1804 Joanna Baillie wrote to the Edinburgh clerk and musical enthusiast George Thomson, responding to a request for song lyrics. Thomson had by then been engaged in editing his *Select Collection* series for over a decade. These elegant volumes of national melodies featured arrangements by composers of the stature of Haydn, while Thomson drew on a variety of literary talent in an attempt to dignify a folk tradition he considered plagued by 'doggrel' and the 'loose and indelicate'.[1] The series was distinguished primarily by an extensive body of material submitted by Robert Burns before the poet's untimely death in 1796. Reflecting this pedigree, Baillie's letter strikes a patriotic chord. 'Sir,' she writes,

> I received your polite letter about a week ago, along with that from my friend Miss Millar. I am always ready to agree to whatever she wishes; but independently of this, to the Friend of Burns and my own countryman, it is impossible to refuse, in such a work as you are engaged in, any little assistance that I am able to give.[2]

Thomson's remodelling of the native song traditions of Scotland, Wales and Ireland for a genteel audience was constituted as a labour of polite cultural reform and is thus another example of the period's improving milieu. Indeed, more remains to be learned from his collaborative literary-musical network, which was positioned on fault lines between folk and polite culture, tradition and improvement.[3] Certainly Baillie's involvement in the coterie of authors enlisted by Thomson signals not only her prominence in the early nineteenth-century literary field, but also her agency as a canon-maker, a distinguished virtuoso recruited to transform the cultural heritage. It also involves her recognition as a Scottish writer. More of Baillie's lyrics would end up in Thomson's Welsh than his Scottish collections, but the letter above is just one of many examples throughout Baillie's writing of the national identity that she maintained despite a permanent move to England as a young woman in 1784.[4] That said, as a playwright writing primarily for the London stage from her home in Hampstead, she does put critical pressure on a category such as 'Scottish Romanticism'.

Baillie's lyrics for Thomson are another artefact in the cultural negotiation of improvement. This chapter, however, focuses on the main body of her work encompassing drama and dramatic theory, arguing that this material sustains a distinctive engagement with the dialectics of improvement. Baillie achieved a reputation as the foremost British playwright of her generation while offering what she described as a 'noble design' for an innovative drama focused unerringly on a 'great moral object'.[5] She sought to refashion the culture of theatrical entertainment in counter-revolutionary Britain into a mechanism of didactic moral instruction. In Chapter 1, poetry emerged as a potential source of moral and cultural renewal working alongside the trajectory of commercial modernisation, while Chapter 2 stressed the protean rhetorical effect of short fiction in reconsidering improvement's complications. The handling of improvement in Baillie results in an emphatically instrumental model of the aesthetic, with the drama itself positioned as a clear source of moral improvement, a way of tackling a range of human failings present in modern as well as 'primitive' societies. At its heart, then, her dramaturgy negotiates the ethics of the theatre and its potential as an edifying as much as an entertaining space. Baillie is unconvinced by the existing, dominant paradigms of improvement: she counteracts both commercial modernisation and cultural politeness to offer up her own, corrective moral trajectory. We are flawed, this suggests, and society exists in motion – perhaps the theatre can offer a benevolent nudge. Ultimately, however, Baillie's work is characterised by a curious mixture of entrepreneurial optimism and disillusioned social critique, the latter of which threatens to dampen the instrumental outcome. At the same time, she wrestles with a formal tension in the performative spectacle of theatre: would staging immorality have the desired moral effect, or steal the show? For all the verve of Baillie's aim to 'improve the mode of [. . .] instruction, and point to more useful lessons' in the theatre, her writing exhibits the difficulty in maintaining a stable vision of improvement.[6]

This is the first major study in Scottish Romanticism to devote substantial space to Baillie, but there is now a rich critical literature on her drama, indicative of the strength of revisionist approaches in the last few decades to both women's writing and theatre in the Romantic period. The feminist criticism of Anne Mellor and Catherine Burroughs has generated a major arterial of this field, complemented by, for example, Michael Gamer's work on Baillie and the Gothic, or Jeffrey Cox's path-breaking historicisation of her plays.[7] Much of the existing work on Baillie is relatable to improving concerns as we will see, but there has yet to be a study that explicitly draws attention to the pluralistic culture of improvement. Baillie's work is particularly susceptible to such an approach, in large part as a result of her view that 'the theatre is a school in which much good or evil may be learned'.[8] This chapter begins with a new perspective on the concept of 'sympathetick curiosity' as the structuring principle of Baillie's work, the basic motor of improvement for both characters and audience. It then reads *Count Basil* (1798) as an example of Baillie's dialectical handling of improvement and a key to her aesthetic politics. This is developed in the following section by a study of *The Family Legend* (1810) that constellates Baillie's management of 'primitive' history in relation to works by Scott and Elizabeth Hamilton. The chapter closes with a discussion of *The Alienated Manor* (1836), Baillie's comedic indictment of modern Britain and her most explicit treatment of improvement as a conflicted and dangerous notion that needed to be recalibrated on behalf of society at large.

'The Drama improves us'

The 'Introductory Discourse' Baillie prefixed to the 1798 first volume of her *Plays on the Passions* is by turns a literary apology, a conjectural history, an aesthetic treatise and an advertising pitch. An author's own theoretical companion to their work is an irresistible source from a critical point of view. Yet Baillie herself highlights a potential mismatch between her plays and her theory:

To conceive the great moral object and outline of a story; to people it with various characters, under the influence of various passions; and to strike out circumstances and situations calculated to call them into action, is a very different employment of the mind from calmly considering those propensities of our nature, to which dramatick writings are most powerfully addressed, and taking a general view upon those principles of the works of preceding authours.[9]

This point about the alienation of theory from practice is of extra salience in the context of drama – where text itself is only a starting point – even if not all of Baillie's works were performed or even intended to be.[10] Nevertheless, the 'great moral object' of the *Passions* series delineated in the 'Introductory Discourse' is an illuminating foundation. Baillie's comment about 'various passions' is slightly misleading, in that the design of each *Passions* play is intended to facilitate the exposition of a single passion – love, hatred, etc. These become legible as archetypal emotional (con)texts, which Baillie wants to develop with a scientific clarity of purpose in order to effect moral improvement. Tragedy, it emerges, is the genre best suited to this agenda – 'fitted to produce stronger moral effect' – because it allows a more unswerving fixation on 'the human mind under the dominion of those strong and fixed passions'.[11]

The 'Discourse' introduces the concept of 'sympathetick curiosity', Baillie's adaptation of eighteenth-century theories of human nature and the mechanism of spectatorship that she argues facilitates her improving drama. Naturally the term has received a good deal of attention in relation to 'sympathy' in Adam Smith, the imaginative, socialising process by which we understand one another. Yet Barbara Judson is among readers who discern a tension inaugurated by Baillie's conjoining of Smithian sympathy with 'curiosity', which introduces an element of voyeurism, titillation and even cruelty into the mix.[12] Baillie, indeed, emphasises the darkness inherent to the process in the conjectural history she provides in the 'Discourse', which explores a collective fascination with suffering (she uses an example of 'the savages of America [. . .] sacrificing their prisoners of war' to prove our 'universal desire' to pay witness to stoic fortitude in extremity).[13] There is thus a note of moral unquiet to the experience of the drama that puts pressure on its supposedly remedial power. At the same time, this 'primitive' basis for spectatorship forces Baillie's didactic drama to negotiate what Victoria Myers calls a 'paradox of primitivism as progressivism', enlisting the unimproved other in the workings of improvement.[14] Or, put differently, improvement moves dialectically, revisiting in order to supplant its origins.

Pressing further on the context for sympathetick curiosity in the 1790s theatre, we might note the economic resonances of the term 'curiosity', which was a keyword in the evolution of tourist and consumer culture.[15] Aileen Forbes argues that curiosity generates a force of '*anti*pathy', in a shift from commonality to individuality that marks the rise of Romantic subjectivity.[16] And if Baillie's work repurposes Smithian sympathy for the Romantic-era entertainment business, it serves a context where, in Andrea Henderson's terms, 'feeling' could be sold as 'an abstract form of wealth'.[17] In fact, Julie Murray claims that 'Baillie accomplishes what Smith himself cannot, by accommodating his moral philosophy to the exigencies of economic man'.[18] Baillie, this implies, completes the project of the eighteenth-century Science of Man by closing the gap between Smith's *Theory of Moral Sentiments* (social sympathy) and *The Wealth of Nations* (individual avarice). Of course, even were such a claim plausible, we should remember that sympathy itself arises out of a complex form of self-interest for Smith – effective, as Murray notes, only insofar as we can imagine *ourselves* into an external situation. In that respect, perhaps the Science of Man was not so incomplete after all. Nonetheless, Murray demonstrates that sympathetick curiosity accommodates a dangerous, 'ungoverned' desire that lurks in 'economic man' in a way that sympathy cannot.[19] Smith, indeed, insists on the necessity of 'flatten[ing]' emotion to an acceptable 'pitch' in concord with one's spectators, so as to avoid eliciting only disgust; curiosity significantly opens the door to fascination as a response.[20] Fundamentally pliant to appetite, curiosity is ideally suited to a consumer society where theatregoers can pay to exercise it in a conducive environment. Baillie thus embraces affect, though the theatre may defuse some of the more 'ungoverned' aspects of this exchange via the recognition of aesthetic distance.[21] Working in the tradition of Smith, Baillie does present sympathetick curiosity as a means of self-control.[22] Still, a threat of contagious, unmoderated passion stalks the boards of her work, significant in the context of a theatrical culture beholden to 'frequent interruptions from the audience that could range from friendly responses to riots'.[23] Moral theatre is supposed to discipline our sympathetick curiosity – and thus our passion – but might it not simply indulge it?

What all of this suggests is that there is a dialectical tension within sympathetick curiosity, the supposed toolkit and medium of Baillie's drama. We are invited to experience the edifying potential of her plays through a negotiation of sympathy and curiosity, which is legible in struggles between our sociability and individuality, our empathy and self-interest, our morality and avarice – even between our modern selves and more primitive urges. Describing how this process generates a moral theatre, Baillie explains that 'The Drama improves us by the knowledge we acquire of our own minds, from the natural desire we have to look into the thoughts, and observe the behaviour of others.'[24] The drama is a means for us to learn about ourselves and about humankind more generally in order to discipline our passions, with a basic interplay between self and other perhaps the most fundamental of the dualities upon which the exercise of sympathetick curiosity rests. Baillie describes the theatre as the ideal locus for moral improvement, due to the licence it grants to indulge sympathetick curiosity in the act of spectatorship, combined with the artificially precise demonstration of human struggle – and thus 'strong and fixed passions' – that a staged fiction admits. Indeed she declares that, 'Formed as we are with these sympathetick propensities in regard to our own species, it is not at all wonderful that theatrical exhibition has become the grand and favourite amusement of every nation into which it has been introduced.'[25] Put simply, the theatre is where we can indulge most powerfully in the full gamut of the human condition. And since it is the basis for all social interaction, sympathetick curiosity is not limited to the act of theatrical spectatorship in Baillie's worldview but also informs the internal workings of her plays, which pose varyingly successful historical encounters. We can exercise our sympathetick curiosity as an audience, in other words, but this dialectical quality of human nature is also inevitably at work within the drama. It governs social interactions at the local level and is also reflected in fraught, macroscopic narratives of improvement, which are reflections at the societal scale of a universal process of becoming that Baillie hopes to redirect.

Baillie's critique of the dangers of the 'stronger passions' targets the modern as much as the primitive, reaching towards a corrective path of moral improvement which idealises simplicity as a core value.[26] As we have seen, 'simplicity' was a fashionable element of the Romantic milieu, celebrated in pastoral poetry as in the picturesque, offering a watchword for dialectical moderation between polite and rustic absolutes in the culture of improvement. In developing its 'simple' ideal, Baillie's work inhabits the logic of improvement as a process of careful reform that remains in close dialogue with its targets. Baillie's central intervention, after all, enlists the commercial theatre in an attempt to purify the ascendant bourgeois hegemony (she considers the 'lowest classes' as substantially beyond the reach of the theatre's 'lessons').[27] To that point, Henderson reads Baillie in a 'dual relation to consumerism', her 'resistance' unable to 'hide the extent to which her project and her understanding of human nature are shaped by its logic', certainly a cogent point in light of the collectable quality of the *Passions* series.[28] Dissecting a range of cultural-historical mores in a popular art form that is highly critical of its own moment, Baillie's emphasis on moral improvement thus plays out the contours of sympathetick curiosity, the improving benefits of which derive from its fulsome engagement with our flawed natures. Still, wholesale pessimism, or even a fascination with the darker sides of humanity, occasionally seem more likely responses than moral learning to these plays that contain a more equivocal view of improvement in general, seeming intermittently unconvinced by either its desirability or plausibility.

Jeffrey Cox situates Baillie as a theatrical innovator with a counter-revolutionary agenda, a writer 'who desired to free the British theatre from the controlling aristocratic dramatic tradition that stretched back to Beaumont and Fletcher but who worried about the people in the theatre'.[29] It is certainly worth reminding ourselves that when the first volume of the *Plays on the Passions* appeared in 1798, Britain was five years into an exhausting war against revolutionary France and under a legitimate threat of invasion, a year that also saw the outbreak of rebellion in Ireland. It is not difficult to draw lines between this climate and Baillie's brand of moral improvement, with its fears about passion.[30] Suggestions in Baillie of a more hesitant attitude towards improvement *per se* should also be understood within this context – innovation and improvement, after all, were perceived to be among the forces driving revolution, even if events in France were considered by mainstream British opinion in 1798 as a lesson in uncivilised chaos as much as progressivism. In this environment, as Baillie imagines history in her early play

Count Basil, the 'great moral object' of her work emerges somewhat gingerly.

Count Basil's Tragic Dialectic

The opening stage direction of *Count Basil: A Tragedy*, one of the triptych of plays in the first volume of the *Passions* series, informs us of '*An Open Street, crouded with People, who seem to be waiting in expectation of some Show.*'[31] This metafictional device serves to confirm Baillie's commitment to the project of sympathetick curiosity, transplanting her audience on to the streets of sixteenth-century Mantua to await the ensuing course of entertainment as instruction. As the setting indicates, the play is an homage to Shakespeare's *Romeo and Juliet* and provides the tragic exploration of love in the volume, counterpointed by a comic treatment of the same in *The Tryal* (Baillie's tragedy on hatred, *De Monfort*, completes the set). The 'pair of star-cross'd lovers' in question are the titular Basil, a military general, and Victoria, daughter of the Duke of Mantua. Passing to the front with his troops, Basil is distracted by Victoria's romantic attentions and is drawn into a painful existential struggle between his duty as a soldier and his feelings for her. Eventually considering himself to have betrayed his men, he commits suicide. This is much to the disappointment of the precocious Victoria, who has been inadvertently furthering her father's machinations all along, by keeping Basil in the domestic drama of the city and away from the theatre of war.

Populating the playhouse metaphor of the '*Open Street*', then, we await the arrival of Victoria's 'grand procession' which will encounter Basil's own 'warlike' pageant.[32] In the meantime, the character of Geoffry, '*an old Soldier, very much maimed in the Wars*' to the tune of a missing arm, provides a kind of mirror-image of the main plot. He recalls with obvious sexual excitement how his 'good service' was once rewarded by 'a mark of favour' from the prince's 'fair consort'.[33] Geoffry is a sentimental bulwark to the war dimension of *Basil*, evidence of a steadfast but humane masculinity that Basil himself cannot sustain. In this memory, he had briefly left the habitus of war, but – crucially – remained safely in the realm of comedy rather than tragedy, since his desire was platonic or at least secure from consummation (he received merely 'a gracious smile').[34] For Basil, however, things are not so simple. It falls to Gauriecio, subordinate to the scheming Duke, to outline Basil's character as it exists before his encounter with Victoria:

> He is a man, whose sense of right and wrong
> To such a high romantic pitch is wound,
> And all so hot and fiery in his nature,
> The slightest hint, as tho' you did suppose
> Baseness and treach'ry in him, so he'll deem it,
> Would be to rouse a flame that might destroy.[35]

This might be acceptable – useful, even – on a battlefield, but it is quixotic in Mantua. Once sent into a tailspin by Victoria, Basil's 'high romantic pitch' can only resolve itself in a disgraceful death, since heroism and 'baseness' are his only options. Love in the city, it seems, is more complicated than war. The effect of love on Basil is thus an immediate experience of self-doubt ('Yes, I believe – I think – I know not well–') that marks the profound loss of social capital he incurs by exiting his enabling milieu.[36]

For her part, Victoria arrives infatuated with her power over men, her ability to 'put a bridle in the lion's mouth, | And lead him forth as a domestick cur'.[37] She too is preoccupied by the act of conquest, but her provocative behaviour contrasts with Basil's sincerity. As Burroughs puts it, 'Unlike the princess, Basil has not yet learned to distinguish between acting an identity and being it'.[38] This aspect of Victoria's character identifies performance with youthful femininity and with her urban realm. It echoes through the play in the outbursts of Count Rosinberg, who describes her as an 'artful woman' and rails against 'women, and their artful snares'.[39] Equally, the Countess Albini remonstrates with Victoria for delighting in an 'ideal tyranny', advising her to build self-efficacy rather than depend on 'unreal' and 'childish pow'r'.[40] Rosinberg's specific use of the term 'arts' is interesting, invoking a lexicon of witchcraft to disparage female power (Basil is 'bewitch'd'), but also the improvement of the polite arts that Victoria embodies as a counterpoint to Basil.[41] In the historical schematic threading its way through Baillie's drama, Victoria is, crucially, polite. The dynamic recurs in *De Monfort*, where the titular character's emotional immaturity encounters and is consumed by the playful duplicity of his antithesis Rezenvelt, whose upward social mobility explicitly designates his behaviour as bourgeois.

Unpacking Smithian sociability, Murray identifies a 'disjunction' between 'unflappable exteriors' and 'recalcitrant interiors'.[42] Polite dissembling may be in part what Baillie's theatre of sympathetick curiosity looks to amend in its recovery of the affective curious, which promises a greater degree of emotional integrity and simplicity. In Victoria's case, certainly, the problematic aspects of her character are associated with a discourse of imagination ('unreal pow'r') and linguistic excess ('graceful eloquence') that feeds into contemporary ideas about young women and their susceptibility to cultural trends driven by popular literature.[43] Of course, to characterise Victoria as 'modern' is not to suggest that performative irony was invented in the Renaissance, or 1689, or 1707, or 1789, or at any other threshold of modernity. It is only to observe that in the Romantic context, she inhabits the trope of a young woman misled by the amusements of 'romance', conjoining sexual indiscretion with imaginative frivolity, fears that tended to orbit around the dangerous influence of the literary genre of the novel but that also extended to the theatre.[44]

The 'star-cross'd' catastrophe looms, replete with a masquerade and balcony devices, Basil and Victoria's encounter freighted as a culture clash between an outdated (masculine) military ideal and a (feminine) culture of modernity in Mantua. In the wider snapshot of the city, Baillie establishes the tyrannical rule of the Duke, who is perverting the social order by denying his subjects the opportunity to 'aim at higher things'.[45] As with Victoria's 'ideal tyranny', the Duke's 'real' version betrays a flawed exercise of sympathetick curiosity: both are antisocial. The Duke can be understood, then, as a millstone around the neck of improvement, a sign of aristocratic backwardness. In that role, however, and in line with Baillie's dual critique of a feudal past and a commercial present, he also represents economic self-interest gone haywire. Plotting Basil's downfall, the Duke explains,

> But int'rest, int'rest; man's all-ruling pow'r,
> Will tame the hottest spirit to your service,
> And skilfully applied, mean service too.
> E'en as there is an element in nature
> Which when subdu'd, will on your hearth fulfil
> The lowest uses of domestick wants.[46]

In order to domesticate Basil's 'hot and fiery' nature, the Duke recommends the application of 'int'rest', the paradigmatic currency of a society to which Victoria belongs and which Basil's rigid honour code cannot comprehend. Indeed, we might even point to 'int'rest' as a lexical juncture between human nature and speculative capital, embodied in what Julie Murray describes as 'economic man' and propelled by the 'curious' polarity in sympathetick curiosity. As the Duke's calculation reaches its climax, Geoffry pleads with a desperate Basil that 'Thy soldier's fame is far too surely rais'd | To be o'erthrown with one unhappy chance.'[47] But Basil inhabits a different generic landscape from Geoffry, ordered by a less forgiving narrative economy – in the gambling terms employed by Geoffry, his entire life has been a process of going all in. This results in a stark inflexibility captured by his declaration that 'I cannot live, therefore I needs must die.'[48] The play then comes full circle when the Duke is betrayed by Gauriecio 'for some int'rest of his own' and finally disparaged as 'a hateful ape, | Detected, grinning 'midst his pilfer'd hoard'.[49] Basil's battlefield high-mindedness is flawed, but the play discovers that the excesses of polite Mantua are at least equally so, since they help to precipitate the Duke's more pernicious brand of violence. After all, if Basil is a relic of aristocratic limited warfare, in the age of Napoleon modernity contains the threat of total war.

The plot of *Basil* plays out a Hegelian dialectic: the old is confronted by the new; an existential struggle ensues in which the old is consumed, the new chastened and modified, with Victoria as the resulting synthesis ultimately deciding to spend her life in 'humble pray'r'.[50] All narrative is dialectical, of course, since all narrative is based in conflict, and Baillie's play is a good example of this. Baillie is scathing about the cultural mores introduced via both Basil and Victoria – as indeed she is about mob violence and elite corruption – in a play full of cynicism. It falls to the Countess Albini's homespun wisdom to generate the salutary alternative, in the ideal of 'a plain domestick dame', an ethics of humane simplicity and emotional control guiding the path of true moral improvement.[51] Here, then, is the chink of light in Mantua's disordered environment, a corrective way forward for a society in which the duplicity of politeness and the concealed savagery of 'int'rest' are really no improvement at all upon Basil's traditional, honour-bound madness. To observe that Albini's wisdom is ineffective, at least as far as Basil is concerned (albeit not as catastrophically so as her counterpart in *Romeo and Juliet*, Friar Laurence), and take this as further pessimism would risk misunderstanding the key function of sympathetick curiosity in the context of tragedy. Put simply, Basil must die for our improvement. The audience's edification is the final dialectical outcome. And indeed Mellor views Victoria's cloistering at the conclusion as a 'return to a counter-sphere, a place where women reign', suggesting that Albini's moral guidance – identified by Mellor with Wollstonecraft – comes to fruition even within the play.[52]

Nevertheless, the act of becoming a nun might be viewed in rather less empowering terms, and there remains space in *Count Basil* for a more openly tragic view of history, with the downbeat ending making improvement seem at best a resigned surrender. All of this may, of course, be educational for the reader/audience, but it does put strain on the disclosure of a positive way forward. What is more, the play operates upon a series of failed communications that act to throw the efficacy of sympathetick curiosity itself into doubt. Observing that Basil flounders because he cannot negotiate the 'performance style' appropriate to the 'urban carnival', Burroughs points to his reliance on a 'hyperbolic' form of speech that is rigidly artificial (unlike the pliable artifice of Victoria), more akin to oration than communication.[53] In that sense, he is an ambassador from the tradition of 'heroic drama' – most notably Dryden's *Conquest of Granada* (1670) – against which Jeffrey Cox sees Baillie setting her teeth, because it was excessively 'aristocratic, rhetorical, and artificial'.[54] The allusions to *Romeo and Juliet*'s balcony sequence in IV.i and V.i highlight this quality. Recounting the first, which takes place offstage, Basil explains how he lingered 'Beneath her window all the chilly night' in silence; while in the latter instance the object of his adoration is present only as '*A light seen in* VICTORIA's *window*'.[55] Basil is thus left to his private bombast in the churchyard, ranting himself deeper into psychological torment – 'To be so near thee, and for ever parted!'[56]

This sense of isolation brings Gauriecio's comments on how to turn Basil's men against him into new relief. Describing the soldiers' vulnerability, Gauriecio explains how fallible our perceptions are:

> [. . .] tho' gen'rous in their nature,
> They yet may serve a most ungen'rous end;
> And he who teaches men to think, tho' nobly,
> Doth raise within their minds a busy judge
> To scan his actions.[57]

This 'busy judge' is a less than reassuring version of sympathetick curiosity, which develops the subjectivity of sympathy and the volatility of curiosity. Combined with Basil's inability to manage *dialogue*, this amounts to a dangerous atomisation of society in which individuals possessed of erratic understanding are easily prejudiced, while Victoria's polite dissembling also perverts the socialising function of sympathetick curiosity. Needless to say, public susceptibility and rhetorical sophistry were disturbing thoughts for a politically volatile 1790s. As we will see below, Baillie claims that one of the main problems with 'strong and fixed passions', such as Basil's love, is that they are little subject to outside forces and thus to mediation, but that danger coexists here with a threat of emotional coercion. The various communication breakdowns, disconnects and manipulations in Mantua all reflect an undesirable illustration of sympathetick curiosity. And even if these are working to cautionary ends, they remain a point of tension, threatening to call into question not simply the chance of improvement in *Count Basil*, but the 'great moral object' of the *Passions* series itself.

Of History and Romance

The Countess Albini provides a jumping-off point for thinking about the way Baillie construes the aesthetic condition of her drama. Albini's very first utterance establishes her ethical authority, in warning her charges against 'false notions of [female] pow'r' encouraged by the artificial ways in which men 'talk of ladies and of love'.[58] She subsequently develops this critique of linguistic excess, in order to challenge Victoria's conceited ideas:

> And does your grace, hail'd by applauding crouds,
> In all the graceful eloquence address'd
> Of most accomplish'd, noble, courtly youths,
> Prais'd in the songs of heav'n-inspired bards;
> Those awkward proofs of admiration prize,
> The rustick swain his village fair-one pays?[59]

I have touched on the way this material envelops Victoria in the trope of a young woman led astray by romance. Associating the delusions of 'graceful eloquence' with Victoria's naivety, this invokes an associational matrix (romance–imagination–childhood) that is among the more general literary emblems of the period. Scott's *Waverley*, famously, takes six opening chapters to establish Edward Waverley's adolescence. Supposedly autobiographical in essence, the early part of the novel finds Waverley 'like a child amongst his toys, culled and arranged, from the splendid yet useless imagery and emblems with which his imagination was stored'.[60] Waverley's attachment to Edmund Spenser as 'romantic fiction' and to Jean Froissart's medieval Romances is linked to idealistic dreaming, 'splendid yet useless', as Scott lays the groundwork for the narrative arc of the novel and Waverley's Jacobite indiscretion. As it happens, Baillie anticipates this version of *Bildung* in accounts of her own youth. Describing herself as 'the worst or one of the worst scholars in the School' at Hamilton, having been uninterested in reading until she discovered Macpherson's Ossian poetry, she remembers how 'Ghost stories told us by the sexton' fired her imagination, acting as potent stimulation to a 'fanciful untaught mind'.[61] These supernatural tales were the stuff of romance, indulged alike by young Baillie and Scott, propelling Edward Waverley into rebellion and warned against by the Countess Albini.

The anxious political climate in Britain at the turn of the nineteenth century helped to underscore questions about the politics and utility of the aesthetic. Approaches to the cultural capital of imaginative literature in the period are, of course, manifold. Scott's appeal to the truths of conjectural historiography is one option. Baillie's full-bodied adoption of didactic instrumentalism – which solves the 'splendid yet useless' quandary by insisting on a profound use-value – is another. Scholars have long recognised the appeal of this method for female authors. In *Britons: Forging the Nation*, for example, Linda Colley explores how a role as 'moral arbiters' could be enabling, while Mellor notes how an expedient ideal ('rational, just, yet merciful, virtuous, benevolent, and peace-loving') provided women with a path to 'literary authority'.[62] There is no question that Baillie's 'great moral object' draws sustenance from some of the same cultural energies as the writing of moralists such as Hannah More, even if Baillie was initially mistaken as male and then construed as an unusually masculine voice for most of the nineteenth century.[63] Improving didacticism could generate a self-flagellating literature that sought to exorcise the threat of the 'literary',[64] but Baillie's approach is to tackle the dubious reputation of the literary head-on. Her work participates in a conventional derogation of romance, but it contains an unequivocal view of the utility of the drama.

Which is not to say that Baillie forswears the idea of entertainment: in fact, she insists that the 'interesting' and the 'instructive' are inseparable. Properly cultivating our instinct for sympathetick curiosity is paramount, however, since,

> If unseasoned with any reference to this, the fairy bowers of the poet, with all his gay images of delight, will be admired and forgotten; the important relations of the historian, and even the reasonings of the philosopher, will make a less permanent impression.[65]

In order to best achieve this aim, she recommends an aesthetics of intimacy, which stimulates our voyeuristic curiosity. For if presented with an 'unhappy perpetrator' under the influence of the passions, who 'would [. . .] not follow him into his lonely haunts'? Under such 'closet' conditions, which are figured both spatially ('the midnight silence of his chamber') and discursively (via soliloquy), the 'gradual unfolding of the passions' can be executed with the greatest precision.[66] The movement in *Count Basil* from public to private space, then, championed by the Countess Albini's praise of 'a plain domestick dame', embodies the formal paradigm of Baillie's theatre. She wants to examine human nature in isolation, to dissect our emotional existence free of the chaos of society and an 'artful cultivation' that too often occludes this formal potential.[67] This involves a suspicion of the devices of plot, which she fears may overwhelm our capacity for interior reflection.[68] If corrected along the right lines, Baillie insists, the theatre offers a powerful tool. In fact, as an immediate outgrowth of our capacity for sympathetick curiosity, drama is uniquely well suited to the curation of this faculty: it touches universal appetites for spectacle and operates with a human immediacy that demands special attention to 'characteristick truth'. 'The most interesting amusement' is primed for didactic renovation – Baillie's 'splendid yet use*ful*' aesthetics – in which the theatre not only ceases to be a frivolous diversion, but becomes an unparalleled educational tool.[69]

There are parallels between the 'Introductory Discourse' and another groundbreaking treatise written (though not published) just a year earlier, William Godwin's 1797 'Essay of history and romance'. The apex of Godwin's piece is in his insistence that

> The writer of romance then is to be considered as the writer of real history; while he who was formerly called the historian, must be contented to step down into the place of his rival, with this disadvantage, that he is a romance writer, without the ardour, the enthusiasm, and the sublime licence of imagination, that belong to that species of composition. True history consists in a delineation of consistent, human character.

Godwin finally declares both romance and history 'almost infantine' modes of representation, but this generic inversion is an important gesture.[70] We do not need to look far in the period for moralistic fears about imaginative literature, a perspective that Barton Swaim finds was especially potent in Scotland.[71] In tandem with the empirical pretensions of 'history', which can be understood to extend across what is now called non-fiction, this could render the pliable category of romance at best 'splendid uselessness',[72] at worst sinister delusion. Yet not only does Godwin argue that romance is a more entertaining medium, he suggests that it actually does a better job at history. Or rather, it would do were it not for the fact that 'romance is a task too great for the powers of man'.[73] Still, 'Nothing is more uncertain, more contradictory, more unsatisfactory, than the evidence of facts', Godwin explains.[74] Freed from an addiction to 'facts' that hamstrings history, which can only ever be a partial, fictitious genre anyway, romance might engage the full capacity of the mind, adopting 'the sublime licence of imagination' to explore in limitless depth the human experience.

The notion that imaginative literature provides a platform for serious debate is now largely taken for granted. There is a complex lineage to Godwin's thinking in the eighteenth century, which it is not possible to rehearse here. Yet Hume stands out as a precursor, both for legitimising the role of the imagination within the discipline of historiography, and in the more radical gesture enacted in his 1739–40 *Treatise of Human Nature*, which potentially lays claim to the imagination – via the subjectivity of belief – as the arbiter of all knowledge.[75] Midway through the 'Introductory Discourse', Baillie writes: 'It was the saying of a sagacious Scotchman, "let who will make the laws of a nation, if I have the writing of its ballads."'[76] Baillie and Godwin are on the same page in their view of imaginative literature here. And in the cases of both Baillie's improving drama and Godwin's salutary romance, the key point is imaginative free rein, the *access* legitimised by fiction. Whether in the naked light of Baillie's 'lonely haunts', or in the move beyond erroneous 'conjectures' towards fuller truth in Godwin, the artifice of art becomes its advantage, going where the historical record never can.[77]

We might understand these arguments in profoundly individualistic terms, as destabilising reality to insist with Hume that the only reliable truth is the truth of the imagination, with each mind potentially a self-contained world. Yet Baillie and Godwin agree that the basic appeal of literature is its exposition of what he calls 'consistent, human character', or she terms 'faithfully delineated nature' – helping us to recognise ourselves in the other, perhaps even to appreciate the other in its own right, depending on where the emphasis falls in the dialectic of sympathetick curiosity.[78] Baillie's theatre makes a conscious appeal to the theatricality, the literariness, of the mind. And just as Hume's counterbalance to the isolation of philosophy is sociability, the collective experience of the theatre as an '*Open Street*' of civic discourse wants to mediate against our atomised existence by improving our capacity for sympathetick curiosity.[79] Situated at the beginning of a new century, Baillie's drama is a form of popular entertainment aimed at counteracting immorality and isolation, including the anomic crisis of commercial modernity understood as a network of self-interested consumers. In doing so, it offers a path of moral improvement in which the theatre supplies the role of the church and the village green as much as the school.

The collision of history and romance destroys Basil, a man birthed in the tribal certainties of war, deconstructed to death by Victoria's performative tyranny and by the analytical focus of the *Plays on the Passions*. Basil is an archetype of the great men of history; he is the product of a two-dimensional narrative modality and possesses an honour code in place of a personality. As Godwin (anticipating Baillie) complains of the rendering of such heroes, 'I am not contented to observe [him] upon the public stage, I would follow him into his closet.'[80] In their different ways, both Victoria and Basil are guilty of artifice, of erroneous forms of theatre. But while she models the dangers of modern romance, he simply cannot survive the intimate unfolding of the passions in Baillie's moral drama. Basil cannot appreciate the passion festering within him, because he is insufficiently versed in the workings of sympathetick curiosity – although we, perhaps, can learn from his mistakes. Still, it is difficult not to feel that the formal catastrophe of the tragic form overshadows the improving confidence of the play, just as a cautionary tale delivered in the medium of sympathetick curiosity is an unstable kind of lesson: the audience, after all, possess their own frailties and complexities, and how reliable is any form of communication? Appealing to a corrective policy of simplicity in the life-world of Mantua, the Countess Albini develops her ideal of a 'plain domestick dame, | Who fills the duties of an useful state'.[81] But is anyone really listening?

Primitive Humanity

Baillie's *The Family Legend* of 1810 is not a part of the *Passions* series but nonetheless bears its mark, offering the audience a set of instructive archetypes on which to fasten their sympathetick curiosity. Indeed, as a document, the 'Introductory Discourse' is as much about universal fundamentals as it is a manifesto for a specific set of works. Referred to by Baillie as 'my Highland Play', *The Family Legend* is an essay on history as modernisation and is the most sustained consideration of primitive culture in her oeuvre.[82] In that respect, it effectively develops upon one half of the social critique in *Count Basil*; *The Alienated Manor*, discussed below, is a complementary work in emphasising a range of modern behaviours. Crucially, as will become apparent, *The Family Legend* has enough atavistic energy to place its ostensibly Whiggish history into doubt, and also to threaten Baillie's own moral inflection of improvement. Any improving project, of course, must negotiate what is improved *upon* or left behind, which in Baillie encompasses a range of targets. Indeed, it is this quality that may encourage us to view improvement in Bakhtinian, dialogic terms, as continually invoking its banished other.[83] To address how Baillie handles the violence and superstitions of clan society in the Scottish Highlands, this section brings *The Family Legend* into contact with related strategies in Elizabeth Hamilton's 1808 novel *The Cottagers of Glenburnie* and in Scott's historical fiction. In short, Hamilton steers restively towards an educational perspective in which the primitive can either be rejected or ameliorated ('improved'). For his part, Scott more fully embraces a third possibility, by means of his celebration of the unimproved in the language of romance. Baillie, I want to suggest, is positioned somewhere between these positions, inclined like Hamilton towards a cautionary view of primitive behaviour, while also mobilising the terms of the aesthetic as a means to salvage something of the past. And in the end, primitive culture is not only sufficiently thrilling but also attractively candid ('simple') enough in *The Family Legend* to complicate the lessons of history. This reflects Baillie's patriotic attachment to an idea of Scotland, as well as the historical moment of 1810. Twelve years after *Count Basil* – with its counter-revolutionary critique of war encountering a volatile public – the Napoleonic Wars were making it increasingly difficult to condemn violence.

At the heart of the distinction between Hamilton and Scott is the term 'culture' itself, described by Raymond Williams in *Keywords* as 'one of the two or three most complicated words in the English language'. It is worth revisiting Williams's etymology. In its earliest forms the word was 'a noun of process: the tending of something, basically crops or animals'. Then, 'From eC16 the tending of natural growth was extended to a process of human development'. There are close affinities between this notion of 'culture' and improvement as it developed in the eighteenth century: both share associations with agriculture and could be interchangeable in the process of 'cultivating' an intellect. Williams goes on to explain that 'Culture as an independent noun, an abstract process or the product of such a process, is not important before lC18 and is not common before mC19.' Here we see the germs of culture as an anthropological object, a 'product' as well as a 'process'. And for the full emergence of the usage that facilitates, for example, 'Scottish culture' – that of the 'independent noun, whether used generally or specifically, which indicates a particular way of life' – Williams looks to what he terms the 'Romantic movement' and particularly a 'decisive change of use in Herder'.[84]

The emerging, Herderian view of 'culture' feeds into aesthetic constructions of local and national character. They, in turn, bear upon a supposed epochal shift from *Gemeinschaft* to *Gesellschaft*, though again it is probably more useful to see it as a revision of extant options, since the abstraction the latter connotes is not a modern preserve. Reading Lockhart's *Peter's Letters to his Kinsfolk*, Duncan suggests that, through the Welsh narrator Peter Morris's modern state (itself an effect of 'cultivation'), Lockhart manages to transpose the national condition from one definition of culture, that of 'an empirical way of life belonging to the natives', to another, aesthetic form: 'the property of our reading, the "soul and spirit of a national literature"'.[85] Such gestures are a possible cure for the dialectical tension in improvement, in creating an aesthetic register capable of sustaining or at least memorialising ethnographic ideas of the unimproved in the modern world. This has long been considered the prime achievement of Scott's Waverley Novels, and is a key part of the cultural landscape in which *The Family Legend* operates.

The fourteen-night run of *The Family Legend* at the Theatre Royal in Edinburgh in January 1810, masterminded by Scott, appears to have been considered by Baillie as among the standout achievements of her career. In the preface that she subsequently published with the play, she acknowledges criticisms of the piece, but holds fast to its 'affectionate reception' in her 'native land'. In fact, she claims to value an expression of patriotic bias above objective critical acclaim: 'I have truly felt, upon this occasion, the kindliness of kin to kin, and I would exchange it for no other feeling.'[86] This becomes topical in light of the play itself, which explores the effects of kinship and superstition on its main character, the chief of the Maclean clan. To quickly synopsise, the play looks back to acrimonious fifteenth-century feuding between the Macleans and the Campbells, the former still deeply superstitious, the latter, led by the Earl of Argyll, models of enlightened rationalism, relatively speaking. With the Macleans hurting from a major defeat, a peace-brokering marriage is arranged between Lord Maclean and Helen, Argyll's daughter. Yet darker elements around Maclean (notably the vengeful Benlora) believe that Helen must be removed to protect the integrity of the clan. *Romeo and Juliet* resurfaces here, highlighted in the observation of a subordinate, 'were she not a Campbell'.[87] After Helen is left to drown on an exposed rock, she is secretly rescued. Maclean and his vassals are then invited to attend a phoney mourning feast hosted by Argyll, at which their treachery is confirmed and Helen unveiled. Maclean is killed, freeing Helen to remarry, this time to an English knight, Sir Hubert de Grey.

Meiko O'Halloran explores a Unionist subtext to all this, with the concluding marriage signalling an end to the primitive ignorance of the Scottish past and with the Campbells an archetype of improved Britishness. Yet, as she notes, the 'compelling primitive violence' of the Macleans is not so easily eclipsed, this despite an insistence on resolution and concord that she finds echoed in Henry Mackenzie's epilogue for the piece as well as Scott's directorial choices.[88] Unearth-ing the same vacillating political energies that characterise Scott's fiction, the play struggles (or perhaps declines) to contain the sub-versive appeal of the primitive. In fact, it discovers a tension between two historiographical options. The simplest method would proceed sequentially: the Campbells, newly united with England, represent the symbolic future of the Macleans, who must be obliterated for his-tory as improvement to assert itself. Alternatively, a more complex process might occur, in which the primitive qualities of the Macleans continue to haunt the forward movement of history, whether in the aesthetic field of 'splendid uselessness' or something more obviously potent, in a messy ongoing dialectic.

Two years earlier, Hamilton's *The Cottagers of Glenburnie* had narrated efforts to improve a remote Highland village. As noted in Chapter 1, Burns's influential portrayal of cottage life in 'The Cotter's Saturday Night' was already something of a historical retrospective by the 1780s. Hamilton's novel fears that the rural piety associated with it has by 1808 been thoroughly eroded, at least in the Highlands. Where Burns's text pictures cottage simplicity as a kind of moral lodestone for the nation, Hamilton wants to regenerate the degraded poor. Chastened improver Mrs Mason's (Anglocentric) perspective is the measuring rule of the novel, setting out the terms of improvement in a text that was actually best remembered in the period for the lazy Mac-Clarty family and their slovenly mantras: '*I cou'd no be fashed*' and 'it does just weel eneugh'.[89] Implicit throughout is the conserva-tive notion that the miserable poor are so through their own neglect. This 'by the bootstraps' defence of privilege underwrites Hamilton's lurid depictions of poverty:

> And here let us remark the advantage which our cottages in general possess over those of our southern neighbours; theirs being so whitened up, that no one can have the comfort of laying a dirty hand upon them, without leaving the impression, an inconvenience which reduces people in that station, to the necessity of learning to stand upon their legs, with-out the assistance of their hands.[90]

Somehow, in the face of this simian grotesque, Francis Jeffrey was impressed by 'the skill with which a dramatic representation of hum-ble life is saved from caricature and absurdity'.[91] In the end, however,

Glenburnie is poised somewhere between an Arcadian state of nature and a condition of vulgar wilderness, as reinforced by local attempts at agriculture: 'None had their outlines marked with the mathematical precision, in which the modern improver so much delights. Not a straight line was to be seen in Glenburnie'.[92] The novel applies the infantilising logic of stadial theory to make Glenburnie a site of uncivilised potential. Still, Hamilton's call to a halcyon past of simple virtue again makes the rhetoric of improvement non-linear, and a more determined pastoral inversion is a nagging presence, summoning the sentiment also expressed by Blake: 'Improvement makes straight roads, but the crooked roads without improvement, are roads of genius'.[93]

Again, Hamilton's readers seem to have found the Mac-Clartys the most compelling aspect of the text.[94] As this suggests, the novel encounters a formal problem in that the allure of the unimproved Highlands is ranged against the drive of improvement. Duncan recognises this situation, in which the dirt that mars the superbly filthy house of Mason's most intractable pupils, the Mac-Clartys (literally the sons of dirtiness), becomes a key signifier of national character.[95] Hamilton herself approaches the problem in the introductory passages of the text, attacking a patriotic inertia in which 'Every hint at the necessity of further improvement is [. . .] deemed a libel on all that has already been done'.[96] Yet the novel's didactic formula jars against its investment in a bathetic Scottish picturesque. Covering the finger-marked walls and sludgy floors of the Mac-Clarty's home, national 'culture' is the antithesis of Mason's janitorial evangelicalism, the idea of Scotland stubbornly rooted in the compost of unimprovement. This is a curious instance of the relativity of dirt, anthropologically defined as matter out of place.[97] It emerges from an imposition of 'culture' as what Williams terms 'the tending of something' and thus, as Duncan notes, 'the antithesis of a national character anchored in a local way of life'.[98] In co-opting two incompatible, alternative definitions of the term, Hamilton's text is split across paradigms, attempting to project both 'cultivation' and ethnographic 'culture'. Squeamish delight in the filth of the Mac-Clartys tempts *Cottagers* towards a full-blown aestheticising gesture, in which the primitive would be reconstituted as romance. Yet Hamilton's stress lies on social engineering, as demonstrated by the Morison family, who are successfully improved. Thus, marvelling at the Mac-Clartys retains more of fascinated disgust than romantic celebration, with Hamilton's Highlands forever on the brink of being cleaned up.

Returning to Baillie's *Family Legend*, there is a linked range of possibilities active within the Maclean clan, who provide the foil to the historical trajectory of improvement embodied in the Campbells. The full potency of their primitive life-world is embodied in the character of Benlora, among the lieutenants driving Maclean to choose clanship over family. From his first appearance, Benlora is intoxicated with the clan rivalry, remembering the quantity of 'hated blood' he has spilled, traumatised by 'two long years' in solitary confinement in a Campbell dungeon, furiously offended by the imposition of his chief's marriage to Helen, 'a bosom worm' who has now produced an heir.[99] In contrast to Benlora's brooding menace, Maclean himself is torn and indecisive – he is described by Benlora as 'of a soft, unsteady, yielding nature'.[100] This makes the chief predisposed to what the play will present as an abrogation of his responsibilities to his wife, his child and society at large. Reflecting upon the characterisation of Maclean in her preface, Baillie defends her decision to complicate 'heroic rules' which disallow any 'mixture of timidity' in 'tragic characters'. She describes Maclean as

> a man of personal courage, brave in the field, but weak and timid in council, irresolute and unsteady in action; superstitious, and easily swayed by others, yet anxious to preserve his power as chieftain; attached to his clan, attached to his lady, and of an affectionate and gentle disposition.[101]

Maclean finally concedes to the authority of his underlings, believing that Helen will not actually be killed. Still, if Benlora figures as the implacable primitive who can only be forbidden or romanticised, Maclean presents at least the possibility of reform, albeit gravely undercut by weaknesses that include residual superstition.

The critical test of Maclean's character comes in II.ii, which takes place in '*A cave, lighted by flaming brands*'.[102] Maclean's vassals have gathered to discuss their course of action, concerned by the import of sinister omens in the visions of 'John of the Isle' and in the 'passing sound' of a mermaid 'o'er the stilly deep'.[103] Lochtarish, another key conspirator, pushes for a secretive murder of Helen, 'This beauteous sorceress [who] our besotted chief | By soft enchantment holds'.[104] Again then, as in *Count Basil*, a military man has been seduced by romantic love, though in this context it is framed as a positive counter-point to the excesses of the clan. For his part, Benlora prefers either 'a public sacrifice' or a shameful deliverance of Helen back to the Camp-bells in order to openly stoke the rivalry, setting up a contrast between his straightforward violence and Lochtarish's fraudulent echo of it.[105] When Maclean arrives and has the ominous signs reported to him, his choice is represented in stark terms as between the 'holy ties' of the clan and his love for Helen.[106] The decisive moment comes when another vassal enters, apparently terrified by the appearance of John of the Isle, who has been 'arrested on his way | By horrid visions'.[107] Maclean exits the cave '*exhausted and trembling*', his will over-come.[108] These supernatural harbingers are interesting, in particular the mermaid's 'fatal song of waves', as if the oral culture of the High-lands is itself the moral deadweight and trigger for the play's primitive violence.[109] Yet the comment of a vassal that 'John of the Isle, by sly Lochtarish taught, | Will work [Maclean] soon to be an oath-bound wretch', suggests the degree to which the supernatural edifice is being manipulated to effect – a form of perverse theatre within the prosce-nium arch of the cave, leveraging the vulnerable aspects of Maclean's sympathetick curiosity.[110] Regardless, Maclean is overawed and from this point forward cannot hope for the salvation of improvement, doomed to share in the fate of Benlora's more determined primitiv-ism, in the condition of a Mac-Clarty rather than a Morison.

Benlora, who glories in 'the gnashing ecstasy of hate', emerges then as the apex for this handling of the primitive.[111] By his exercise of unrestrained emotion – his complete lack of interest in the dialectical compromises that enable the Campbell-led future – he falls foul of the admonitions that structure Baillie's *Passions* series. Maclean's ultimate failures to control his superstition, ambition and clannish loyalty are related crimes. There is again a public/private dynamic unfolding in this play: in the moral dilemma presented to Maclean, and in various combinations of public display and private emotion. Helen seems to provide an admirable model, in her willingness to act 'in steady, willing, cheerful duty' despite a lack of real affection for Maclean, suggesting that if disconnects between interiority and exteriority are inevitable, then behaviour should be moderated in the interests of civility.[112] Then again, in line with Baillie's habitual suspicion of dissimulation – of acting in bad faith – in the characters of Lochtarish, Victoria (*Count Basil*) or Rezenvelt (*De Monfort*), the straightforwardness of Benlora's position, however brutal, emerges with a certain moral power. In the end, when the Macleans are exposed in the castle of Argyll, Benlora retains all the grandeur of his authentic primitivism, crying to his fellows 'Rouse ye, base Macleans!' in an echo of Macbeth's final call to Macduff, accusing Lochtarish of having caused their disgrace in a debasing of honest clan hatred.[113]

Unbroken, Benlora is mortally wounded in the final skirmish and screams in warrior ecstasy of his return to the earth, having once and for all escaped the terrible threat of the Campbell dungeon.[114] The final words fall to Argyll, whose civilised authority is established in his declaration that 'Upon the guilty | Our vengeance falls, and only on the guilty.'[115] Regretting the cost of these internecine conflicts, Argyll launches into a vision of the future, when 'mountain warriors' shall be deployed in 'foreign climes', while 'gazing southron' celebrate their

> [. . .] hardy brothers of the north;–
> The bold and gen'rous race, who have, beneath
> The frozen circle and the burning line,
> The rights and freedom of our native land
> Undauntedly maintain'd.[116]

Suddenly, then, we have fast-forwarded hundreds of years into the era of the Napoleonic Wars, with Highland regiments now celebrated as the battle-hardened defenders of ancient British freedoms across the globe. The spectacular intrigue of Baillie's cave scene and Benlora's anti-heroism have already suggested that the 'dirt' of the primitive past is escaping a sequential historical equation (the modern supplanting the premodern) to an even greater degree than does the filth of Hamilton's Mac-Clartys. And Argyll's final speech paints an image of the 'warlike pipe' and 'plaided bands' that is as overt an aestheticisation of Highland militarism as any in the period.[117]

Maclean's final degradation, in lying to the Earl of Argyll, is framed as 'a lesson to every ingenuous mind more powerful than his death', reminding us of the didactic thrust of Baillie's drama.[118] Equally, the historical perspective of *The Family Legend* positions commercial modernisation as a salutary force with a degree of confidence that is lacking from *Count Basil*. Even so, the Macleans, and Benlora in particular, refuse to remain a cautionary example, moving into a more complicated relationship with history, aestheticised as a group of men discussing magic in a cave, reconstituted as military might on nineteenth-century battlefields. The effect turns on the appeal of Benlora's passion, in which unadulterated hate overlaps with integrity, placing the affective, 'curious' polarity of sympathetick curiosity in the ascendency and threatening to make moral improvement secondary to the thrill of appetite. When discussing the necessity of limiting the distractions of plot in her work, Baillie turns to spectacle – 'shew and decorations' – to ward against the drama becoming 'tiresome'.[119] Yet this involves granting the primitive an aesthetic power here that helps it to transcend its role as the denigrated other of history. Regarding Scott's Waverley Novels, critics have long tussled over whether a compelling representation of the primitive defuses or renews the struggles of history, with the past recoverable in some combination of 'threat' and 'regret', which as we have seen involves complex questions of reception, narrative determinacy and aesthetic utility.[120] In *The Family Legend*, the explicit fast-forward to the contemporary battlefield leaves little doubt over the ideological appropriation of the past that is taking place. And in this light, Baillie's condemnation of the Macleans is swamped in a deeper lesson: the improvements of the modern world do not replace but actually rely upon primitive violence. The past must retain an element of threat in order to be usefully co-opted. Human nature endures: the Macleans and the Campbells are two sides of a coin.

The Family Legend attempts simultaneously to improve the Highlands, with the Campbells promising the way forward, while also indulging in the outlandish delights of the Macleans. It does seem doubtful whether the audience's exercise of sympathetick curiosity will condemn rather than marvel at divisive, independent Benlora, his raw power triumphing over the civil decency of Argyll, Helen and her new English husband. Baillie's aim to rationalise emotion struggles with the contagious experience of the theatre here, partly a sign of the patriotic complication (another brand of 'strong and fixed passion') of the Scottish source material, following on from the 'Introductory Discourse' itself, which summons a patriotic rusticity characterised as the 'rough forest of our native land'.[121] *The Family Legend* probably stops short of the aesthetic legerdemain by which Scott distils the national past into a half-remembered melody in *Guy Mannering*, prevented from doing so by its greater investment in improving didacticism, which binds it to an altogether guiltier enjoyment of 'dirt'. Even so, the compellingly unimproved Macleans are a challenge to the Whiggish model of history as modernisation, just as the cautionary example of Benlora teeters on the brink of a tragic anti-heroism quite at odds with Baillie's educational agenda. Of course, Maclean passion may have been more useful than Campbell politeness as ideological fodder in 1810. Still five years shy of Waterloo in an era of total war, an outright denial of violence might look like wishful thinking, even naive or unpatriotic.

Bad Improvements

The Alienated Manor is probably not among Baillie's most successful works. Still, energetic and occasionally funny, it is an appropriate place to conclude this discussion, since it brings improvement explicitly to the fore via the discourse of the picturesque as it was applied to the landscaping of estates in the period. As it unfolds, this *Passions* comedy on jealousy branches from the subject of 'elegant, tasteful, parkish' groundworks to amplify the overlapping, plural quality of improvement, which is presented in a distinctly calamitous form.[122] It first appeared in Baillie's three-volume *Dramas* of 1836, technically outside the date-range of the present book, though the author explained that 'the greater number of the Dramas' therein had 'been written many years ago'.[123] The plot concerns the deepening jealousy of a country gentleman, Charville, who is mistakenly convinced that his young wife is engaged in an adulterous intrigue with another man. A fairly conventional series of misunderstandings propels the comedy, most of which is beyond my concern here. More interesting is the presence on Charville's estate of 'SIR LEVEL CLUMP, *an Improver*' and 'SMITCHENSTAULT, *a German Philosopher*'.[124] As it emerges, Charville's envy is the companion of a perverse attitude to money, as instanced in his willingness to ruin another man at the gambling table, both reflections of what Regina Hewitt has called 'possessive individualism'.[125] Yet these characters fill out the historical context in which Charville's moral failings are revealed, with the landowner's personal crisis becoming the nerve centre for a dangerous convolution of improving discourse in the early nineteenth century. This is not limited to picturesque landscaping or German philosophy or commercial mania, but includes examples such as 'foreign mail, or the changing of an old turnpike road'.[126] Equally, the character of 'SANCHO, *a Black*', introduces an element of crazed resentful energy, speaking in stylised pidgin English, attempting to murder Charville on his master's behalf, and ending up on his knees in relieved worship of one of the (white) leads.[127] Sancho's struggles foreground issues of slavery, servitude, race and education within the play's conundrum of improvement, orbiting around Charville, the greedy and jealous landowner. This is all indicative of a modernity in which the notional project of improvement overhangs a set of unhealthy cultural perversions, necessitating – of course – the intervention of Baillie's moral corrective in the form of a remedial drama.

Sir Level Clump's toxic worldview is established early on, the improver driven (like Charville) by an impulse for mastery, in an overwhelming obsession with his 'plan' for the estate. 'If there be no plan, there is no meaning in what you do; *ergo*, no taste', is the way Clump puts it.[128] Capable of finding beauty only in 'the rules of art', Clump's version of 'the modern taste' is improvement at an extreme, in which the regulated and the new are the only signifiers of value.[129] There are echoes of this character throughout Baillie's oeuvre, perhaps most plainly in Mr Royston in *The Tryal*. Royston is an idiot driven by fashion and competition to oversee 'a world of alterations going at Royston-hall', having 'dug up the orchard, and pull'd down the old fruit wall, where that odd little temple used to stand', in an act of improving philistinism.[130] For his part, Clump is the logical outcrop of Charville's crass infatuation with capitalist accumulation, with a concurrently withered sensibility that renders nature a blank page for the exercise of a 'plan'. If there is an outward contrast between Clump and the bathetic German philosopher Smitchenstault, due to the latter's vacuous nods to 'de free plan of nature', both are actually beholden to progressive casuistry, parasites exacerbating Charville's unhealthy persona, literally hollowing the foundations of country life by consuming the 'good bin of claret' from the wine cellar.[131]

Baillie brings Clump into contact with Charville's neighbour Crafton, who acts as the mischievous but salutary alternative to these dangerous extremes of modernity. Indeed, where *The Family Legend* attempts to negotiate the primitive, *The Alienated Manor* is in some sense its mirror-image, and the two plays taken together fill out a dual critique of past and present that is consolidated by *Count*

Basil. Insisting that the estate (his former home) would be better if Clump 'let it alone altogether', Crafton characterises the hierarchy of improvement in very different terms from Clump.[132] Where the improver sees the distinction between the existing parkland and his plan as between 'a rude, untamed clown' and 'a gentleman', Crafton contrasts 'a savage chief' with 'a posture-master'.[133] Clump's improvements are explicitly decorative: he is dismissive of the idea of planting potatoes, even of improving 'corn-fields in the first place, to get money for other improvements', preferring 'to cut down the wood on one part of the ground, to pay for beautifying the other' in an unsustainable version of improvement.[134] In aesthetic terms, Henderson observes that Clump's ideas model Lancelot 'Capability' Brown's naturalistic school of English landscaping, signalling the degree of artifice in this method when juxtaposed against the evolved language of the picturesque spoken by Crafton. Baillie thus 'shows how the principles of the picturesque take the ideals of Brownian landscaping one step further', amplifying its commitment to the naturalistic to a level more in line with Baillie's drama (where, as Henderson notes, an emphasis on 'nature' turns out to be 'an even more fashionable commodity' than the 'sophisticated').[135]

If Clump is pre-picturesque, then, his practice marks an earlier point in the evolution of naturalism, as indicated in his plan to build a folly or a 'ruin' to introduce the correct degree of attenuated sublimity into Charville's vista.[136] While defining improvement narrowly as 'a range of practices from enclosure to clearance', Hewitt finds *The Alienated Manor* exploring how 'the picturesque was often used to justify' such activity.[137] Still, as part of Baillie's oeuvre, the play largely endorses the updated vision of naturalism iterated by Crafton. In truth, Clump, Crafton and Baillie are all located at points within an aesthetic paradigm that places the unimproved and the improved in tension, coordinated by their relationship to the leitmotif of 'simplicity', which was powerful enough to justify almost any intervention in the period – literary, landscaping or otherwise. Thus Crafton's mockery of Clump turns on the correct understanding of simplicity, Crafton seeking to renew its connection to nature, where the tellingly named Level Clump's 'improving simplicity' renders everything 'plain, and smooth, and orderly' in a process of stale degeneration.[138]

With Clump as one of its agents, Charville's destructive commer-cialism is an antithesis to the 'anti-Georgic tendency' of the pictur-esque (however much that itself is a posture) and a sign of a culture of improvement that is out of kilter with the dialectical median of simplicity.[139] We might detect a simultaneous indictment of polite-ness in Charville, subject as he is to a kind of calculating vulgar-ity, but the play seems rather to be using him to signal the way in which commercial improvement and politeness did not always map on to each other. Indeed, Mrs Charville, Crafton and others engage in a polite game-playing which in a tragedy Baillie might disapprove of, but they mostly retain the narrative's approval. The fundamental problem for Charville is that he is cut off from the negotiated emo-tion of society – deficient in the exercise of sympathetick curiosity – predicating his commercial greed and his romantic jealousy (there may be a pun on 'alienated man' in the title). When explaining how it is that 'strong and fixed passions' swell out of control in the 'Intro-ductory Discourse', Baillie comments that they proceed 'from small beginnings' and develop 'seemingly unprovoked by outward circum-stances'.[140] The major problem with passionate characters is their isolation: emotion needs to be transactional in order to be healthy. Politeness, as in *Count Basil*, can be another sign of alienation, a mirror-image of primitive breakdowns in sociability and commu-nication, but in this context it would help Charville negotiate the modern world. Unequipped to recognise the passion souring within himself, Charville is in a desperate situation, since his jealousy is only lightly subject to the workings of 'outward circumstances'. As I have noted, there are considerable tensions in the socialising process of sympathetick curiosity. Still, this problem of emotional self-reliance underpins Baillie's efforts to effect a long-term moral culture, which attempts to build the underlying toolkit with which individuals coun-ter their passion, whether that passion is expressed in clan murder or tasteless gardening.

Unlike in *Count Basil*, *The Alienated Manor*'s comedic form allows for Charville's errors to be corrected through what Hewitt calls the emergence of 'adaptive alternatives' to his aberrant behaviour, with the agency of sympathetick curiosity – the human traits that enable improvement – effective within as well as outside the text.[141] As seen above, Baillie claims that tragedy is the best vehicle for her moral agenda, since it takes the audience farthest into the dangerous condition of the passions. Yet comedy may actually be a more effective 'school' for her, since it is less apt to veer into anti-heroic, sublime immorality.[142] Indeed, although any insight whatsoever that these dramas contain might feasibly be constituted as a lesson, it is not at all clear that the experience of the theatre at large – and not just tragic denouements – can be piloted reliably towards edification. In this case, Baillie's 'simple' moral panacea, figured largely in the character of Crafton, is the alternative to the missteps of a commercial modernity in which improving hubris is an expression of violent passion. *The Alienated Manor* is thus another expression of Baillie's mobilisation against a range of flawed social structures, her aim to repackage the Romantic theatre into a vehicle for a superior form of improvement, with an archetypal moral journey enabled by sympathetick curiosity permeating the text on both a thematic and a formal level. It hopes to leave its audience, constituted of a broadening range of moneyed consumers under threat from a variety of ideological perversions, feeling with Crafton that 'We shall all be wiser, and, I hope, better, for what has just passed, and therefore have no cause to regret it.'[143] Still, the whole *Passions* project remains internally fraught, due in part to the plural involvedness of improvement and indeed human nature, not to mention the relativity of morality, with Baillie's pessimism never far away, threatening to smother the outcome. Perhaps the fundamental point, however, is again the alienation of theory and practice: in drama, as in literature more widely, lessons are not wholly controllable.

* * *

In the early passages of *The Alienated Manor*, Clump and Crafton discuss the improver's misfiring attempts to 'operate upon' the Laird of Glenvorluch's estate in Lochaber.[144] Despite being granted '*carte blanche*' for his plans, Clump finds the Highland landscape unimprovable, as emblematised by a 'perverse sprite of a stream' that 'would neither serpentine, sweep, nor expand in any direction, but as it pleased its own self'.[145] Suddenly, then, we are back in the territory of the implacable primitive of *The Family Legend*, introduced again by way of the Scottish Highlands. If one approach to such resistance is to transpose the primitive into the realm of art, Clump takes the opposite tack. Confounded, he presents the nobles with a copy of his plan, now 'hanging in the library, to show what the place ought to be, if it will not'.[146] The act of improvement itself is negated, this visual representation providing a memento of what might have been rather than a recuperation of what once was.

As seen across the examples in this chapter, Baillie's drama is immersed in the complexities of improvement as they were understood in the Romantic era, when there were many competing ideas about what form improvement should take. If her theatre is a school, then one of its lessons appears to be that sometimes improvement is either impracticable or undesirable, and Baillie's drama may itself be susceptible to this insight. Her pessimistic social critique – not to mention the rhetorical loading of the 'simple' and the natural, ideals that may advocate inaction as much as moderated improvement – threatens an exasperated conservatism from time to time. The cumulative force of communication breakdown in *Count Basil*, compelling primitive energy in *The Family Legend*, and the various forms of improving hubris in *The Alienated Manor* put pressure on even the most carefully calculated historical intervention.

Stressing the contribution of Baillie should help to challenge the category of Scottish Romanticism in diasporic, gender and genre terms, encouraging a more inclusive perspective on the canon than has sometimes been evident. A leading innovator in British theatrical culture during decades of political instability and war, Baillie places ideas of improvement front and centre in her drama. Baillie mocks philosophical pretensions about the primacy of the imagination through the character of Smitchenstault in *The Alienated Manor*, who announces that 'De imaginations is all dat we do know: de veritable real *true* is a foolish notion'.[147] But she leaves little doubt over the privileged role that sympathetick curiosity grants to the medium of imaginative literature, with drama as its purest expression. It is the force of Baillie's gesture to the power of literature to bring about change that lays claim to our sympathy, or at least curiosity.

Notes

1. See George Thomson to Robert Burns, September 1792, in *The Works of Robert Burns*, ed. Currie, vol. 4, pp. 1–3 (p. 2).
2. See Joanna Baillie to George Thomson, 18 February 1804, in *Collected Letters of Joanna Baillie*, ed. Slagle, vol. 1, pp. 93–4 (p. 93).

3. The main, Scottish portion of Thomson's collections – originally titled *A Select Collection of Original Scotish Airs* – continued to appear until 1846, as the editor modified and reissued his various volumes. For more on Thomson's work, see *Burns's Songs for George Thomson*, ed. McCue; McCue, 'George Thomson'; and McKeever, 'Simplicity, Rightly Understood'.
4. See McCue, 'George Thomson', p. 149.
5. See Joanna Baillie, 'Introductory Discourse', in *Plays on the Passions*, ed. Duthie, pp. 67–113 (pp. 113, 106). Hereafter cited as ID.
6. ID, p. 104.
7. See Mellor, 'Joanna Baillie and the Counter-Public Sphere'; Mellor, 'A Criticism of Their Own'; Burroughs, *Closet Stages*; Gamer, 'National Supernaturalism', reprised as ch. 4 in Gamer, *Romanticism and the Gothic*; and Cox, 'Staging Baillie'. Cox was also influential at an early stage in the revision of Baillie with *In the Shadows of Romance* (1987).
8. ID, p. 104.
9. ID, p. 106.
10. Slagle's *Baillie: A Literary Life* includes a chronology that details productions of Baillie's plays (pp. 25–33). Baillie's primary interest was in writing for the stage – in the 'Introductory Discourse', she insists that stage drama is 'a more valuable and useful production' than closet drama (ID, p. 109).
11. ID, pp. 93, 86.
12. Judson, 'Sympathetic Curiosity'. Sean Carney views the work of both Baillie and Smith as plagued by 'a surplus value' of 'antisocial desire' ('The Passion of Joanna Baillie', p. 227).
13. ID, p. 70. For more on torture and 'savagery' in Scottish Enlightenment moral philosophy, including Smith, see Berry, *Idea of Commercial Society*, pp. 142–6.
14. See Myers, 'Baillie's Theatre of Cruelty', p. 105.
15. See here Leask, *Curiosity and the Aesthetics of Travel Writing*.
16. Forbes, 'Baillie's Theater of the Passions', pp. 38, 41.
17. See Henderson, 'Passion and Fashion', p. 201, reprised in Henderson, *Romanticism*, p. 131.
18. Murray, 'Governing Economic Man', p. 1044.
19. Ibid. pp. 1045, 1051–4.
20. Smith, *Theory of Moral Sentiments*, p. 27.
21. See Carney, 'The Passion of Joanna Baillie', p. 233.
22. See Smith, *Theory of Moral Sentiments*, pp. 27–8.
23. Cox, 'Staging Baillie', p. 160.
24. ID, p. 90.

25. ID, p. 83.

26. ID, p. 101.

27. ID, p. 103.

28. See Henderson, *Romanticism*, pp. 128–9.

29. Cox, 'Staging Baillie', pp. 163–4.

30. See here Watkins's reading of *De Monfort* in *Materialist Critique*, pp. 39–59. This includes the suggestion of a 'formal-generic' component to this historical 'crisis', Romantic drama 'at once weighted with nostalgia and desire for the once powerful social world that had brought it to prominence', while also feeding off the new 'social energies' of the period (p. 40).

31. Baillie, *Count Basil: A Tragedy*, in *Plays on the Passions*, ed. Duthie, pp. 115–213 (p. 119). Hereafter cited as CB.

32. CB, I.i.2, 70.

33. CB, 'Persons of the Drama' and I.i.38–9.

34. CB, I.i.43.

35. CB, II.iii.29–34.

36. CB, II.i.42.

37. CB, II.iv.25–6.

38. Burroughs, *Closet Stages*, p. 137.

39. CB, IV.iii.150, 254.

40. CB, II.iv.37–8, 44.

41. CB, IV.iii.80.

42. Murray, 'Governing Economic Man', p. 1060.

43. CB, II.iv.38, 12.

44. See Richardson, *Literature, Education, and Romanticism*, pp. 185–6. Burroughs has a discussion of 'the stage as an instrument of social corruption' centred on unruly female sexuality (*Closet Stages*, pp. 44–6). On John Witherspoon's influential critique of the morality of the theatre in mid-eighteenth-century Scotland, see McLean, 'Hugh Blair and the Influence of Rhetoric', p. 148.

45. CB, II.iii.135.

46. CB, II.iii.35–40.

47. CB, V.i.66–7.

48. CB, V.ii.22.

49. CB, V.iii.182, 192–3.

50. CB, V.iii.171.

51. CB, II.iv.34.

52. Mellor, 'Joanna Baillie and the Counter-Public Sphere', pp. 565, 566.

53. Burroughs, *Closet Stages*, pp. 138–9.

54. Cox, 'Staging Baillie', p. 150.

55. CB, IV.i.16 and p. 201.

56. CB, V.i.43.

57. CB, III.ii.22–6.

58. CB, II.i.94–5.

59. CB, II.iv.11–16.

60. Scott, *Waverley*, p. 18; see Scott, 'General Preface to the Waverley Novels', p. 411.

61. See Slagle, *Baillie: A Literary Life,* pp. 48–52.

62. See Colley, *Britons*, p. 276; and Mellor, *Mothers of the Nation*, pp. 142, 11.

63. See Slagle, 'Evolution of a Writer', pp. 15–16; and Burroughs, *Closet Stages*, pp. 99–100.

64. O'Connell, *Ireland and the Fiction of Improvement*, p. 5.

65. ID, p. 76.

66. ID, p. 73; and Baillie, 'To the Reader' [prefixed to vol. 3 of *Plays on the Passions*], in the 1851 *Dramatic and Poetical Works*, pp. 228–35 (pp. 232–3).

67. ID, p. 79.

68. ID, p. 76.

69. ID, pp. 82–3.

70. Godwin, 'Essay of history and romance', in *The Political and Philosophical Writings of William Godwin*, ed. Philp, vol. 5: *Educational and Literary Writings*, ed. Clemit, pp. 291–301 (p. 301).

71. Swaim, *Scottish Men of Letters*, pp. 27–8.

72. Scott, *Guy Mannering*, p. 302.

73. Godwin, 'Essay of history and romance', p. 301.

74. Ibid. p. 297.

75. See Allan, 'Winged Horses, Fiery Dragons, and Monstrous Giants'; Duncan, *Scott's Shadow*, p. 133; and Hume, *Treatise of Human Nature*, for example pp. 82–3.

76. ID, p. 103.

77. Godwin, 'Essay of history and romance', p. 300.

78. ID, p. 81.

79. Hume, *Treatise of Human Nature*, pp. 172–5.

80. Godwin, 'Essay of history and romance', p. 294.

81. CB, II.iv.33–4.

82. Baillie, *The Family Legend: A Tragedy, in Five Acts*, in *Baillie: A Selection of Plays and Poems*, ed. Gilroy and Hanley, pp. 125–202. This edition hereafter cited as FL. See in the same edition, Baillie, 'To the Reader' (1810), pp. 127–31 (p. 131).

83. See Bakhtin, *The Dialogic Imagination*.

84. Williams, *Keywords*, pp. 87–90.

85. Duncan, *Scott's Shadow*, p. 63. See Lockhart, *Peter's Letters to his Kinsfolk*, vol. 3, pp. 301–38.

86. Baillie, 'To the Reader' (1810), p. 131.

87. FL, I.i.37.

88. O'Halloran, 'National Discourse or Discord?', pp. 46, 48.

89. Hamilton, *Cottagers*, pp. 118, 114. Mrs Mason is presumably an homage to the benevolent teacher of the same name in Wollstonecraft's *Original Stories from Real Life*.

90. Hamilton, *Cottagers*, p. 107.

91. See Jeffrey's review of *The Cottagers of Glenburnie* in *The Edinburgh Review* for July 1808, p. 402, also provided as an appendix to Perkins's edition at pp. 341–52.

92. Hamilton, *Cottagers*, pp. 100–1.

93. Blake, *The Marriage of Heaven and Hell*, in *The Complete Illuminated Books*, pp. 107–33 (p. 116).

94. See Kelly, *English Fiction of the Romantic Period*, p. 92.

95. Duncan, *Scott's Shadow*, p. 71.

96. Hamilton, *Cottagers*, p. 48.

97. See here Mary Douglas's influential *Purity and Danger*.

98. Duncan, *Scott's Shadow*, pp. 71–2.

99. FL, I.i.64, 69, 87.

100. FL, I.i.134.

101. Baillie, 'To the Reader' (1810), pp. 129–30.

102. FL, II.ii (p. 154).

103. FL, II.ii.48, 55–6.

104. FL, II.ii.7–8, 88–9.

105. FL, II.ii.92, 99.

106. FL, II.ii.209.

107. FL, II.ii.254–7.

108. FL, II.ii (p. 162).

109. FL, II.ii.168.

110. FL, II.ii.271–2.

111. FL, II.ii.75.

112. FL, II.iii.17.

113. FL, V.iii.46.

114. FL, V.iv.79–83.

115. FL, V.iv.124–5.

116. FL, V.iv.139–41, 148–53.

117. FL, V.iv.143.

118. Baillie, 'To the Reader' (1810), p. 130.

119. ID, p. 76. See here Cox, 'Staging Baillie', pp. 150–1.

120. Pittock, *Scottish and Irish*, p. 215.
121. ID, p. 79.
122. In the absence of a modern edition, the text of *The Alienated Manor* here is the first edition, in *Dramas*, vol. 1, pp. 121–249. Hereafter cited as AM. See I.i (p. 125).
123. See the 'Advertisement' to Baillie, *Dramas*, vol. 1, pp. v–vii (p. v).
124. AM, p. 122.
125. Hewitt, 'Improving the Law', p. 50.
126. AM, II.i (p. 151).
127. AM, p. 122; V.ii (pp. 235–8).
128. AM, I.i (p. 126).
129. AM, I.i (pp. 129, 124).
130. See Baillie, *The Tryal: A Comedy*, in *Plays on the Passions*, ed. Duthie, pp. 215–98 (II.i.104–11).
131. AM, II.i (p. 158); II.v (p. 180).
132. AM, I.i (p. 128).
133. AM, I.i (p. 126).
134. AM, IV.iii (p. 222); I.i (pp. 131–2).
135. Henderson, *Romanticism*, pp. 145–6, 147. See Bermingham in *Landscape and Ideology* on Uvedale Price's critique of Brown, which mounts a similar attack to Crafton's (pp. 66–7).
136. AM, II.i (p. 159).
137. Hewitt, 'Improving the Law', p. 52.
138. AM, I.ii (p. 143); IV.iii (p. 216).
139. See Andrews, *The Search for the Picturesque*, p. 9.
140. ID, p. 86.
141. Hewitt, 'Baillie's Ecotopian Comedies', para. 8.
142. See Judson, 'Sympathetic Curiosity', p. 52.
143. AM, V.iii (p. 249).
144. AM, I.i (p. 129).
145. AM, I.i (pp. 126–7).
146. AM, I.i (p. 129).
147. AM, V.iii (p. 246).

Chapter 4

The Story of John Galt's Scottish Novels

There is a set piece in John Galt's 1823 novel, *The Entail*, that illustrates the protagonist's tortured obsession with a plot of ancestral land. Following his dispossession as a young man, Claud Walkinshaw has made recovering his hereditary estate the 'actuating principle of his life'. This is reflected in his visits to a viewpoint that overlooks the now-reclaimed Kittlestonheugh acreage:

> On gaining the brow of the hill, he halted, and once more surveyed the scene. For a moment it would seem that a glow of satisfaction passed over his heart; but it was only a hectical flush, instantly succeeded by the nausea of moral disgust; and he turned abruptly around, and seated himself with his back towards the view which had afforded him so much pleasure. In this situation he continued some time, resting his forehead on his ivory-headed staff, and with his eyes fixed on the ground.[1]

Claud's 'nausea of moral disgust' prevents him from being able to look upon the estates he has idolised at such a high cost – a determination to secure this legacy having prompted him, among other things, to disinherit his first-born. Holding the 'ivory-headed staff' (p. 183) that we learn is adorned with the meaningful symbol of a lone silver eye, this pedlar-turned-Glasgow-grandee experiences a profound moral unease towards the end of a life of what Galt calls 'gathering' (p. 150): the accumulation of wealth. Claud is largely motivated by his fanatical pride in hereditary status, and the sense of just deserts in this passage is aimed primarily at that weakness via the one of simple avarice. Yet both faults serve a wider meditation in *The Entail* on the pitfalls and unintended consequences of improvement. In fact, this moment of shame emerges from a novel that deals with a whole series of social, political and moral anxieties occasioned by Scotland's Age of Improvement. Galt's writing is often characterised by its acute sense of the material advantages contingent upon the trajectory of modernisation. But while the project of *The Entail* sees his historical analysis vividly disintegrate – through both formal and thematic means – into pessimism, this is an amplification of tensions already inherent within his oeuvre, as demonstrated in the *Annals of the Parish* of 1821.

If Scottish literature of the early nineteenth century owes much to the cultural influence of the capital city of Edinburgh, Galt is a writer for whom Scotland's western urban centre is still more important. Building on his roots in Irvine and Greenock, Galt's work particularly reflects the experience of the west, concentrated around the emerging imperial trading hub of Glasgow. As Glaswegian merchants gorged themselves on the profits of colonial markets – becoming 'an oligarchy, as proud and sacred, in what respects the reciprocities of society, as the famous Seignories of Venice and Genoa' (*Entail*, p. 109) – a rapid transformation of the west seemed to focus the recent history of the Lowlands. Galt's brand of fiction as social history in the 1820s provides one of the most overt literary engagements with improvement in the period, picturing a totalising range of effects orbiting around commercial modernisation. Improvement, as we have seen, was a 'leitmotif' of the Scottish Enlightenment's account of commercial modernity;[2] and at the same time a malleable ideal that was applicable to diverse and contradictory models of progress. It provided the explanatory narrative for a reality in a permanent condition of becoming and, by the early decades of the nineteenth century, remained tied (incompletely) to the consolidation of the British state in both material and ideological terms. Galt's interest lies in the ground-level application of improvement's logic, in its characteristic victories and tragedies as a medium of long eighteenth-century life. The dialectical shape of improving discourse is clearly foregrounded in his Scottish novels, which render struggles such as that between luxury and morality, with a spatial politics that has imbibed enough of political economy to understand the scaling effects of market forces and that measures the resilience of the local and the national as counterbalances to globalisation.

Galt's fiction particularly lends itself to Raymond Williams's theoretical approach. If improving priorities were increasingly 'dominant' during the period, then we can constellate the cultural milieu relationally. The Scottish context occasions many forms of 'emergent' cultural production in the period, but the 'residual' category is of particular application here in considering the negotiation of local cultural forms both within and against the developing imperial hegemony. Williams notes that

> The residual, by definition, has been effectively formed in the past, but it is still active in the cultural process, not only and often not at all as an element of the past, but as an effective element of the present.[3]

Such residual cultural formations are often at the forefront in Galt. His Scottish novels are at pains to explore the capacity of the modernising imperial framework to cope with, and to sustain, the presence of localised, historically rooted and distinctive cultural forms. These native modes of cultural expression, which Galt largely resists the temptation to idealise, maintain a difficult relationship to improvement. This is expressed on many levels, including in conflicts between 'sober presbyterian simplicity' and new anglicised registers of speech;[4] in lingering, feudal attachments to the land; in fashion, as women 'lay aside the silken plaidie over the head, the which had been the pride and bravery of their grandmothers'; even through changing Christian names that render 'our Jennies, Jessies, and our Nannies, Nancies' (*Annals*, p. 49). Galt explores this situation with a fragile optimism, potentially yielding to a Gothic typology of haunting, as the national imaginary breaks down. Reflecting on the vigorous encroachments of capital into a society increasingly understood as a series of symbiotic localities, residual culture offers Galt an effective way of citing the moral ambiguities inherent in a new, dominant network of macroeconomic power. Again, however, he does not erase the blemishes of the residual cultures being affected by improvement. Indeed, he is deeply suspicious of tendencies towards atavism and sets out to problematise sentimental ideas of the local and the national that were emerging at the same moment as the politics of space were changing irrevocably. In this context, while national character can function as a subtle moral security in Galt's portrayal of the brink of modernity in the west of Scotland, it can also be reduced to a sinister, twisted force percolating through the new commercial world.

The foregoing chapters have identified key aesthetic innovations in poetry, short fiction and drama in which a range of ideas about improvement were embedded. For their part, Galt's idiosyncratic novels probe especially at the controversial dialogue between commerce and morality in improvement, at times casting the modernising project as eroding the cultural and ethical integrity of the Scottish nation, at others wondering if 'culture' itself is not a deadweight to the march of capital. Again, sociable and commercial exchange were twin arterials in the culture of improvement emerging during the eighteenth century. Adam Ferguson signals a complementary structure in isolating 'conversation' and 'production' as the chief motors of improvement:

> In the bustle of civil pursuits and occupations, men appear in a variety of lights, and suggest matter of inquiry and fancy, by which conversation is enlivened, and greatly enlarged. The productions of ingenuity are brought to the market; and men are willing to pay for whatever has a tendency to inform or amuse.[5]

Both 'conversation' and 'production' remain drivers of this historical trajectory for Galt, but he acknowledges the potential for a less seamless relationship. His novels present a sophisticated account of commerce, with an eye on the experience of towns such as Greenock and Irvine in the area immediately to the south-west of Glasgow – nearby Port Glasgow having been a hub for the arrival of rum, sugar, tobacco and other colonial goods. And in the introduction to her edited volume on Galt, Regina Hewitt notes the affinities between Galt's work and the pessimistic strain in Scottish Enlightenment historiography epitomised by Ferguson, who in less sanguine moments contributed to a literature of suspicion around the effects of 'luxury'.

Certainly Galt is attuned to the potential moral and cultural costs of improvement. In fact, as *The Entail* reveals, if localised cultures cannot be accommodated in this context, the outcome risks a chaotic mess in which an overcompensating historical consciousness prohibits what good improvement can offer. Galt frames this as a revenge of the human propensity for 'story', notionally banished by his characteristic version of the novel ('theoretical history'). I want to suggest that in *Annals of the Parish*, Galt's ironic prohibition of 'story' already bears a tragic element, while as we will see, much of that narrative energy has actually been absorbed by the history of improvement itself. Yet if that grand narrative has questionable aspects in *Annals*, it is truly perverted by clumsy attempts at cultural reconciliation in *The Entail*. Hewitt wants to stress Galt's analysis of the 'dynamics' of society above his evaluation of what she calls the 'progress plot', but this chapter focuses on their intersection, engaging with the author's reworking of the novel into an experimental test-case for the mechanisms of rapid change and its cultural impact at both a local and national level, with narrative itself the contested ground of history.[6]

The acuity with which Galt's fiction navigates the history of improvement should establish it as a key vehicle for the ongoing conversation around Scottish Romanticism.[7] Galt's sophisticated vision of Scottish history testifies to a distinctive experience with international dimensions, just as improvement transcends borders, and just as Galt's work as a leading colonialist (and improver) in Canada introduces a transatlantic perspective. His writing naturally serves the attempt to clarify a porous national voice within and beyond the 'four-nations' approach to British literature. It brings out a full dialectical engagement with improvement in Romantic literature, moving well beyond the symbiotic 'romantic critique' of modernisation emphasised by Makdisi to demonstrate why our base definition of Romanticism must encompass a more holistic view.[8] By considering Scottish Romanticism as a varied, modal set of literary works coordinated around the idea of improvement, we can open up this perspective and reap the full benefit of its example. Indeed, while Galt's unorthodox literary method might be viewed as acutely counter-Romantic – he is even more suspicious than Scott of the aesthetic and its literary apex in 'romance' – his oeuvre should instead encourage a supple taxonomic discipline, unbeholden to overt or Wordsworthian idealism of the imagination. Beginning, then, with the theoretical basis of Galt's fiction, this chapter moves through *Annals of the Parish* and *The Entail* to trace the development of his penetrating fiction of improvement.

'The shape and glamour o' novelles'

The early decades of the nineteenth century were marked by shifting cultural taxonomies. This evolving field is reflected in Galt's Scottish novels through characters' comments on recent changes in taste. These often-comedic observations serve as a reminder of an unstable though potentially lucrative context. Particularly prone to a sneering brand of this is the Walkinshaw matriarch, 'the Leddy', probably the heroine of *The Entail*, who responds to the love intrigues of her young family by regretting 'thir novella and play-actoring times' (p. 261). Expounding on what she considers to be a sea change in the attitudes of the upcoming generation, the Leddy points to the influence of literary vogue:

> When we reflek how the mim maidens now-a-days hae delivered themselves up to the Little-gude in the shape and glamour o' novelles and Thomson's Seasons, we need be nane surprised to fin Miss as headstrong in her obdooracy as the lovely young Lavinia that your sister Meg learnt to 'cite at the boarding-school. (p. 230)

Devilish and intoxicating, literature takes on a sinister role in this commonplace judgement.[9] With particular fears for young women, the Leddy (who betrays her own literary interests with the reference to Lavinia) voices an important position in the contemporary debate.[10] Suspicions of moral impropriety were persistently involved in the working-out of authorship status and the valuation of genres. Such doubts were exacerbated by the gendered perception of the novel. As Alan Richardson explains, 'Writers on female behaviour and education in the eighteenth and early nineteenth centuries were much concerned with the novel, a genre which had become widely identified with women as both its principal consumers [. . .] and producers.' This led to a variety of strategies on the part of writers, some of whom found themselves in awkward rhetorical positions. For example, Jane West, Hannah More and Mary Wollstonecraft all 'wrote novels while condemning the genre as a whole'.[11] In the case of Galt, an insistence on representing his practice as a kind of historical sociology can be understood as an attempt to masculinise the form – emphasising it as a site of pseudo-scientific enquiry and self-improvement, with the pedagogical weight of a 'vehicle of instruction'.[12] While remaining short of Joanna Baillie's instrumental view of the drama, Galt is then another advocate for the use-value of the aesthetic, albeit his work will not shake off its fundamental mistrust of storytelling and thus of its own métier.

These questions of utility emerged from a period in which the basic structures of literary production were in flux. As the book trade became increasingly market-oriented and authorship unhooked itself from the practice of patronage, the task of generating cultural capital entered a new phase. Still predating the comfortable model of a professional man of letters, Galt was sensitive to the prestige of his labour. Indeed, while largely lacking the aristocratic pretensions of Scott, he was equally at pains to distance himself from the image of a lower-status trade. After all, 'The eighteenth-century book trade was a barter industry that had once been associated with the stationers' guild. Booksellers frequently commissioned volumes, particularly novels, and paid by the word.'[13] It is important to remember the novelty of a man like Scott, who was able to navigate the social strata of hereditary privilege while earning a living as a working writer. Entering into this environment, the role of Scott's publisher (and the man behind the *Edinburgh Review*), Archibald Constable, was significant. Constable helped to dignify the profession by paying high fees, functioning as a kind of socio-economic buffer between a fading patronage system and the free market.[14] Indeed, as *laissez-faire* economics penetrated more deeply into Scottish society at all levels, the literary field provides us with a useful criterion for studying the process. The burgeoning marketplace can be considered an improved system, replacing patronage as part of the same historical motor as changes in land ownership or agricultural practice. Literary production was itself a hostage to, and beneficiary of, the same processes of improvement.

Writing in his *Literary Life* against this background, Galt explains, 'I think no ingenuity can make an entirely new thing. Men can only combine the old together; join legs and arms and wings as he may, only the forms of previously created things can be imitated.'[15] Distancing himself from the quasi-divine power of the imagination central to the Romantic ethos for which Coleridge is a spokesman, he enunciates what could be described as a pure Associationist aesthetic.[16] True creation is discarded as an idealistic myth; rather, the work of the writer is in reworking pre-existing materials into new configurations, however monstrous. This flaunts Galt's debt to the strain in Enlightenment philosophy for which Hume represents a vanishing point. He takes the logic of association and applies it to the creative process. Though this might appear to involve a diminution of art, and of the human mind *per se*, Galt makes it clear that he believes quite the opposite, that the form of literary endeavour he outlines deserves to be considered extremely highly.[17] Moreover, this renunciation of the entirely 'creative' faculty remains in tension, as demonstrated in instances where he seeks to reintroduce elements of 'art' into his practice:

> It is imagined that I have drawn entirely on my recollection, both for the incidents and characters of my most valuable pictures; and it has been alleged that I have had very little recourse to that kind of invention, composition, which constitutes the vitality of art [. . .] There is a universal harmony in Nature, and in the imitation and perception of this divine impress consist the excellence and the glory of art. One may extract by observation the elements, as it were, of works of art, but the discernment of the eternal and universal harmony is essential to their formation.

Here we find Galt searching for an adequate vocabulary to describe his work, anxious to protect himself from accusations of mere 'recollection'. 'Harmonising' emerges as a possible solution, in a passage where he also disclaims having first-person experience of his novels' lower-class subject matter – a point that bears both social and cultural capital.[18] The stress is very much on 'representation' rather than 'creation', yet a tension is clear. Galt is keen to appropriate value through his lack of pretension to a spurious transcendental creativity, yet reluctant to downplay the artistic endeavour clearly so central to his writing.

Regina Hewitt stresses Galt's 'sense of obligation to contribute to society', with an attendant suspicion of literary work as pompous and socially redundant.[19] We also should not underestimate the canny aspect of his approach, which saw Galt 'capitalise on the growing interest in social history'.[20] He was also a businessman. In the contested 1820s and subsequently, however, Galt's rejection of the 'creative' faculty in favour of the 'recreative' opened him to a form of high-cultural criticism:

> We see quite enough of real life without sitting down to the perusal of a dull account of the commonplace course and events of existence. The writer who imitates life like a Dutch painter, who chooses for his subjects turnips, fraus, and tables is only the copyist of inferior objects; whereas the mind that can create a sweet and beautiful though visionary romance, soars above such vulgar topics and leads the mind of readers to elevated thoughts.[21]

This complaint from Susan Ferrier represents a significant historical view of Galt. Attention to the 'commonplace' is construed as a vulgar substitute for 'visionary romance', with Galt's writing merely hackwork from a lesser talent. In 1959 Eric Frykman was also mistaking a set of literary mores for a shortcoming in ability when he concluded that Galt, 'was embarrassed by an uneasy feeling that invention was dishonest. It was not only that his imagination was limited: he also distrusted the higher power of creative, as opposed to documentary, truth'.[22] It would be naive to accept an author wholly on their own terms, but 'recreation' is entirely the point for Galt, who advertises a rigorous approach to social machinations, bound up in a tense rejection of the frivolity of romance.

As part of this, Galt's fiction is juxtaposed against the developing *Bildungsroman* form with its stress on the individual. Instead, his concern resides with a network of causation: individual will is incorporated within a vast matrix of interlocking connections from which it cannot and must not be extricated.[23] Personal agency becomes quickly subsumed within a universal narrative – that of 'improvement'. If this endorses a sense of conformity in which heroic or rebellious activity is fatal, it also feeds a sophisticated view of social history as a kind of mass kinesis, heavily influenced by Enlightenment thinkers including Adam Ferguson.[24] By the same token, it anticipates Thomas Carlyle's lament for a society that has 'lost faith in individual endeavour', though without that obviously negative emphasis.[25] Alongside stresses on 'instruction' and 'imitation', the systemic perspective underpins Galt's claim on the innovative literary form that he terms 'theoretical history'. Resonating with the Enlightenment conjectural historiography of which it is in some respects the closest literary analogue, the term neatly encapsulates his proposed aesthetic programme. Theoretical histories are to perform a speculative interrogation of social, political and cultural conditions not strictly based on specific factual examples, yet striking at a particular kind of certifiable reality. In contrast to the Coleridgean or Keatsian nod to the creative imagination as a guarantor of truth, Galt justifies his tales by way of the same arguments that were applied to Enlightenment reconstructions of ancient history: a reasoned likelihood of truth based on a careful examination of macroscopic patterns. While Scott's historical fiction drew heavily on the same historiography, Galt's approach is to claim a more complete or faithful conjectural methodology. As he wrote, 'It is not in this age that a man of ordinary common sense would enter into competition in recreative stories, with a great genius who possessed the attention of all. I mean Sir Walter Scott'.[26] The term 'recreative stories' is interesting, seeming to confirm the limits of the mind: even the monolithic Scott is only capable of secondary 'recreation'. Given that direct competition with Scott would be commercial suicide, Galt formulates a rival position as 'a man of ordinary common sense', carving out a space in the literary field as the producer of fiction-as-science, a form of robust social analysis. This empirical flavour sanctions the memorable comment on his literary productions, in which Galt announces that 'the best of them are certainly deficient in the peculiarity of the novel', lacking 'a consistent fable' or 'story'.[27]

A wilful rejection of 'story' is central to Galt's theoretical method, which seeks to remain entirely immanent to history as the record of improvement's material and cultural phenomena. Rejecting the overarching and complex plotting of romance as purveyed by Scott,

> Galt cleaves to a trompe-l'oeil mimicry of those secular narrative forms, admitted to the fold of historiography in the late Enlightenment, that have transmitted the historical record without the conspicuous imposition of a plot: memoir, anecdote, local annals or chronicle, the 'statistical account'.[28]

This formal condition helps to make Galt such an important novelist (retaining the term) of improvement, since he is concerned with replicating not only the subject matter but also key non-fictional textual forms of the culture (we should also mention periodicals here).[29] In practice, of course, Galt's limitation of the fictional is far from watertight, and indeed the proximity between romance plotting and conjectural history's faith in archetypal experience prefigures the studied collapse of his aesthetic framework in *The Entail*. Yet it is probably most faithfully realised in *Annals of the Parish*, which is a direct reflection of Sinclair's first *Statistical Account* in both subject matter and narrative style. Appropriating the *Account*'s formal mediation through the eyes of parish ministers and its miscellaneous concern with local enquiry, Galt produces a striking echo, even ironic replica, of improvement's sacred text.[30] If the *Account* was designed as both a record and instrument of improvement, then *Annals of the Parish* seeks to delve further into the experience of these processes dynamically unfolding at ground level. Although the model of *Annals* is never exactly replicated, it provides an informative basis for Galt's ensuing literary career, as reflected in his publication of subsequent important texts under the moniker of the 'Author of Annals of the Parish'.[31] Furthermore, as specifically a precedent for the more expansive project of *The Entail*, *Annals* will allow us to identify the growing tensions in Galt's rendering of Scotland.

Enlightened Fiction

At the beginning of *Annals of the Parish*, Galt's best-known novel, Micah Balwhidder is placed as the parish minister for Dalmailing (p. 1). It is 1760, the year of George III's ascension to the British throne. This contiguity is fundamental to the construction of the work, in which small-scale local events are linked to wider national and global affairs, all part of the same interlocking system. Balwhidder's appointment is a contentious one, reflecting the agitation over patronage in the Kirk that remained a source of widespread disaffection throughout the period. Balwhidder, who is a member of the Moderate party, is selected by a patron, in a process that was at odds with the popular Evangelical desire for parishioners to choose their own minister (p. 5). This is a notable signposting at the opening of the text, establishing the terms of a contest between residual culture and improvement. The community eventually forgets the perceived imposition of the appointment, yet the suggestion that Balwhidder represents the modernising wing of the Kirk at this stage is interesting, since he will presently struggle to comprehend or endorse the pace of social change. This is apparent in subsequent episodes such as his complaint about a young minister's 'Englified' language: by this point Balwhidder's taste for the 'plain auld Kirk of Scotland' has lost touch with 'the younger part of the congregation' (p. 132). A significant generational gap has opened up in Scottish society, alienating the minister's investment in residual cultural forms. While, often after the fact, Balwhidder achieves a largely positive outlook on improvement during the epoch traced by *Annals* – his providentialist faith in God's plan affording significant reassurance – his attachment to expressions of residual particularism weakens his relationship to the institutional force of the Moderates and to improvement in general. Though by no means a defensive Scottish patriot (note the personal identification with George III), the minister is consistently troubled by the local impact of improvement, even if, as Martha Bohrer argues, he himself is 'unconsciously' improved along with his community.[32] Surveying this pattern, the novel is the elderly Balwhidder's retrospective meditation upon his time in Dalmailing, laying particular emphasis on cumulative improvements. A hostage to the forces of a globalised imperial economy, the village experiences a steady penetration of its rural way of life by technological, cultural and political innovation.

Improvement, in *Annals*, exists in something like its normative Enlightenment form, as a process of incremental social modification, with prosperity the root cause of a clustering of effects that ranges from manners to dress and speech to religious faith. As is to be expected, it is not without its controversies in shaping the life-world that Balwhidder dimly understands is coming into being before his eyes. Key to Galt's contribution to the literature of improvement is his demonstration of the way that instance and system interact, introducing the narrative of improvement as a persistent subtext to everyday life, just as the segmented, annalistic form of the text itself insists on the parts of a whole. The driving forces of improvement are both local and universal, specific and general. Thus *Annals* subtly mixes human agency with the apparently inexorable material forces drawing Dalmailing into modernity. When Lord Eglesham is catapulted from his coach to land head-first in a midden, this occasions the improvement of the road; yet the text's litany of similar occurrences quickly subsumes the human prompt, which becomes incidental in a general trend that perhaps all along rendered the process inevitable.[33] This presents a sophisticated image of the shades of utility and futility to single events in history, a perspective that the notionally unimportant village setting helps to amplify, as it plays host to modernity's arrival. It also foregrounds an issue of free will – what can an individual signify in the Age of Improvement? For his part, Balwhidder sees the agency of providence at work, that altogether more passive language of progress, with God having abashed Eglesham's pride (pp. 41–3). Yet as the reader is invited to perceive, the true invisible forces at work in Dalmailing are those of modernisation and globalisation, narrative effects of an unimaginable network of constituent agents. Particularly exposed to these influences through their pivotal imperial trade position, the local communities of the west of Scotland are establishing firmer links with a broader geographical zone.

Confronted by this steady change, Balwhidder's sporadic verdicts on the process show him wrestling between his instinctive conservatism and a somewhat lagging respect for innovation, the text exhibiting a deep sensitivity to the dilemma of improvement:

> At the time, these alterations and revolutions in the parish were thought a great advantage; but now when I look back upon them, as a traveller on the hill over the road he has passed, I have my doubts. For with wealth come wants, like a troop of clamorous beggars at the heels of a generous man, and it's hard to tell wherein the benefit of improvement in a country parish consists, especially to those who live by the sweat of their brow. (p. 50)

This description of improvements under the rubric of 'alterations and revolutions' is significant, the latter term invoking the political unrest that at various points plagues Balwhidder's ministry. In certain lights, improvement can be as disquieting as radical discontent for the rural minister. Duncan is correct to point out the text's demonstration of the positive influence of commercialisation, Galt in one instance exemplifying Adam Smith's theory of capitalism's 'invisible hand' at work (the historical precursor to the dubious 'trickle-down effect').[34] And indeed, in this context, attempts to hold rigidly on to the past might very well be immoral. Yet the text demands something more than patronising amusement in response to Balwhidder's point that improvement also brings 'wants', which, via the double meaning, indicates not simply unnecessary luxuries but also a sense of moral deficiencies creeping into hardworking rural life. Smith himself flags such concerns when discussing the social impact of the division of labour. Specialisation is capable of producing workers 'as stupid and ignorant as it is possible for a human creature to become', and involves a worrying decline from the collective martial responsibility that Smith cites in classical models.[35] Furthermore, as Balwhidder's complaint about 'Englified' language makes clear, elements in the improving trajectory may pose a threat to a localised way of life specifically associated with residual cultural integrity. Indeed, in spatial terms, they may erase the local as formerly known: distinctive, uneven places becoming nodes in a transnational system of exchange that is financial and cultural at once.

The vigour of modernisation in *Annals* renders Balwhidder's professional duty of spiritual care primarily a matter of conservation, with his Presbyterian variety of moral improvement providing succour against change rather than being a viable alternative means of progress. 'We were, doubtless, brought more into the world, but we had a greater variety of temptation set before us' (p. 152), he reflects. These fears again chime with the pessimistic side to Enlightenment historiography, Adam Ferguson having fretted that 'many of the boasted improvements of civil society, will be mere devices to lay the political spirit at rest, and will chain up the active virtues more than the restless disorders of men'.[36] Wary of social decay and an erosion of patriotic citizenship in the face of 'civility', Ferguson goes further than Smith in representing the division of labour as a dangerous force. However, in Galt at least it is important to recognise that this corruption is not merely with regard to universal values. Running through his Scottish novels is the fear that improvement necessarily involves a dilution of local specificity, which is enough to give Galt pause *even though* that specificity had always been imperfect. William Robertson wrote that 'Commerce tends to wear off those prejudices which maintain distinction and animosity between nations. It softens and polishes the manners of men.'[37] Robertson couches the process largely in positive terms, yet the dilemma is clear. Must the 'polishing' of 'manners' and the supersession of 'prejudice' come at the price of national identity? In the case of *Annals*, Ann Roberts Divine observes how the experience of Meg Gaffaw – who is described as 'a daft woman' (p. 70) and a 'natural' (p. 159) and is thus a ready incarnation of the community's *völkisch* conscience – enforces a dark aspect to the progress narrative, since her social isolation contributes to an inability to adapt to the new world. Even if the changes in Dalmailing are taken to be an unequivocal good, the question remains of who specifically benefits and who is left behind by improvement? Indeed, might the market economy sometimes entrench rather than transcend disadvantage?

This picture of a fatal, categorical indisposition to history will recur in *The Entail*; in *Annals* the coding of Meg's suicide by drowning at the cotton mill (p. 160) is clear: it is the passing of the 'old ways, of which she is both practitioner and symbol'.[38]

Galt foregrounds a vacillation over the effects of improvement when discussing the writing of *Annals* in his autobiography. Recounting a visit to the village of Inverkip, he meditates on the 'progress [that] had been made in turning it inside out':

> The alteration was undoubtedly a great improvement, but the place seemed to me neither so picturesque nor primitive as the old town, and I could not refrain from lamenting the change, as one sighs over the grave of an old man.[39]

Annals goes to some lengths to highlight the benefits of improvement in Dalmailing, but adequate space remains for the text to register its threatening aspects. P. H. Scott further confirms this latitude by noting the Rousseau essay that Galt associates with his endeavour, which concerns the question, 'Has the progress of the arts and sciences contributed more to the corruption or purification of morals?'[40] By diminishing the 'picturesque' and the 'primitive', these processes of 'alteration' exert a disquieting agency upon this figuring of a national heartland. Balwhidder's own conservation of national character seems to offer a level of reassurance, but the antagonisms cannot be ignored. Bohrer argues that the minister 'illustrates the moral sentiments necessary for the humane functioning of *laissez faire* capitalism', yet there is a suggestion that this ethical stability is a direct product of the local systems that are acted upon by improvement.[41] A faith in residual culture maintains the power to upset the positive trend, the fading of the 'old man' of traditional practice a cause for concern.

Furthermore, Galt's analysis of commerce itself is not homogeneous. To take an example: Balwhidder's second wife, Lizy Kibbock, embodies an entrepreneurial spirit in the text and though the minister is disturbed when she transforms the manse into 'a factory of butter and cheese', her industriousness has a roundly positive effect in the community: it 'made many a one beak his shins in comfort, that would otherwise have had but a cold coal to blow at' (p. 33). And yet Lizy's work is rooted in a form of pre-industrial labour organisation – cottage industry – that is quite different from the local cotton mill, which signifies an urban way of life associated with 'unhealthy melancholy' (p. 136), and which is vulnerable to speculative capital in a way that, on one occasion, brings 'sore distress' for the workers and their families (p. 199). That particular crash impels the establishment of a Savings Bank, and thus the ascendant dialectic of improvement continues, but it is clear that industrial modernity will not be without its tragedies.

The text's fidelity to the form of the yearly record is significant, above and beyond facilitating Galt's charting of the ongoing, local manifestations of global improvement. This is also a material reflection of his publishing experiences. Apparently tailor-made for serialisation (though *Annals* was not itself published in serial form), Galt's theoretical history flaunts the shaping influence of his role writing for *Blackwood's*, with compact, relatively self-contained units unfolding the story. Frank Hallam Lyell notices this point with regard to Galt's vocal denials of the novel form.[42] Certainly the segmented format helps to underwrite the supposed refusal of a 'consistent fable' across the piece, even if the 'theoretical' tenor of these annalistic passages has less to do with their length and more to do with an assault on the romance contents of prose fiction *per se*, with 'story' itself the sign of a literariness that Galt purports to find disreputable.

Still, recent criticism has elaborated on Galt's use of the short form as a rebuttal to the increasing dominance of the novel and its characteristic tendencies. Bohrer contextualises his stressing of community above individuality within the genre of 'tales of locale', which deny the 'romantic reconciliation of class differences as advanced in the novel', Galt picturing instead 'a community that functions as part of a material, global economy'.[43] Also coordinating Galt's denial of novelistic romance via genre is Caroline McCracken-Flesher, who focuses on the form of the 'sketch', where 'inadequate narrators' combine with 'shifting perspectives' to illustrate 'the wonderful impossibility of plot, or of "fable" with its limitations to meaning'.[44] And, working along similar lines, Duncan describes serialised narratives as particularly amenable to 'the effects of fragmentation and heterogeneity'. Yet, taking a different tack to McCracken-Flesher, he submits that 'incompletion' in Galt has the potential to invite a kind of 'participatory narration' that demands the reader's collaboration in assembling a story's 'virtual community' – in other words, he construes fragmentation as generating rather than withholding narrative.[45] As noted in Chapter 2, early nineteenth-century novels themselves drew on the fragmentary possibilities of short fiction. Nevertheless, the formal architecture of *Annals* clearly participates in Galt's denial of 'story' as a key thrust of this experimental fictional method. If open-ended short fictions sit alongside the theoretical history as another rebuttal of the novelistic vending of romance, then perhaps a work such as *Annals* partakes of something of both forms. While not as radically disrupted as, for example, McCracken-Flesher's models, the serial history of *Annals* offers an integral, even flagship example of Galt's undercutting of the rising *Bildungsroman*.

Again, *Annals* is also a formal homage to the literature of improvement. The contemporary periodical press, alluded to both directly and obliquely by the narrative, was a key site for improving debates. Not least in this was Balwhidder's own preferred reading material, the *Scots Magazine*, whose 'eclectic mix of subjects' and 'annual January summary of the foregoing year's foreign affairs' are far from coincidental.[46] Across the yearly unfolding of the minister's life, however, there is a profound debt to Sinclair's *Statistical Account* and not merely in terms of improving ideology, statistical enquiry or segmented analysis. The imposition of Balwhidder's slightly eccentric narration is also a nod to Galt's source, which contains an entertaining variety of personalities. For example, in her study of the *Old Statistical Account* (Galt is writing a decade before the appearance of the second *Account*), Maisie Steven notes that the contributor for Fala and Soutra in the Lothians 'resorts to sarcasm' with a complaint that, 'It is only fashionable for the lower classes of people to attend the church. The higher orders are above the vulgar prejudice of believing it is necessary to worship the God of their fathers.'[47] Galt uses the persona of Balwhidder to satirise the idiosyncratic vision of Scottish improvement immortalised by the parish ministers of the *Account*. By the same token, Balwhidder enables Galt to demonstrate the non-transparent interface between an individual and the world.[48] Unstably swaying between an acknowledgement of the importance of human activity and a faith in God's plan, the minister functions as a caricatured and inverted version of the reader's implied experience, in which the hard reality of improvement occasionally gives way to 'romantic' ideas such as fate and predestination.[49] It is this fluid, ironic perspective that permits *Annals* its complex judgemental framework, manoeuvring us through a doubled perspective, chronicling how a worldview fits itself to circumstances, alongside the limitations, inconsistencies and consolation inherent in the process.

Mathew Wickman suggests that Balwhidder's attempts to rationalise a hugely complex global reality are presented as necessarily imperfect, that the text ultimately explodes a systematic understanding of the world. A denial of simplicity certainly rings true as part of Galt's assertion of vast, cryptic involvedness in place of the simplistic threads of 'story', and Wickman neatly identifies the ironic limitations imposed on Balwhidder's worldview. Yet while he argues that the rendering of localised experience within a coherent network *per se* must resolve itself as an insufficient kind of myth-making, this risks underestimating globalisation itself, the complexity of which may be inconceivable without rendering it illusory.[50] Indeed, we may be inclined to insist that *Annals*'s notion of a 'great web of commercial reciprocities' (p. 197) only signifies an inevitable and primordial condition being rendered tangible: the idea of a truly isolated system on earth, whether economic, ecological or otherwise, being a fantasy.

The metaphor of the web nicely foregrounds what emerges as the tense narrativity of improvement in the text, which, for all its denial of 'consistent fable', serves up a remarkably tight version of history. Indeed, there is a strong sense in which the theoretical history has not dispensed with 'story' at all but, rather, that improvement itself monopolises that function for Galt's fiction of social and economic change, a subject area in which, he implies, the usual methods of novelistic storytelling are unsuitable. Viewed in this light, the theme of interconnectedness in *Annals* begins to provide a further, perhaps even inadvertent, reflection back on to Galt's programmatic literary approach. In this purest emanation of the theoretical history, the globalising imperial economy may be itself a methodological suppressor of romance – consuming, by demystifying, the enigmatic imaginative spaces it requires. Just as the 'old ways' are smothered by a tide of exchange, so, too, lyrical and mythic perspectives are lost, as 'theoretical' becomes the only valid form of history. Improvement, in this account, at once annihilates 'story' and reconstitutes it as the spectacle of its own cultural and material processes. The character of Colin Mavis suggests this condition, as a pastoral poet who works as a mill clerk, described by Divine as 'a shepherd poet misplaced in an industrial age'.[51] Colin's eventual literary success is less a challenge to, than a confirmation of, the new order, coming as it does only once he has been incorporated by improved modernity (pp. 173–4). In dialectic terms, the thesis of improvement has trumped the antithesis of romance. And in this rendering of an age of limitless connection, some versions of 'story' may be a faded possibility as much as a redundant excess, what Carlyle would call the 'Age of Machinery' replacing heroic narratives with those of system.[52]

Balwhidder's statistical account of Dalmailing stays remarkably faithful to its aesthetic agenda, offering up an account of modernity as a process of constant, worldwide revelation that seems to preclude 'story' as traditionally understood. Epitomising Galt's denial of plotting, the text formulates an innovative narrative methodology by appropriating discourses of empirical analysis found in its non-fictional precedents, and thus, as Duncan comments, resists the engagement of an 'allegorical mode'.[53] Disclaiming the imposition of an external meaning upon events, *Annals* navigates the world according to Balwhidder through a methodical, journalistic sequence of events: exploring the complex terrain of a globalising economy described through Newtonian rubric. Balwhidder's own attempts at allegory – his faith in the workings of providence – form a pseudo-comic foil to the text's own position, in which meaning is an internal, metonymic product of the ongoing workings of socio-economic improvement. Yet while *The Entail* will see Galt's refusal of 'story' vividly collapse, there are also studied chinks in the non-fictional armour of *Annals* above and beyond the necessary shortcomings in Galt's paradoxical literary ideal, as in the baleful imagery of orphaned children waiting 'on the green' (p. 200), their father having been ruined by the failure of the cotton-mill company. Duncan notes this as a sign of capitalism's 'spasmodic contractions' threatening to impose a sinister grand narrative.[54] Certainly the defining term, improvement, constantly inclines to become a national myth. However, despite such tensions and Balwhidder's alternative viewpoint – with religion itself apparently motivated by an archaic need for 'story' – the novel goes to some lengths to ensure a secular, non-allegorical explanation for itself.

Annals of the Parish is probably the text that best exemplifies Galt's literary theory in practice, his ideal of a non-fictional fiction. Right on cue, reviewers documented the supposed realism of the work, including John Wilson who, according to Blackwood, described it as 'not a book but a fact'.[55] Looking back on the piece, Galt later insisted he 'had no idea it would ever have been received as a novel', and that it was 'as different from a novel, as a novel can be from any other species of narrative', describing it as a 'treatise on the history of society'.[56] Appropriating a mode of empirical enquiry from influences including the *Statistical Account*, Balwhidder's tale charts the dramatic experience of improvement in a pinpointed area of the west of Scotland – marking its emergence as a new type of locality, a segment or circle of influence in an ever-expanding network of consolidating imperial power. Improvement, *Annals* suggests, is a largely benevolent force. Yet seeing beyond Balwhidder's stubborn faith in God's plan, the reader faces a more ambiguous situation. Partly construed as the loss of the local as a site of cultural particularism, of stability – perhaps even of imaginative freedom – globalisation brings an uncertain energy to bear.

Dramatising the rise of a network of constant interrelation, or 'history', topos and methodology act as one in *Annals*: a global awareness negating the shadowy ideological space for romance or 'story'. Galt presents allegorical modes of understanding as a surplus hangover in a new society that is saturated by raw information, as fact trumps fiction. There is an unavoidable irony, of course, in that this supposedly naked image of history constantly resolves itself into one of the most significant grand narratives of all: the inexorable rise of the modern, commercial world as described by improvement. In this way, the human infatuation with 'story' has not been obviated so much as displaced. As it unfolds, like its inspiration in the *Statistical Account*, Galt's text ably demonstrates a distance between the 'enlightened' project of Balwhidder's historical chronicle and the interjection of his personal urges, prejudices and opinions. In this respect, *Annals of the Parish* grants the history of improvement a human touch, allowing us to recognise the impact of rapid change upon an individual. The minister moves from a position of perceived dangerous novelty at his appointment to become a cultural relic, exemplifying the dizzying speed of improvement in the period and beginning to hint at the challenges it brings.

National Crisis

'LET GLASGOW FLOURISH!' runs the civic motto that closes *The Entail* (p. 364). The city is especially central here. The novel asserts that if Edinburgh is the legal and cultural capital of Scotland, Glasgow is its commercial powerhouse: a town of 'Fatted calves, and feasting Belshazers' (pp. 355–6). Just beyond its halfway point, the novel informs us that 'a general spirit of improvement [. . .] was then gradually diffusing itself over the face of the west country' (p. 205). Change is foregrounded, then, within a text that charts an entire historical trajectory and asks a series of questions about what it means. Alyson Bardsley theorises that *The Entail* 'criticizes the fervor of collective identity it associates with nationalism and renders its pursuit tragic and ridiculous'.[57] In parts the text does render ideas, or rather 'stories' of the nation as septic and ironically self-serving expedients, which lead to isolation and social breakdown. Yet if this represents a dismissal or critique of nationalism *per se*, it must be understood within the context of the history of improvement. Unfolding a series of personal and collective crises in a text that porously reflects and ridicules the state of the literary tradition, this novel is Galt's extended essay on the Scotland of his day. It is a text in which improvement and nostalgia both take on a very ambivalent character indeed.

The Entail wastes no time in beginning to construct the intricate framework that threatens to form the text into a full-blown allegory of national history. Indeed, the tale of the Walkinshaw family is so roundly figurative that it might seem heavy-handed, if that density was not exactly the point. The saturation of the novel with touchstone historical allusions creates a realm in which these have become an obsessive and counter-productive language, a perverse expression of 'story' that accompanies the history of improvement. Claud is a victim of his father's involvement in Scotland's attempt to become an independent imperial power through the Darien scheme, and his rise to regain his ancestral estate charts a long history of improvement, with attendant moral emergencies. Given Darien's position as a key perceived motivator behind the Act of Union, Claud's poverty and subsequent 'gathering' carry a heavy national-symbolic load. In her role as early protector of Claud, the servant Maudge Dobbie embodies the final vestige of his family's prior standing, and is the source of 'goblin lore and romantic stories' of the national past. However, at this stage the boy displays a predilection for the (here Anglocentric and metropolitan) fiction of economic accumulation: he 'early preferred the history of Whittington and his Cat to the achievements of Sir William Wallace' (pp. 3–4).

Yet the description of patriotic Scottish history as a quasi-mythical area to which Claud's avaricious taste is disinclined is slightly misleading. For central to the problem of his life is an infatuation with his family's lost status that is represented as irrational or foolishly idealistic. As Galt writes, 'avarice with him was but an agent in the pursuit of that ancestral phantom which he worshipped as the chief, almost the only good in life' (p. 76). His sacrificial pursuit of former glories occasions the disinheritance of his favourite and eldest son – a transgression against 'the natural way' (p. 57) – as only the most prominent example in a life where emotional ties and even personal gratification are muted. A throwback to a period of feudal allegiance – or as his wife puts it, the 'papistical and paternostering' times (p. 259) – Claud's goal places an inappropriate historical burden upon the commercial environment of modernising Scotland. Economic overdrive on its own might be challenging, but the novel suggests that a brand of cultural conservatism is making things worse. Consigned to the substance of improvement by the sociological realism of Galt's theoretical history, 'story' erupts as a variegated threat here, with titanic change bearing a troublesome counterpart in a retreat to the cultural past. In fact, with his eldest and youngest sons demarking the alternative possibilities presented to eighteenth-century Britain – Jacobite Charles and Hanoverian George – Claud's motives are symptomatic of a misalignment of society, his family emblematising a culture divided between incompatible and antagonistic polarities: 'humanity' is butting against 'economy' (both financial and emotional) by virtue of a miscarrying historical narrative.

The world of the novel is being suffocated by an arid legal culture. This is, after all, a text narrated by a lawyer, one that takes as both its title and its central plot device a constrictive legal fiction: the entail. The entailing of land was highly topical in the early nineteenth century, by which time approximately 50 per cent of Scotland was held under this system. With the Abolition of Heritable Jurisdictions Act of 1746, following the Jacobite Rising, the reform of land law represented a key thrust to the modernisation of society. Yet entails offered an interesting succour to the process, providing 'a grant bind-ing heirs through a legal device to the same degree that feudal law had bound them, but on the terms of the new commercial society'.[58] In a sense, then, the entail is itself a throwback to a former stage of history – perhaps even a Gothic remnant – and is thus the appropri-ate tool for Claud's retrospective passion.[59] Indeed, the legal fiction was attacked by Adam Smith as a sacrifice of the future to the past, in a passage that may have provided inspiration for Galt's novel: 'They are founded upon the most absurd of all suppositions [. . .] that the poverty of the present generation should be restrained and regulated according to the fancy of those who died perhaps five hun-dred years ago.'[60] Awkwardly locking land into large estates, the device is an impediment to modernisation for Smith, who notes, 'It seldom happens [. . .] that a great proprietor is a great improver.'[61] Devine complicates Smith's view by noting the effect of legislation in 1770 that 'partially alleviated' the 'rigidity' of the entail system, and by stressing 'the strongly interventionist role of many landown-ers'.[62] Still, as an 'instrument that articulates the trace of the feu-dal in the commercial', the entail represents the culture clash with which the novel is concerned, being one of its dangerous, even mon-strous results.[63] If the medieval English fable of Dick Whittington is featured as a narrative seed for modern British commercialism, the entail as a pre-British leftover inverts this perspective. Positioned as the symbol of a historical crux, it is the unifying emblem of the text's epistemological battles, variously expressed as emotion versus commerce, religion versus law, history versus romance, or nature versus its abomination. Consider, for example, the lawyer Keelevin's attempts to persuade Claud against his plan to entail his lands and thus pervert the normal patrilineal succession. He complains that 'there's no Christianity in this'. Claud's reply is succinct: 'But there may be law, I hope' (p. 57).

If one of the divisions the text makes is between a modernising commercial society and a residual west coast Presbyterianism, end-less legal disputation pervades the whole. Unrestrained commercial-ism emerges as a weaponised form of self-interest, but so too are more traditional social relations – such as family lineage – tainted in a Hobbesian social commentary. Lawyers are shown to have a decid-edly unethical power, positioned at the heart of the social model, 'grasping, as they do, the whole concerns and interests of the rest of the community' (p. 55). Duncan observes a literary quality to this attack on legal casuistry:

> *The Entail* articulates a sharp critique, from the empirical-realist per-spective of a West-country merchant class, of an Edinburgh *noblesse du robe* which misrecognizes commercial society through its promotion of an ideology of feudal nostalgia. This (crypto-Jacobite) Edinburgh ascen-dancy includes not just the law but the literary culture which disciplines the city's professions and institutions, exemplified by the cultural indus-try of romance revival.[64]

We should stress that this 'West-country merchant class' are them-selves targeted by a text that is also suspicious of excessively financial motives. Indeed, Galt is partly exploring the workings of capitalism in the absence of Smith's curative 'sympathy'. Within its framework of legalese, the novel is punctuated by commercial modes of expression, with even metaphysical machinery described under the rubric of commerce: 'Life is but a weaver's shuttle, and Time a Wabster, that works for Death, Eternity, and Co. great whole merchants' (p. 279).

Yet Duncan rightly identifies the demonisation of an Edinburgh that is the foil to a Glaswegian commercial ideal, incorporating the law and literature in a denunciation that it is hard not to sense is aimed personally at Scott. This attack plays on a suspicion of Edinburgh as 'the intellectual city' (p. 179), invoking the city's aca-demic culture and 'metaphysical refinement' (p. 187) in a sweeping mockery of east coast pretentiousness, but a particular component shines through. Mirroring Claud's inappropriate commingling of feudalism and commercialism, the 'awfu' folk wi' the cloaks o' dark-ness and the wigs o' wisdom frae Edinbro" (p. 203) signify an incur-sion into the present, a key element defiling the contiguity of Scottish society in a perverse mixed modernity. Figured by the act of writing as centred on the entail itself, this 'romance revival' invites an anach-ronistic worldview into the domain of improving Scotland, infecting the all-pervasive subtext of improvement with more overt forms of 'story'. Consequently, when Keelevin is fretting about the morality of the entail, Claud's dismissal of him with 'Ye're, as I would say, but the pen in this matter' (p. 72) actually emphasises the lawyer's problematic agency. In a sense, then, *The Entail* can be said to mount a dual attack on the legal culture, at once the servant of a ruth-less commercialism, and the sinister remnant of a previous epoch. Within this blighted context, the division between Scotland's two main urban centres is a significant device, with commercial Glasgow and romantic Edinburgh symbolising a fragmented national subjec-tivity. Whether by virtue of an inappropriate nostalgia or an absence of sympathy, the society of *The Entail* is stiflingly inadequate. The recurring slogan of the text – 'sufficient for the day is the evil thereof' (p. 14) – ironically articulates its problematic, in which a flawed pres-ent is little able to suffer the baggage of a fading past.

In this litigious environment, many of Galt's characters suffer from emotional dysfunction. Even the narrator claims, with ambigu-ous comic intent, to have no experience or understanding of love (p. 305). Claud's ungrateful treatment of his carer Maudge signals the first of a chain of failed or overloaded sympathetic ties in the work. In particular, the breakdown of mother-child relationships (repeated through the Leddy's sequence of family feuds) signals an emotional crisis. As the text's vessel for the romantic stories of national his-tory, Claud's specific neglect of Maudge (he later repents having 'stifled the very sense o' loving kindness within me' (p. 150)) hints at broader betrayals – perhaps the Act of Union, or cultural alien-ation over the period. Claire A. Simmons also notes an irony here, in that despite his 'feudal ambitions', Claud's treatment of Maudge goes against his traditional feudal obligation to her, another result of the text's systematic mismarriages.[65] Yet while Claud's experience has Faustian resonances – representing 'a spectacle of moral bravery' (p. 140) for the narrator – his wife appears more simply devoid of human sympathy. A remarkably shallow woman who acts out of theatrical compunction, even in the face of a son's serious illness her concern is superficial (p. 134). When, later in the text, James Walkin-shaw provides a kind of internal critique, complaining of his family's destructive selfishness as captured in the term 'interest' (p. 239), he only registers a fraction of the novel's crisis. This is a text plagued by widespread dissociation. The historical trajectory personified in Claud has undermined the cultural order and isolated the modern subject. The characters are sectioned off into incompatible groupings that fail alone, whether divided along regional and ideological lines, or in miniature among one family. The situation is nicely summarised in Watty Walkinshaw's picture of the last man eating a solitary meal: 'for ye ken if a' the folk in the world were to die but only ae man, it would behove that man to hae his dinner' (p. 147).

In short, improvement and national culture are tragically at odds in *The Entail*; the line and the circle are fundamentally incompatible. As the novel unfolds, Galt's meditations upon 'story' become more openly conflicted. Claud's (note the pun on a 'clod' of earth) hereditary project is at the centre of a text that explores contrasting epistemologies by way of opposing narrative modes, introducing a pattern of romance fatality that inverts what Duncan calls the 'modality of contingency and accident' that we recognise from *Annals*. An alternate, wilful form of 'story' escalates to counterpoint the Newtonian evolution of society (itself already primed to collapse into the narrative determinacy of improvement). While the simmering allegorical matrix of national imagery immediately suggests this alternative mode, it is principally signified by the entail itself, which 'works itself out in a systematic, overdetermined contradiction of human agency'.[66] Claud is born into a claustrophobic symbolism that he both perpetuates and corrupts. He sets the stage for this with his early neglect of Maudge, an act that resonates throughout the novel. There is a fatal misreading in his behaviour, which neglects the personified (and thus negotiable) bearer of residual culture for an abstracted, destructive ideal of the same. While rejecting William Wallace for the rags-to-riches myth of Dick Whittington appears to signal a lack of interest in romantic ideas of Scottish nationhood, the text resolves Claud's status obsession into the most intransigent kind of idealism, an inflexible grand narrative that imbibes the charged feudal romance of Whittington's archetypal rise. The novel thus tropes nationalism as a perverse, 'romantic' obsession with family inheritance which turns commerce itself into a Gothic pursuit. Fixating on a hollowed-out version of his cultural inheritance, Claud misses the human, sympathetic element that might have sutured the national condition, inviting in a dark version of Scottishness that haunts the text thenceforth. In epistemological terms, he steps beyond the paradigm of theoretical history in engaging with the substance of romance at all, but the impersonal, debased version that Claud brings to the narrative renders the situation truly ruinous, permanently souring the unfolding of history. Thus, while Balwhidder's flexible and sympathetic imposition of 'story' via his religion proves a harmless superfluity in modern Scotland, Claud's static form of imagined nationhood brings catastrophic results for the nation as family.

The substance of Galt's literary project cannot tolerate Claud's attempt to manipulate history in service of his ideal via the key device of the entail, and the damaged version of theoretical history it produces is a dangerous terrain. The shadow of narrativity in the conjectural form expands into an aggressive force, as the non-novel collapses into its central pathology. Thus, in the text, characters are killed off by the impact of important revelations, the workings of 'story' grown malevolent. This includes Charles Walkinshaw, whose 'romantic' emotional inability to engage in bourgeois commerce is a sign of the divided nation summoned by Claud (pp. 125–42). Ultimately, navigating this deformed modernity requires extreme flexibility, apparent in a character like the Leddy, whose capriciousness allows her to maintain 'a firmer grip on mundane reality'.[67] Freed from the constraints of a concrete will, she transcends the fatal machinery, as signified in her frequent reworking of historical detail (see especially pp. 285–7). Yet while the Leddy moves effortlessly within the narrative – protected by the comparatively elastic fabric of theoretical history – Claud and Charles Walkinshaw are suffocated by a tragic modality that is owed to the destructive feudal revival. Keith M. Costain argues that Claud 'suffers tragically in an essentially comic world', yet the Leddy's might actually be the more exceptional experience.[68] The sporadic incursions of the narrator, using a direct address to the reader, themselves figure the text's intermittent disruption of the theoretical historical form, scything across its generational unfolding of national history with a jolt of the fictive (see p. 99). Galt emphasises the literary bent to these concerns throughout, seen for example in Lady Plealand's inability to read her psalm-book on Charles's death, with the performances of literature inextricably involved in the text's consideration of history as a contest over forms of 'story' (p. 142).

The alternate romance mode percolating through the novel erupts in the third volume, which has traditionally baffled or disappointed critics.[69] An evident change in tone here has been put down to the interference of William Blackwood, yet we must consider how the text's agenda develops regardless.[70] By this point, Galt has established a main opposition of family factions through the residences at Kittlestonheugh and Camrachle. The former hints at

modern Scotland or North Britain, 'where every thing was meth-
odized into system', the latter traces of a residual national experience, where 'the fields were open, and their expanse unbounded'
(p. 220). Now the suppressed family line stemming from Charles
and based at Camrachle – linking together Jacobitism, Highlandism
and emotional susceptibility – comes into greater focus as the narrative leaves Glasgow and travels north. Mrs Eadie's oracular predictions play upon the incursion of the alternative modality, as the
increased prominence of the 'romantic' branch of the family imposes
its own narrative forms (pp. 340–1). The text at once parodies and
brings Claud's anachronistic ideal to fruition here, as it removes
into a Highland landscape saturated with the trope-heavy material
of romance. Eadie's observation that her prophetic 'gift' stands in
contrast to the rational, material world is cogent. She explains that
'it comes not to us till earthly things begin to lose their hold on our
affections', signalling the continuing location of forms of residual
culture as fundamentally antithetical to life in the intractable material revolutions of the modernising world, and thus maintaining the
text's fatal dichotomies (p. 283). Indeed Peter Womack cites the idea
of 'Second Sight' as a recurrent formula for such oppositions, a (particularly Hebridean) tradition contributing to the Highlands' suit-
ability 'as a refuge from the tyranny of the evidential'.[71] Paralleling
Claud's attempted imposition of 'will' (in both senses of the word),
Eadie's Second Sight is so anachronistic as to require death, another
strain in the fruitless concoction of Scottishness as romance.

Firmly establishing the territory of a romanticised national subjectivity in this sequence, Galt explores the darker potential to such
a space: a fatal severance from or debasement of reality, rather than
imaginative addendum. Yet if the faulty archaism of both Eadie and
Claud are principal targets of Galt's critique, we must remember
that this is only a part of his pessimistic analysis. Nostalgia, greed
and haplessness have come to dominate a society failing to resolve a
healthy sense of itself against processes of rapid change, with culture
itself becoming a foolish brand of 'story' facing down improvement.
Scotland has never recovered from Darien, it seems, and the Age of
Improvement is a cycle of national trauma.

As the third volume's modal deviation draws to a close, Galt's
national chronicle eddies among sneering parody and comic resolution. James Walkinshaw's final inheritance may be designated as

a therapeutic union, recombining the dissonant formations of the nation, yet the vigorous irony of the final section makes this suspect. The novel closes with the Leddy's final interference via the outcome of her will, with that textual device a corrective likeness of the entail itself, part of the Leddy's unique capacity as an author of events (pp. 362–3). The Leddy's triumph, then, apparently counters the text's fatality as experienced by Claud and others, in which 'human power [is] set at nought by the natural course of things' (p. 115). In one sense, *The Entail* finally attains the coherence its world has so lacked, allowing for a renewal of the cultural economy within the modern commercial framework. Yet the imbrication of the final inheritance plot in the ridiculed Highland narrative – not to mention its entanglement within Galt's chronic distrust of 'story' – acts to question whether this is truly a resolution. For Juliet Shields, the novel achieves 'the reconciliation of past and present and the synthesis of heroic sentiment with commercial interest' through the agency of key female characters (Mrs Eadie and the Leddy) working either outside or against a misfiring patriarchy. That gendered perspective is interesting, but Shields's assertion that Galt seeks to 'revive the heroic virtues and ardent sensibility associated with Jacobitism' misses his cynical sense of humour.[72] *The Entail* renders such sentimental recuperation distinctly absurd and it is insufficient to address what has become a national crisis.

If *Waverley* seems a nagging presence here, this is because the novel implies a vicious critique of Scott's aesthetic reconstruction of Scottish history. Claud's feudal project, with its roots in the failed colonial enterprise of the Darien scheme, predates the intense and sustained experience of improvement in Scotland that would begin later in the eighteenth century. Yet implicit in *The Entail*'s tragic history, and centrally figured in Claud's subsequent decision to entail his lands, are responses to improvement that seek to idealise elements of the national past and of the localised cultures that appear under threat. This constitutes a dark view of modernity's ethnological turn, presenting national 'culture' as a reactionary answer to the process of 'cultivation'. And though the Darien prehistory here suggests that eighteenth-century improvement had always been tainted by a brand of erroneous nostalgia, Galt's novel is also of its time in reflecting on the state of Scottish fiction in the 1820s. Two years after *Annals of the Parish*, Galt's theoretical history frames the Walkinshaw saga as a noxious injection of 'story' into the modern world, a kind of historical overcompensation that muddies the cultural landscape. Again, with Scott's historical romances the obvious target, *The Entail* condemns the agency of 'romance revivalism', though this can be understood to extend across a much larger sense of cultural nostalgia: history as improvement might be challenging enough, but it is a comical mess when in thrall to the unimproved, whether this is in the realm of land ownership or in the nation's literary culture.

While *Annals* had seemed to imply that the novelistic form of 'story' was no longer relevant in the modern world, it returns here in a mangled form. Whether or not *The Entail*'s third volume reflects Blackwood's literary advice, the effect is satirical. The storytelling materials of romance flare up in caricature only to confirm their inadequacy – though not their impotency – in *The Entail*. And yet it is not simply this sentimentality but also improvement itself that is to blame, as Galt develops his concerns from *Annals* over the impact that dramatic change can have on cultures that are locally constituted. The world of *The Entail* may not rule out a more constructive version of this historical process, but as things stand, improvement is a process of endlessly firefighting unforeseen consequences. National modernity, in the end result, is not dialectical but temporally confused, not culturally diverse but incongruous, not communal but competitive, with the cast of self-interested relatives at the reading of the Leddy's will providing a final acrid note (pp. 358–61).

In fact, *The Entail* leaves us with a macabre sense of Scottish culture. A series of key episodes surround Watty Walkinshaw's attitude to death. Published in the same year as Hogg's *The Three Perils of Woman*, *The Entail*'s treatment of Watty has elements that resonate with the Gothic mode of Hogg's writing (the chaotic amplification of the third volume is also a shared feature). In general, Watty's condition as a 'natural' makes him an erratic component of the Walkinshaw symbolism. With his 'glaiks and gleams o' sense' (p. 193), Watty provides a comic foil as a kind of idiot savant, only vaguely aware of how accurately he exposes his family's ill intentions. Watty is a skewed distillation of emotional honesty repressed elsewhere, and his volatile presence condenses the 'accidental' formula of theoretical history. In this role he functions as a medium for, and embodiment of, Claud's frustrated plans, a figure of the modality his father foreswore, which can now only impact on the patriarch as unsolicited 'story'. In a particularly dark passage, however, Watty moves from intense grief upon his wife's death in childbirth to an unfeeling disregard for her corpse. Only pages after displaying an 'astonishment of sorrow', he resolutely announces his lack of interest in the body: "'There's nane o' my Betty Bodle here. [. . .] I canna understand [. . .] what for a' this fykerie's about a lump o' yird? Sho'elt intil a hole, and no fash me."' Requesting that her body be unceremoniously shovelled away, Watty refuses or is unable to engage with the death, instead insisting that her being has transferred into the person of his infant daughter (pp. 114–17). The subsequent passing of the child, his second 'Betty Bodle' (a death Watty refuses to acknowledge until confronted by 'a kirkyard smell frae the bed'), occasions the subsequent reimagining of his wife upon another proximate vessel, this time a niece (p. 167). This pattern of death, repressed grief and incestuous reincarnation reflects bleakly on the nation so loudly figured by the Walkinshaw family.

The faulty imagined communities of Claud's ancestor worship or Watty's unsettling reinventions of his dead wife paint a picture of the nation-state in which central processes of memorialisation have become warped.[73] Bardsley argues that '*The Entail* develops the theme of a reciprocal inadequacy between categories and their exemplary instance and the bearing of that philosophical problem on the constitution of collectivities'.[74] Certainly Galt's text is suspicious of the narrative acts involved in figuring the nation, including in the consumer medium of the novel. Yet this critique is located within a knotty historical context. Transported across the rapidly improving long eighteenth century, the Walkinshaws have become disjointed; so incoherent, in fact, that they are plagued by delusions and hauntings. George Walkinshaw's wife spends 'nearly twenty years almost as much dead as alive' (p. 303) and her situation reflects a larger crisis, in which culture broadly understood is failing to collaborate with the clustering of effects legible as improvement. In temporal terms, culture's notionally static and cyclical qualities will not mesh with improvement's commitment to change. Partly a (reductive) pastiche of Scott, *The Entail*'s engagement with history compulsively denies any simple process of cultural remediation. Indeed, the literary imagination, with its addiction to romance and to 'story' at large, constitutes much of the problem. As James enlists Highland troops to fight Napoleon *en route* to the 'just' inheritance of the Kittlestonheugh estates (p. 340), Galt is laughing in the face of such mythic ideological recovery, which is another kind of phantasm or revenant. *The Entail* reveals the enthusiastic appropriation of a Highland Scottishness for the British Empire as a farcical and bewildering scheme. Instead, Galt's most ambitious theoretical history refuses to produce any answers.

Prefiguring Marx's insight into the unrelenting great plot of bourgeois commercialism, Galt presents this as only one of a series of miscarrying narratives.[75] Tracing the impact of a new global milieu upon an already complex and flawed culture, he produces one of the most pessimistic and compelling novels of the period. *The Entail*'s ambivalent view of the past reflects Galt's idiosyncratic liberal Toryism. It is a fine memento of an 1820s marked by ideological revision, and an appropriate emblem for Galt's importance to a Scottish Romanticism understood via its relationship to the thorny, dialectical history bubbling under the unifying keyword of improvement. *The Entail*'s competing narrative threads nicely illustrate an interlocking system of societal change, a whole body of incremental developments and contrasting attitudes that Galt makes synonymous with national history. If, as I have suggested, the commercial remains at the heart of this particularly west coast dynamic, the dangers of a single-minded accumulation of wealth are distilled in grasping George Walkinshaw, whose seduction by money foregrounds the dangers of that particular working fiction.[76] Yet this narrowly commercial point concedes to a larger one: when the goals of improvement must share history with the stubborn set of values and desires we term culture – as of course they must – the result, if we are not careful, is a punch-drunk drama, a community moving in many directions at once. Compromise seems to be the missing term in *The Entail*'s long eighteenth century, its mediation replaced only by private disappointment as narrative at large lets Scotland down.

Galt's theoretical history is a significant contribution to the debate over the form and function of the aesthetic in the early nineteenth century. It self-describes as an instrumental, 'recreative' form and comes decked out in the trappings of social history. And indeed, *The Entail*'s diversion from the stricter model of the theoretical history epitomised by *Annals* actually ends up reinforcing Galt's strictures about the dangers of 'story'. (In that regard, Galt's literary agenda seems diametrically opposed to the aesthetic idealism, not to mention national essentialism, we will see celebrated by Thomas Carlyle in the next chapter.) To take a wider view: as noted previously, the long eighteenth century saw culture as 'a noun of process' joined by a new definition of culture as a phenomenon bound to the canonical works, social customs and historical consciousness of the 'people'.[77] These competing ideas remained in dialogue with one another, and Galt's novels track something like this dynamic as a permanent condition of modernity. As *Annals of the Parish* and *The Entail* demonstrate, the processes of improvement operate on existing conditions in a tectonic collision of cultivation and culture – both of which, of course, involve acts of storytelling. It might seem ironic that these writings betray such an acute sense of narratology, given Galt's provocative claim that they are not in fact 'stories', or at least not novels. Yet the experimental perspective of the theoretical history illuminates the condition of prose fiction. These texts establish a distinctive methodology in their approach to recent history, providing a range of insights into a seismic experience of change in the west of Scotland and further afield. In doing so, they mark the importance of the dialectics of improvement to the Scottish novel of the 1820s.

Notes

1. Galt, *The Entail*, ed. Gordon, pp. 12, 147–8. Further citations of this edition are given in parentheses in the main text.
2. Berry, *Idea of Commercial Society*, p. 17.
3. Williams, *Marxism and Literature*, pp. 121–7.
4. Galt, *Annals of the Parish*, ed. Kinsley, p. 132. Further citations of this edition are given in parentheses in the main text.
5. Ferguson, *History of Civil Society*, p. 175.
6. See the introduction to Hewitt (ed.), *Galt: Observations and Conjectures*, pp. 1–29 (pp. 2–8).
7. The forthcoming Edinburgh Edition of the selected works of John Galt (general editor: Angela Esterhammer) is a timely development.
8. See Makdisi, *Romantic Imperialism*, pp. 6–7.
9. See Swaim on this distrust of imaginative literature lingering on beyond the eighteenth century, in *Scottish Men of Letters*, pp. 27–8.
10. Lavinia being the daughter of Latinus in Virgil's *Aeneid*, the subject of a prophecy advising her father to reject all Latin suitors (allowing her ultimately to marry Aeneas). See pp. 160–1.
11. Richardson, *Literature, Education, and Romanticism*, pp. 185–6.

12. Galt, *Autobiography*, vol. 2, p. 210.
13. Tuchman with Fortin, *Edging Women Out*, pp. 25–6.
14. Murdoch and Sher comment on Constable's 'liberal payment policy' in 'Literacy and Learned Culture', p. 133.
15. Galt, *Literary Life*, vol. 1, p. 229.
16. Galt's notion of the creative process is more closely aligned with what Coleridge terms the 'fancy'. See *Biographia Literaria*, p. 305.
17. With reference to *Annals*, Galt comments, 'No doubt it has what my own taste values highly, considerable likeliness' (*Literary Life*, vol. 1, p. 155).
18. Ibid. pp. 144–6.
19. Hewitt, 'John Galt, Harriet Martineau', pp. 347, 358–9.
20. Simpson, 'Ironic Self-Revelation', p. 88.
21. Cited in Lyell, *Novels of John Galt*, p. 223.
22. Frykman, *Galt's Scottish Stories*, p. 220.
23. See also Trumpener, *Bardic Nationalism*, p. 152.
24. P. H. Scott illustrates the debt in *John Galt*, p. 36.
25. Carlyle, 'Signs of the Times', p. 444.
26. Galt, *Autobiography*, vol. 2, p. 210.
27. Ibid. p. 219.
28. Duncan, *Scott's Shadow*, p. 217.
29. Duncan discusses Galt's relationship with the periodical press in 'Altered States', pp. 53–63; on the author's dealings with *Blackwood's*, see Morrison, 'Galt's Angular Magazinity', pp. 257–73.
30. For more on Galt and statistical accounts, focusing on his colonial endeavours in Canada, see McNeil, 'Time, Emigration', pp. 303–8.
31. See Gordon, 'Galt and Politics', pp. 120–1.
32. Bohrer, 'Galt's *Annals*', pp. 106–13.
33. Trumpener remarks of Galt's *The Provost* (1822) that it shows 'how the machinery of change, once put into operation, camouflages [human] agency as the movement of history' (*Bardic Nationalism*, p. 156).
34. Duncan, *Scott's Shadow*, p. 227.
35. Smith, *Wealth of Nations*, vol. 2, pp. 781–8.
36. Ferguson, *History of Civil Society*, p. 210.
37. Robertson, *History of the Reign of Charles the Fifth*, vol. 1, p. 47.
38. Divine, 'The Changing Village', p. 125.
39. Galt, *Autobiography*, vol. 2, p. 227.
40. Scott, *John Galt*, p. 28.
41. Bohrer, 'Galt's *Annals*', p. 101.
42. Lyell, *Novels of John Galt*, p. 50.
43. Bohrer, 'Galt's *Annals*', p. 114.
44. McCracken-Flesher, 'The Sense of No Ending', p. 74.

45. Duncan, 'Altered States', pp. 55, 61–2. See also Robert Morrison pulling back the frame to discuss the potential in magazines for surrounding articles to extend and modify meaning ('Galt's Angular Magazinity', p. 268).

46. Bohrer, 'Galt's *Annals*', pp. 105–6.

47. Steven, *Parish Life*, p. 165.

48. See also Duncan, *Scott's Shadow*, p. 226.

49. Simpson suggests that, '[w]ith his manifest contradictions and complexities, [Balwhidder] may well represent the double vision of Scottish Presbyterianism with its conflicting emphases on pre-determination and practical energy' ('Ironic Self-Revelation', p. 80).

50. Wickman, 'Of Tangled Webs', paras. 1–10.

51. Divine, 'The Changing Village', p. 123.

52. Carlyle, 'Signs of the Times', p. 442.

53. Duncan, *Scott's Shadow*, p. 223.

54. Ibid. pp. 228–30.

55. Oliphant, *Annals of a Publishing House*, vol. 1, p. 451.

56. Galt, *Literary Life*, vol. 1, p. 155; *Autobiography*, vol. 2, pp. 219–20.

57. Bardsley, 'Novel and Nation', p. 540.

58. Schoenfield, 'Family Plots', pp. 62–3.

59. See also Berry, *Idea of Commercial Society*, p. 45.

60. A sentiment very much alive in Paine's criticism of hereditary government in *Rights of Man*, for example p. 174.

61. Smith, *Wealth of Nations*, vol. 1, pp. 384–5.

62. Devine, *Transformation of Rural Scotland*, pp. 64, 61.

63. Schoenfield, 'Family Plots', p. 62. For more on entails, including in Galt's novel, see Fielding, 'Earth and Stone', pp. 159–66.

64. Duncan, *Scott's Shadow*, pp. 238–9.

65. Simmons, 'Feudal Days', p. 181.

66. Duncan, *Scott's Shadow*, pp. 239–40.

67. Costain, 'Mind-Forg'd Manacles', p. 184.

68. Ibid. p. 169.

69. Frykman complains of 'concessions to popular taste' in the heightening of melodramatic and supernatural elements, suggesting that Galt is attempting to cash in on Scott's popularity (*Galt's Scottish Stories*, pp. 137, 158). For a different view, see Trumpener on the novel playing out the eighteenth-century shift from 'Defoean realism' to 'Ossianic elegy and Mackenziesque sentimentalism' (*Bardic Nationalism*, p. 154).

70. See Gordon's introduction to Galt, *The Entail*, ed. Gordon, pp. vii–xvi (p. xiii).

71. Womack, *Improvement and Romance*, pp. 89–94.

72. Shields, *Sentimental Literature*, pp. 160–5.

73. See Anderson, *Imagined Communities*.
74. Bardsley, 'Novel and Nation', p. 562.
75. See Berman, 'Tearing Away the Veils', para. 9.
76. Trumpener observes 'Galt's foregrounding of economic factors as the most important long-term motor of plot and character development' (*Bardic Nationalism*, p. 154).
77. Williams, *Keywords*, pp. 87–90.

Coda: 'There is no end to machinery'

If you think my silence requires any apology you will please observe the date, which says more for my despatch and agility as a correspondent then were I to write a hundred quarto volumes to prove it. I only received yours of the 27th this morning in town, and since then I have performed a journey that some years ago took Moses forty long years to make out, to say nothing of the various appendages and encumbrances I had along with me, and a pair of hackney horses, who, I'm sure, were worse to drive than all the stiff-necked children of Israel. So much for the improvement of modern times!

This letter from Susan Ferrier to her younger brother, written 'betwixt tea and cards' on May Day 1810, marks the osmosis of improvement into Scottish society at the outset of the nineteenth century – a subject now of polite repartee, an ingrained vernacular worldview.[1] It is from this context that the argument of the previous chapters emerges, that improvement was decisively at work in a series of aesthetic innovations comprehensible under the aegis of an updated Scottish Romanticism. For the Edinburgh novelist Ferrier, improvement is the root cause of 'modern times', a progressive source code that contracts time and space, with forty years now a day's journey in the landscape. The cost is in 'appendages and encumbrances', the process less synonymous with R. Buckminster Fuller's 'ephemeralization' – in which technology simplifies life towards a utopian vanishing point – than might be expected.[2] Equally, Ferrier reminds us of the less quantifiable collateral effects of improvement: time-travel is exhausting, for one thing. This does not mean that improvement, in its plural forms orbiting around commercial productivity, had ceased to be a fundamentally desirable ideal in 1810. Rather, it is a sign of the complex dialectical unfolding of improvement as a phenomenon, possessed of a myriad forms and contested at all levels. Scottish literary Romanticism is of lingering value as a testing ground for this characteristic of our world.

These four case studies, stretching chronologically from Burns's 1786 *Poems* to Hogg's later contributions to *Blackwood's* across 1830–31, fill out some of the potential of improvement as a literary-historical phenomenon. Its influence is to the fore in Burns's poetics of 'simplicity' as in the discursive commerce of Romantic short fiction; in Baillie's theatre of social renewal as in Galt's (non-)novel of an improving nation. The full gamut of improving discourse, from progressive evangelism to primitive revolt, and from determinism to chaos, is active in this literature in a holistic view of the culture clash and condition of rapid change we call modernity. Each of these examples also involves improvement in a conception of the literary aesthetic: medium of secular belonging, vehicle of indefinite exchange, educational tool, theoretical guide to history. This conjunction rounds out the logic of improvement as an approach to Romanticism *per se*: not simply a key theme or environmental background for literary texts, but also of real consequence to the period's formal innovations.

Improvement, again, as this book has underlined, was conceived in the period as an unstable field of thought and action with commercial modernisation at its centre. We must avoid innocently replicating the Enlightenment's stadial and teleological view of history, even if (or rather, especially since) it continues to shape contemporary ideas about modernity and history. It is certainly worth underlining the contingency of improvement as the *y*-axis of this particular mapping of time. These literary texts do much to illuminate that point, by registering the dialectical and rhetorical complexity of improvement as much as its momentous force. For all the path-dependency of a society constituted upon improvement, many of the values it incorporates remained and remain contested. And acknowledging the enormous achievements won in the service of improvement should not preclude a more complicated discussion. Equally, among the things I hope this study has registered are the limits to a macroscopic view of improvement. Understanding its systematic logic is a necessary task. But thinking in localised, incidental terms may allow for more creative and disruptive outcomes, in historical scholarship as in the present, shifting history further from a linear path (whether tragic or victorious) into the realm of narrative, 'made' and thus available to be remade. Without discounting the basic insight of materialistic determinism, clearly the totem of improvement has (in the broadest sense of the word) a 'cultural' quality that is susceptible to mediation. This is, of course, a pressing concern for our own period of geopolitical instability, when environmental factors including man-made climate change are sharpening the debate over what we call and how we achieve 'improvement'.

There are signs in the literary field between 1786 and 1831 of an improvement with aspirations to be a kind of *mathesis universalis*, a comprehensive science of civilisation not at all limited to the secular, but covering in fact 'religion, law, politics, agriculture, and sheep farming'.[3] The broad meanings of the term 'commerce' in the eighteenth century offer one way to conceptualise this latitude, as relevant in Adam Ferguson's terms to 'conversation' as to financial exchange proper.[4] Regarding the equally expansive notion of the unimproved, by the period in question the term 'enthusiasm' had come to stand for a number of aberrant behaviours inconsistent with the basic tenor of polite, improved modernity, applicable to Elspat MacTavish's attachment to the past in Scott's 'The Highland Widow', to the 'romance and enthusiasm' perpetrated by the mystic Mrs Eadie in Galt's *The Entail*, and to Benlora's hatred in Baillie's *The Family Legend*.[5] Enthusiasm was often of a specifically religious form in an image of dangerous evangelical fervour, providing a way of signalling the fundamentally sober, common-sense appeal of the moderate and the modern.[6] Still, modernity contains its own enthusiasms. The texts at hand record a complex, passionate debate both for and against improvement in its various forms. What Marshall Berman argues of *The Communist Manifesto*, then – at once product of, paean to, and devastating attack on an intoxicating and carnivalesque modernity – was already true of Romantic literature.[7]

Pure Light

In the closing years of the 1820s, Thomas Carlyle published a significant trio of review essays in the *Edinburgh Review*, which postulate a Britain riven between the inhuman mores of Enlightenment and a degraded popular culture, looking to ideal truth (*'pure light'*) and its secular expression in poetry as a means of salvation.[8] These essays are a further instalment of the dialectical purchase of improvement in the period, veering as they do between despondency and hope, assured on one hand that 'the time is sick and out of joint', on the other that 'the happiness and greatness of mankind at large has been continually progressive'.[9] Carlyle is instinctively appalled by the dominant logic of improvement, though his faith in an imminent literary-spiritual revolution – for all its narrative of sublime transformation – might be viewed as somewhat rehabilitating rather than dispensing with the idea. In that sense, there are parallels between these reviews and the redemptive varieties of the aesthetic in Burns and Baillie, where pastoral 'simplicity' and didactic theatre are moral lodestones by which to untangle the dialectics of improvement towards a more positive vision. As becomes clear, however, Carlyle's argument entails a rejection of the Scottish Enlightenment and indeed of the greater part of the literature surveyed in this book. Taken collectively, his three essays perform a kind of canon-making work, antagonistic to my argument and useful as a counterpoint.

In the 'State of German Literature' (1827), Carlyle mounts a defence of German idealism and the apparently cognate achievement of Johann Wolfgang von Goethe upon a stadial or rather cyclical model of history. This plays the re-emergence of ideal truth – in which a distinction between religious faith and the capitalisation 'Art' is moot – as an echo in Germany of the Elizabethan models of Milton and especially Shakespeare, though now mixed with modern 'French clearness'.[10] Indeed, 'so closely are all European communities connected, that the phases of mind in any one country [. . .] are but modified repetitions of its phases in every other'.[11] This is an epochal moment for 'an era of such promise and such threatening'.[12] The atheistic threat personified by Hume (who is cast as the *ne plus ultra* of Lockean associationism) is displaced by a transcendental ontology that ensures 'true nationality', since poetry is both the wellspring and guardian of national character.[13] At the same time, Carlyle rejects a sensationalised popular culture in, for example, the plays of August von Kotzebue, which represents merely passing 'forms of Unreason', following here in a path trodden by William Wordsworth, who in 1800 had taken aim at 'sickly and stupid German tragedies'.[14] When the essay turns to Immanuel Kant and to a 'Reason' that is 'of a higher nature than Understanding' as the answer to society's ills, Carlyle's reader may be left wondering whether this is not merely a better (or more Christian) form of unreason: belief, in other words.[15] However, in the end what the text sets out is really a version of high Romanticism, in which the proper national ideals are mediated by great poetry: Kant not Kotzebue, Goethe not the Gothic. This gesture involves a negation of the 'Scotch school' as followers of John Locke, and might constitute a kind of post-North-Britishness both in its intellectual politics and its conception of national culture: Carlyle, notably, is writing on behalf of 'we of England'. That said, it is tempting to suggest a displaced Scottish topos in the address to Germany, a nation that the ignorant regard as 'a *belle sauvage* at best'.[16] This leads us towards the figure who becomes a sputtering test-case for the emergence of truth into nineteenth-century Britain: Robert Burns.

Carlyle's 1828 review of John Gibson Lockhart's *Life of Robert Burns* deals with its ostensible subject in one paragraph (Lockhart's book has 'insight' but lacks 'depth').[17] What follows inflects the regretful admiration of the poet which had been popularised by James Currie in 1800; this despite a complaint about Currie's 'patronising, apologetic air'.[18] Putting Burns in the same sentence as Shakespeare is Carlyle's highest praise, and indeed he ranks Burns as the undisputed 'first of all our song-writers'.[19] Nevertheless, Burns's oeuvre represents only 'a poor mutilated fraction of what was in him', and it is this calamity that the majority of the essay attempts to explain.[20] Carlyle's elegant, meandering prose means that different positions are taken up only to be qualified or overturned. His first sentence introduces the supposed lack of remuneration of this poet who eventually settled into a career in the excise, 'quarrelling with smugglers and vintners': what a 'waste'.[21] This point is developed to target both 'the Dumfries Aristocracy' and 'the Edinburgh learned', the latter of whom 'were in general more noted for clearness of head than for warmth of heart'.[22] Yet perhaps even a royal pension might not have saved Burns, who was primarily undermined by a 'want of unity in his purposes'.[23]

Many of Burns's difficulties were an effect of social class, his Edinburgh sojourn and experience of 'rich men's banquets' having opened galling horizons.[24] Still, while the 'dissocial' world at large must be admonished for its lack of patronage, Carlyle also discounts all external factors: Burns was treated better than most great men, and money is anathema to artistry anyway ('he *cannot* serve God and Mammon').[25] In fact, 'we question whether for his culture as a Poet, poverty, and much suffering for a season, were not absolutely advantageous'.[26] The ostensible point here is that 'Burns was nothing wholly, and Burns could be nothing, no man formed as he was can be anything, by halves'.[27] Yet Carlyle circles around the economics of art and the utility of disadvantage, producing in the end a kind of paradox, in which Burns's struggles and failures as both man and poet are integral to the spectacle of his greatness. Character and poetry are entirely coterminous here, on show 'equally in word and deed'.[28] Yet it is the life more than the works of Burns that are to be his testament: 'the grand unrhymed Romance of his earthly existence'.[29] It is in this theatrical register – 'a tragedy, and one of the deepest' – and not lyric poetry that Carlyle comes to rest, with the 'mutilated fraction' of Burns providing the antidote to 'an age the most prosaic Britain had yet seen'.[30]

Our engagement with this fallen icon requires a tinge of regret, of self-examination and of moral censure, all summed up in the phrase: 'We love Burns, and we pity him'.[31] Loving and pitying Burns is the catharsis upon which Carlyle's post-North-Britishness is to be based, a celebration of this martyr whose shortcomings and victories are, in the last measure, our own. Indeed, 'Perhaps no British man has so deeply affected the thoughts and feelings of so many men', Carlyle writes, with the poet beginning to embody the global sweep of the empire itself.[32] Burns's influence is a fundamental 'increase of nationality' that restores the '*pure light*' of Scotland.[33] Scottish culture had been singularly un-Scottish before Burns ('almost exclusively French'), especially Hume, who did not really exist in the normal sense at all, occupying a metaphysical space in which 'he not so much morally *lived*, but metaphysically *investigated*'.[34] If, as Colin Kidd has argued, Enlightenment historiography made Scotland's pre-Union history a blank spot on the historical map, here it is the eighteenth century that is an absence, waiting for Burns's re-engagement of 'human affection'.[35] This situation was part of a wider lack of 'literary patriotism' that had plagued British letters, an 'attenuated cosmopolitanism' that needed to be replaced with a different model of global sentiment.[36] Walter Scott is a welcome sign of the new direction, in which national character is freed from the Enlightenment doctrine of circles of influence (by which patriotism extends outwards from our individual locales) into a more essential *and* portable form. 'Our literature no longer grows in water, but in mould', Carlyle proclaims, but the Burns cult is a blueprint for Britain's seafaring empire and a means of proclaiming national 'truth' worldwide.[37]

This 'true Poet and Singer' who deserves our 'pitying admiration', standing in heroic opposition to an entire 'age' of 'scepticism, selfishness and triviality', is a maladjusted modern saint.[38] Such eschatological language prepares the ground for the final instalment of this triptych, Carlyle's 1829 review-essay 'Signs of the Times'. Here the review premise is at an extreme, with the works listed going entirely unmentioned in the main text and functioning instead as scenery or bibliography.[39] Carlyle's celebrated polemic against modernity – a great 'Age of Machinery' in which 'all is by rule and calculated contrivance' – opens, ironically, by ridiculing a contemporary revival of the jeremiad genre in a spate of 'lugubrious predictions'.[40] Regardless, what the essay depicts is a massive corruption of society by 'machinery', which is a kind of 'abbreviating process' that favours the systemic and the inanimate, in a pattern that is equally as applicable to the prevalence of institutions ('hives') as to institutional ways of thinking, involving a concurrent dissolution of the individual that is not merely 'external and physical' but 'internal and spiritual also'.[41] As this suggests, the tract derives its energy from a lurid description of, even painful infatuation with, the evil at hand – it is typical of the genre of the jeremiad in this respect, while of course anticipating Marx and the *Manifesto*'s 'appreciation of capitalism'.[42] Carlyle entertains a Whig history that acknowledges the 'wonderful accessions' made by material improvement, though the concentration of wealth is a worry, but such latitude finally has little place in this historiography.[43] In the 'State of German Literature', he had accepted that 'commerce in material things has paved roads for commerce in things spiritual', but that possibility is now overwhelmed by the tendency of modern improvements to reinforce the hegemony of the machine.[44]

Locke and Hume are once again the villains of the piece, the former establishing a fundamentally 'material' worldview, the latter taking this 'and the world into bottomless abysses of Atheism and Fatalism'. Thomas Reid and the Common Sense philosophers had 'a dim notion that much of this was wrong', but their intervention was a hopeless panacea, itself mechanical, unable to escape the terms of the Lockean world, which as it turns out are writ large in the emergent industrial complex.[45] Carlyle bitterly resents the status of 'Profit and Loss' as the end-goal of all endeavour; the taxonomy of commercial modernisation in a 'calculation of the Profitable' is for him a profound kind of irreligion.[46] Yet it is here that his argument develops a wrinkle. For all its depiction of a society ruled over by system, the essay apparently resists a deterministic model of history (this despite Carlyle's adoration of Newton).[47] 'By arguing on the "force of circumstances"', it explains, 'we have argued away all force from ourselves'.[48] Mechanical forces are in fact *not* the driver of history, which is actually an effect of the transcendent actions of individuals (the chief example given is the Crusades, which were propelled entirely by 'Religion' and 'the passionate voice of one man').[49] In this way, modern history as mechanism is a myth, a form of collective self-delusion, for a society awaiting the re-emergence of heroic individual endeavour in the *'true light'* of a Kant, Goethe or even a Burns, the latter of whose achievement (of course) was entirely at odds with historical circumstances.

'In the management of external things we excel all other ages; while in whatever respects the pure moral nature, in true dignity of soul and character, we are perhaps inferior to most civilized ages', Carlyle writes.[50] His answer to this condition is significantly *not* Smith's sympathy, the associational paradigm of virtue, since an emphasis on collectivity is at the root of the problem. Society faces an imbalance of the 'Mechanical' and the 'Dynamical', which signify systematic knowledge and ideal truth respectively. This is not a zero-sum game: too much of the Dynamical and we get fanaticism and superstition.[51] Yet in the current moment Britain must look to its arbiters of ideal truth: religion and its virtuoso disciple, literature. Carlyle resents the emergence of the newspaper as a secular sacred text, but literature – and specifically poetry – remains the most plausible vehicle of spiritual renewal, especially given his theologically heterodox attack on all 'institutions and establishments'.[52] Unfortunately, nineteenth-century literary culture is 'a fierce clashing of cymbals', falling far short of the 'pure melodies'[53] that would conclusively reveal the dynamical nature of both 'Science and Art'. As Carlyle says of great achievements, 'These things rose up, as it were, by spontaneous growth in the free soil and sunshine of Nature. They were not planted or grafted, nor even greatly multiplied or improved by the culture or manuring of institutions.'[54] The individual mind must be freed to mediate the national spirit, in a process of spiritual and aesthetic renewal that, rhetorically at least, is too miraculous to be described in terms of moral improvement, emerging in preference, or as a redemptive counterpart, to narrowly scientific, technological and commercial varieties of progress.

What then does all this signify in light of the foregoing? 'There is a deep-lying struggle in the whole fabric of society; a boundless, grinding collision of the New with the Old', Carlyle announces, in one of the most distinct expressions of the Age of Improvement. The answer to this dialectical, 'constant intercommunion' is a compensatory literature of certainty, bearing truth that is national by virtue of transcending, even confounding, the national milieu, in a revolutionary turn that is presented less as dialectical than transformational.[55] Carlyle's argument thus inverts my own, by denying the complex, productive relationship between improving discourse and the aesthetic to see only suffocation and heroic liberation. In doing so, he cancels any historical basis for artwork at all – however much Burns's 'grand unrhymed Romance' in the Scottish Lowlands, or Carlyle's own intoxication with the nineteenth century, repudiates the point.

Each of the four major case studies in this book finds texts wrestling with improvement and with the politics of the literary. Carlyle's polemical prose is another example of this tendency, adapted in his case to diminish almost the entire culture of eighteenth- and nineteenth-century Britain in a radically ungenerous act of canon-making. The texts covered in this book attempt to manipulate the literary in and out of history, charging its volatile politics with interpreting, embodying and reimagining a mesh of phenomena intelligible in the period as improvement. At one end of this spectrum, Carlyle provides a major intervention in debates about the function of the aesthetic in the Romantic period with a national idealism that is more emphatic that any of the emergent forms of that tendency in my case studies. Indeed, his essays consecrate 'Art' as the transcendent language of the nation-state and harbinger of modern faith. In doing so, they suggest Terry Eagleton's comment upon the 'natural' effect of ideology, which makes 'forms of consciousness' appear 'magically absolved from social determinants'.[56] As far as improvement itself is concerned, Carlyle burlesques this set of material and cultural forces in his notion of mass sacrilegious delusion, but he does raise the possibility of a meaningful literary contribution. *'Pure light'* is a very limited vision of literature's relationship to the dialectics of improvement, but it lends definition to the more complicated landscape in this book, emerging from its shadow.

Notes

1. Susan Edmonstone Ferrier to Walter Ferrier, 1 May 1810, in *Memoir and Correspondence of Susan Ferrier*, ed. Doyle, pp. 44–6.
2. See Fuller's 1938 *Nine Chains to the Moon*.
3. Hogg, 'Robin Roole', in *Contributions to Blackwood's*, ed. Richardson, vol. 2, pp. 216–29 (p. 218).
4. See Furniss, 'Reading John Anderson's Will', p. 184; and Ferguson, *History of Civil Society*, p. 175.
5. Galt, *The Entail*, p. 222. Jon Mee tracks meanings of 'enthusiasm' in the period, including its association with poetic inspiration, in *Romanticism, Enthusiasm, and Regulation*.
6. See Ahnert, *Moral Culture*, pp. 10–11.
7. See Berman, 'Tearing Away the Veils'.
8. Carlyle, 'State of German Literature', p. 307.
9. Carlyle, 'Signs of the Times', pp. 457–8.
10. Carlyle, 'State of German Literature', pp. 333, 335.
11. Ibid. p. 337.
12. Ibid. p. 306.
13. Ibid. p. 308.
14. Ibid. p. 313; and Wordsworth, preface to *Lyrical Ballads*, vol. 1, pp. v–xlvi (p. xix).
15. Carlyle, 'State of German Literature', p. 348.
16. Ibid. pp. 321, 346, 313. In general, if there is a rustic, 'Northern' aspect to Carlyle's redemptive essentialism that links Germany and Burns, this remains implicit in these essays, which are on the surface little enamoured with the 'rude and humble' (see 'Burns', p. 274). Compare, here, John Ruskin's 1853 'The Nature of Gothic' from *The Stones of Venice* (vol. 2, pp. 151–231), described by Fiona Stafford as

a 'diatribe against the deadening mechanization of modern society', which is engaged in 'finding inspiration in the wild North' (see 'The Roar of the Solway', p. 42).

17. Carlyle, 'Burns', p. 269.
18. Ibid. p. 268.
19. Ibid. p. 287.
20. Ibid. p. 273.
21. Ibid.
22. Ibid. pp. 301, 298.
23. Ibid. p. 306.
24. Ibid. p. 309.
25. Ibid. pp. 305–6, 309–10.
26. Ibid. p. 308.
27. Ibid. p. 306.
28. Ibid. p. 282.
29. Ibid. p. 290.
30. Ibid. p. 271.
31. Ibid. p. 237.
32. Ibid. p. 287.
33. Ibid. p. 288.
34. Ibid. pp. 288–9.
35. See Kidd, *Subverting Scotland's Past*; Carlyle, 'Burns', p. 289.
36. Carlyle, 'Burns', p. 288.
37. Ibid. p. 289.
38. Ibid. pp. 306, 311.
39. They are *Anticipation; or, an Hundred Years Hence*; Mackinnon, *The Rise, Progress, and Present State of Public Opinion in Great Britain*; and Irving, *The Last Days*.
40. Carlyle, 'Signs of the Times', pp. 442, 441.
41. Ibid. pp. 442, 444. Alistair Livingston contextualises this argument in the Dumfriesshire landscape around Craigenputtock, where Carlyle had moved in 1828 ('The Galloway Levellers', p. 100).
42. Berman, 'Tearing Away the Veils', para. 6.
43. Carlyle, 'Signs of the Times', p. 442.
44. Carlyle, 'State of German Literature', p. 307.
45. Carlyle, 'Signs of the Times', pp. 445–6.
46. Ibid. pp. 450, 453.
47. Ibid. p. 453.
48. Ibid. p. 457.
49. Ibid. p. 450.
50. Ibid. p. 452.

51. Ibid.
52. Ibid. pp. 455, 450.
53. Ibid. p. 455.
54. Ibid. p. 449.
55. Ibid. p. 459.
56. Eagleton, *Ideology: An Introduction*, p. 59.

Bibliography

A. S., 'On Improvements in Scotland. From the Political Herald', *The Edinburgh Magazine, or Literary Miscellany* (December 1786): 426–30.

A. S., 'To the Editor of the Political Herald; On Improvements in Scotland', *The Political Herald, and Review*, 17 (1786): 346–52.

Ahnert, Thomas, *The Moral Culture of the Scottish Enlightenment, 1690–1805* (New Haven: Yale University Press, 2014).

Aitchison, Peter, and Andrew Cassell, *The Lowland Clearances: Scotland's Silent Revolution, 1760–1830* (Edinburgh: Birlinn, 2012).

Alexander, J. H., 'Literary Criticism in the Later "Noctes Ambrosianae"', *The Yearbook of English Studies*, 16 (1986): 17–31.

Alker, Sharon, and Holly Faith Nelson (eds), *James Hogg and the Literary Marketplace: Scottish Romanticism and the Working-Class Author* (Farnham: Ashgate, 2009).

Allan, David, '"Winged Horses, Fiery Dragons, and Monstrous Giants": Historiography and Imaginative Literature in the Scottish Enlightenment', in Ralph McLean, Ronnie Young and Kenneth Simpson (eds), *The Scottish Enlightenment and Literary Culture* (Lewisburg: Bucknell University Press, 2016), pp. 19–36.

Allen, Walter, *The Short Story in English* (Oxford: Clarendon Press, 1981).

Anderson, Benedict, *Imagined Communities: Reflections on the Origin and Spread of Nationalism*, 2nd edn (London: Verso, 1991).

Andrews, Corey E., *The Genius of Scotland: The Cultural Production of Robert Burns, 1785–1834* (Leiden: Brill Rodopi, 2015).

Andrews, Malcolm, 'The English Cottage as Cultural Critique and Associationist Paradigm', in Peter Brown and Michael Irwin (eds), *Literature and Place 1800–2000* (Oxford: Peter Lang, 2006), pp. 49–68.

Andrews, Malcolm, *The Search for the Picturesque: Landscape Aesthetics and Tourism in Britain, 1760–1800* (Aldershot: Scolar Press, 1989).

Anticipation; or, an Hundred Years Hence (London, 1829).

Baillie, Joanna, *The Collected Letters of Joanna Baillie*, ed. Judith Bailey Slagle, 2 vols (Madison: Fairleigh Dickinson University Press, 1999).

Baillie, Joanna, *Dramas*, 3 vols (London: Longman, Rees, Orme, Brown, Green and Longman, 1836).

Baillie, Joanna, *The Dramatic and Poetical Works of Joanna Baillie* (London: Longman, Brown, Green and Longmans, 1851).

Baillie, Joanna, *Joanna Baillie: A Selection of Plays and Poems*, ed. Amanda Gilroy and Keith Hanley (London: Pickering and Chatto, 2002).

Baillie, Joanna, *Plays on the Passions (1798 edition)*, ed. Peter Duthie (Peterborough, ON: Broadview Press, 2001).

Baird, John D., 'Two Poets of the 1780s: Burns and Cowper', in Donald A. Low (ed.), *Critical Essays on Robert Burns* (London: Routledge and Kegan Paul, 1975), pp. 106–23.

Bakhtin, M. M., *The Dialogic Imagination: Four Essays*, ed. Michael Holquist, trans. Caryl Emerson and Michael Holquist (Austin: University of Texas Press, 1981).

Bardsley, Alyson, 'Novel and Nation Come to Grief: The Dead's Part in John Galt's *The Entail*', *Modern Philology*, 99 (2002): 540–63.

Barrell, John, *The Idea of Landscape and the Sense of Place, 1730–1840: An Approach to the Poetry of John Clare* (London: Cambridge University Press, 1972).

Barrell, John, *The Spirit of Despotism: Invasions of Privacy in the 1790s* (Oxford: Oxford University Press, 2006).

Barnard, Toby, *Improving Ireland? Projectors, Prophets and Profiteers, 1641–1786* (Dublin: Four Courts Press, 2008).

Benchimol, Alex, 'Periodicals and Public Culture', in Murray Pittock (ed.), *The Edinburgh Companion to Scottish Romanticism* (Edinburgh: Edinburgh University Press, 2011), pp. 84–99.

Benchimol, Alex, and Gerard Lee McKeever (eds), *Cultures of Improvement in Scottish Romanticism, 1707–1840* (London: Routledge, 2018).

Bentman, Raymond, 'Robert Burns's Declining Fame', *Studies in Romanticism*, 11.3 (1972): 207–24.

Berman, Marshall, 'Tearing Away the Veils: The Communist Manifesto', *Dissent: A Quarterly of Politics and Culture*, 6 May 2011, <http://www.dissentmagazine.org/online_articles/tearing-away-the-veils-the-communist-manifesto> (accessed 27 June 2019).

Bermingham, Ann, *Landscape and Ideology: The English Rustic Tradition, 1740–1860* (London: Thames and Hudson, 1987).

Berry, Christopher J., *The Idea of Commercial Society in the Scottish Enlightenment* (Edinburgh: Edinburgh University Press, 2013).

Blackwood, William, 'On Parliamentary Reform and the French Revolution, No. IX: Consequences of Reform', *Blackwood's Edinburgh Magazine*, 30 (September 1831): 432–47.

Blake, William, *The Complete Illuminated Books*, introduction by David Bindman (London: Thames and Hudson, 2000; repr. 2009).

Bohrer, Martha, 'John Galt's *Annals of the Parish* and the Narrative Strategies of Tales of Locale', in Regina Hewitt (ed.), *John Galt: Observations and Conjectures on Literature, History, and Society* (Lewisburg: Bucknell University Press, 2012), pp. 95–118.

Bourdieu, Pierre, *The Field of Cultural Production: Essays on Art and Literature*, ed. Randal Johnson (Cambridge: Polity Press, 1993).

Briggs, Asa, *The Age of Improvement, 1783–1867* (1959) (Abingdon: Routledge, 2014).

Broun, Dauvit, 'Britain and the Beginning of Scotland', *Journal of the British Academy*, 3 (2015): 107–37.

Burke, Edmund, *Reflections on the Revolution in France* (1790), ed. J. G. A. Pocock (Indianapolis: Hackett, 1987).

Burns, Robert, *The Letters of Robert Burns*, ed. J. De Lancey Ferguson, 2nd edn, ed. G. Ross Roy, 2 vols (Oxford: Clarendon Press, 1985).

Burns, Robert, *The Oxford Edition of the Works of Robert Burns, Vol. 1: Commonplace Books, Tour Journals, and Miscellaneous Prose,* ed. Nigel Leask (Oxford: Oxford University Press, 2014).

Burns, Robert, *Poems, Chiefly in the Scottish Dialect* (Kilmarnock: printed by John Wilson, 1786).

Burns, Robert, *Poems, Chiefly in the Scottish Dialect* (Edinburgh: Printed for the author, and sold by William Creech, 1787).

Burns, Robert, *The Poems and Songs of Robert Burns*, ed. James Kinsley, 3 vols (Oxford: Clarendon Press, 1968).

Burns, Robert, *Robert Burns's Songs for George Thomson*, ed. Kirsteen McCue (Oxford: Oxford University Press, forthcoming).

Burns, Robert, *The Works of Robert Burns; with an Account of his Life, and a Criticism of his Writings* [. . .], ed. James Currie, 4 vols (Liverpool: Cadell, Davies and Creech, 1800).

Burnes, William, 'A manual of religious belief, composed by William Burnes for the instruction of his children', Robert Burns Birthplace Museum, object no. 36699.

Burnett, John, 'Kilmarnock and the Kilmarnock Edition', *Burns Chronicle* (2015): 27–38.

Burroughs, Catherine B., *Closet Stages: Joanna Baillie and the Theater Theory of British Romantic Women Writers* (Philadelphia: University of Pennsylvania Press, 1997).

Butler, Marilyn, 'Burns and Politics', in Robert Crawford (ed.), *Robert Burns and Cultural Authority* (Iowa City: University of Iowa Press, 1997), pp. 86–112.

Butler, Marilyn, *Romantics, Rebels and Reactionaries: English Literature and its Background, 1760–1830* (Oxford: Oxford University Press, 1981).

Byron, Lord, *The Complete Miscellaneous Prose*, ed. Andrew Nicholson (Oxford: Clarendon Press, 1991).

'A Bystander', 'Sir H. Parnell on Financial Reform', *Blackwood's Edinburgh Magazine*, 30 (September 1831): 457–74.

Carlyle, Thomas, 'Burns', *The Edinburgh Review*, 48 (December 1828): 267–312.

Carlyle, Thomas, 'Signs of the Times', *The Edinburgh Review*, 49 (June 1829): 439–59.

Carlyle, Thomas, 'State of German Literature', *The Edinburgh Review*, 46 (October 1827): 304–51.

Carney, Sean, 'The Passion of Joanna Baillie: Playwright as Martyr', *Theatre Journal*, 52.2 (2000): 227–52.

Carruthers, Gerard (ed.), *The Edinburgh Companion to Robert Burns* (Edinburgh: Edinburgh University Press, 2009).

Carruthers, Gerard, *Robert Burns* (Tavistock: Northcote, 2006).

Carruthers, Gerard, and Don Martin (eds), *Thomas Muir of Huntershill: Essays for the Twenty First Century* (Edinburgh: Humming Earth, 2016).

Carruthers, Gerard, and Alan Rawes (eds), *English Romanticism and the Celtic World* (Cambridge: Cambridge University Press, 2002).

Çelikkol, Ayşe, *Romances of Free Trade: British Literature, Laissez-Faire, and the Global Nineteenth Century* (Oxford: Oxford University Press, 2011).

Chandler, James, *England in 1819: The Politics of Literary Culture and the Case of Romantic Historicism* (Chicago: University of Chicago Press, 1998).

Cobbett, William, 'Gold!', *Cobbett's Weekly Register*, 64.9 (24 November 1827): 555–9.

Coleridge, Samuel Taylor, *Biographia Literaria; or, Biographical Sketches of My Literary Life and Opinions* (1817), ed. James Engell and W. Jackson Bate (Princeton: Princeton University Press, 1983).

Colley, Linda, *Britons: Forging the Nation 1707–1837* (New Haven: Yale University Press, 1992).

Cooney, Seamus, 'Scott and Cultural Relativism: "The Two Drovers"', *Studies in Short Fiction*, 15.1 (1978): 1–9.

Costain, Keith M., 'Mind-Forg'd Manacles: *The Entail* as Romantic Tragicomedy', in Christopher A. Whatley (ed.), *John Galt 1779–1979* (Edinburgh: The Ramsay Head Press, 1979), pp. 164–94.

Cox, Jeffrey N., *In the Shadows of Romance: Romantic Tragic Drama in Germany, England, and France* (Athens: Ohio University Press, 1987).

Cox, Jeffrey N., 'Staging Baillie', in Thomas C. Crochunis (ed.), *Joanna Baillie, Romantic Dramatist* (London: Routledge, 2004), pp. 146–67.

Craig, Cairns, *Out of History: Narrative Paradigms in Scottish and English Culture* (Edinburgh: Polygon, 1996).

Craig, David, *Scottish Literature and the Scottish People, 1680–1830* (London: Chatto and Windus, 1961).

Crawford, Robert, *Devolving English Literature*, 2nd edn (Edinburgh: Edinburgh University Press, 2000).

Crawford, T., *Burns: A Study of the Poems and Songs*, 2nd edn (Edinburgh: Oliver and Boyd, 1965).

Cunningham, Allan, *Paul Jones; a Romance*, 3 vols (Edinburgh/London: Oliver and Boyd/Longman, Rees, Orme, Brown and Green, 1826).

Daiches, David, 'Scott's Achievement as a Novelist', in D. D. Devlin (ed.), *Walter Scott: Modern Judgements* (London: Aurora, 1970), pp. 33–62.

D'Arcy, Julian Meldon, *Subversive Scott: The Waverley Novels and Scottish Nationalism* (Hagatorgi: University of Iceland Press, 2005).

Davis, Leith, 'Re-presenting Scotia: Robert Burns and the Imagined Community of Scotland', in Carol McGuirk (ed.), *Critical Essays on Robert Burns* (New York: G. K. Hall, 1998), pp. 63–76.

Davis, Leith, Ian Duncan and Janet Sorensen (eds), *Scotland and the Borders of Romanticism* (Cambridge: Cambridge University Press, 2004).

Devine, T. M., *Clearance and Improvement: Land, Power and People in Scotland, 1700–1900* (Edinburgh: John Donald, 2006).

Devine, T. M., *Scotland's Empire 1600–1815* (London: Allen Lane, 2003).

Devine, T. M., *The Transformation of Rural Scotland: Social Change and the Agrarian Economy, 1660–1815* (Edinburgh: Edinburgh University Press, 1994).

Dick, Alexander, *Romanticism and the Gold Standard: Money, Literature, and Economic Debate in Britain 1790–1830* (Basingstoke: Palgrave Macmillan, 2013).

Dick, Alex J., 'Walter Scott and the Financial Crash of 1825: Fiction, Speculation, and the Standard of Value', in Ian Haywood (ed.), *Romanticism, Forgery, and the Credit Crunch*, Romantic Circles Praxis Series (2012), <www.rc.umd.edu/praxis/forgery/HTML/praxis.2011.dick.html> (accessed 27 June 2019).

Divine, Ann Roberts, 'The Changing Village: Loss of Community in John Galt's *Annals of the Parish*', *Studies in Scottish Literature*, 25.1 (1990): 121–33.

Douglas, Mary, *Purity and Danger: An Analysis of Concepts of Pollution and Taboo* (London: Routledge and Kegan Paul, 1966).

Drayton, Richard, *Nature's Government: Science, Imperial Britain and the 'Improvement' of the World* (New Haven: Yale University Press, 2000).

Duncan, Ian, 'Altered States: Galt, Serial Fiction, and the Romantic Miscellany', in Regina Hewitt (ed.), *John Galt: Observations and Conjectures on Literature, History, and Society* (Lewisburg: Bucknell University Press, 2012), pp. 53–71.

Duncan, Ian, *Modern Romance and Transformations of the Novel: The Gothic, Scott, Dickens* (Cambridge: Cambridge University Press, 1992).

Duncan, Ian, *Scott's Shadow: The Novel in Romantic Edinburgh* (Princeton: Princeton University Press, 2007).

Duncan, Ian, 'Urban Space and Enlightened Romanticism', in Murray Pittock (ed.), *The Edinburgh Companion to Scottish Romanticism* (Edinburgh: Edinburgh University Press, 2011), pp. 72–83.

Dwyer, John, *Virtuous Discourse: Sensibility and Community in Late Eighteenth-Century Scotland* (Edinburgh: John Donald, 1987).

Eagleton, Terry, *Ideology: An Introduction*, 2nd edn (London: Verso, 2007).

Esterhammer, Angela, '1824: Improvisation, Speculation, and Identity-Construction', *BRANCH: Britain, Representation and Nineteenth-Century History*, ed. Dino Franco Felluga, <http://www.branchcollective.org/?ps_articles=angela-esterhammer-1824-improvisation-speculation-and-identity-construction> (accessed 27 June 2019).

Ferguson, Adam, *An Essay on the History of Civil Society* (1767), ed. Fania Oz-Salzberger (Cambridge: Cambridge University Press, 1995).

Ferguson, J. De Lancey, 'Cancelled Passages in the Letters of Robert Burns to George Thomson', *Burns Chronicle and Club Directory* (1929): 90–103.

Ferguson, J. De Lancey, 'The Immortal Memory', *The American Scholar*, 5.4 (1936): 441–50.

Ferrier, Susan, *Memoir and Correspondence of Susan Ferrier*, ed. John A. Doyle (London: John Murray, 1898).

Fielding, Penny, '"Earth and Stone": Improvement, Entailment and Geographical Futures in the Novel of the 1820s', in Alex Benchimol and Gerard Lee McKeever (eds), *Cultures of Improvement in Scottish Romanticism, 1707–1840* (London: Routledge, 2018), pp. 152–69.

Fielding, Penny, *Scotland and the Fictions of Geography: North Britain 1760–1830* (Cambridge: Cambridge University Press, 2008).

Fielding, Penny, *Writing and Orality* (Oxford: Clarendon Press, 1996).

Forbes, Aileen, '"Sympathetic Curiosity" in Joanna Baillie's Theater of the Passions', *European Romantic Review*, 14.1 (2003): 31–48.

Fordyce, James, *Sermons to Young Women* (London: Millar and Cadell, 1766).

Frykman, Eric, *John Galt's Scottish Stories: 1820–1823* (Uppsala: Lundequistska Bokhandeln, 1959).

Fuller, R. Buckminster, *Nine Chains to the Moon* (Philadelphia: Lippincott, 1938).

Furniss, Tom, 'Reading John Anderson's Will: Improving Human Nature, Science and Scotland in a Commercial Society', in Alex Benchimol and Gerard Lee McKeever (eds), *Cultures of Improvement in Scottish Romanticism, 1707–1840* (London: Routledge, 2018), pp. 173–90.

Galt, John, *Annals of the Parish; or the Chronicle of Dalmailing during the Ministry of the Rev. Micah Balwhidder, Written by himself* (1821), ed. James Kinsley (London: Oxford University Press, 1972).

Galt, John, *The Autobiography of John Galt*, 2 vols (London: Cochrane and McCrone, 1833).

Galt, John, *The Entail; or, The Lairds of Grippy* (1823), ed. Ian A. Gordon (Oxford: Oxford University Press, 1984).

Galt, John, *The Literary Life and Miscellanies of John Galt*, 3 vols (Edinburgh/London: Blackwood/Cadell, 1834).

Galt, John, *The Provost* (1822), ed. Ian A. Gordon (Oxford: Oxford University Press, 1982).

Gamer, Michael, 'National Supernaturalism: Joanna Baillie, Germany, and the Gothic Drama', *Theatre Survey*, 38.2 (1997): 49–88.

Gamer, Michael, *Romanticism and the Gothic: Genre, Reception, and Canon Formation* (Cambridge: Cambridge University Press, 2004).

Gidal, Eric, *Ossianic Unconformities: Bardic Poetry in the Industrial Age* (Charlottesville: University of Virginia Press, 2015).

Gidal, Eric, and Michael Gavin, 'Introduction: Spatial Humanities and Scottish Studies', *Studies in Scottish Literature*, 42.2 (2016): 143–50.

Gilpin, William, *Observations, Relative to Picturesque Beauty, Made in the Year 1776, on Several Parts of Great Britain; Particularly the High-Lands of Scotland*, 2 vols (London: R. Blamire, 1789).

Godwin, William, *The Political and Philosophical Writings of William Godwin*, ed. Mark Philp, 7 vols (London: Pickering, 1993), vol. 5: *Educational and Literary Writings*, ed. Pamela Clemit.

Gordon, Ian A., 'Galt and Politics', in Elizabeth Waterson (ed.), *John Galt: Reappraisals* (Guelph: Ampersand, 1985), pp. 119–28.

Haywood, Ian (ed.,) *Romanticism, Forgery and the Credit Crunch*, *Romantic Circles Praxis Series* (2012), <http://www.rc.umd.edu/praxis/forgery/index.html> (accessed 27 June 2019).

Hamilton, Elizabeth, *The Cottagers of Glenburnie; and other Educational Writing*, ed. Pam Perkins (Glasgow: Association for Scottish Literary Studies, 2010).

Harris, Bob, and Charles McKean, *The Scottish Town in the Age of Enlightenment 1740–1820* (Edinburgh: Edinburgh University Press, 2014).

Harris, Jason Marc, *Folklore and the Fantastic in Nineteenth-Century British Fiction* (Aldershot: Ashgate, 2008).

Hegel, Georg Wilhelm Friedrich, *The Science of Logic* (1812–16), trans. and ed. George di Giovanni (Cambridge: Cambridge University Press, 2010).

Hemans, Mrs [Felicia], 'We Return no More!', *Blackwood's Edinburgh Magazine*, 28 (July 1830): 40.

Henderson, Andrea, 'Passion and Fashion in Joanna Baillie's "Introductory Discourse"', *PMLA* (March 1997): 198–213.

Henderson, Andrea, *Romanticism and the Painful Pleasures of Modern Life* (Cambridge: Cambridge University Press, 2008).

Hewitt, Regina, 'Improving the Law: Property Rights and Self-Possession in Joanna Baillie's "The Alienated Manor"', *The Wordsworth Circle*, 38.1/2 (2007): 50–5.

Hewitt, Regina, 'Joanna Baillie's Ecotopian Comedies', in Regina Hewitt (ed.), *Utopianism and Joanna Baillie, Romantic Circles Praxis Series* (July 2008), <https://www.rc.umd.edu/praxis/utopia/hewitt/hewitt.html> (accessed 27 June 2019).

Hewitt, Regina, 'John Galt, Harriet Martineau, and the Role of the Social Theorist', in Regina Hewitt (ed.), *John Galt: Observations and Conjectures on Literature, History, and Society* (Lewisburg: Bucknell University Press, 2012), pp. 345–72.

Hewitt, Regina (ed.), *John Galt: Observations and Conjectures on Literature, History, and Society* (Lewisburg: Bucknell University Press, 2012).

Hogg, James, *Contributions to Blackwood's Edinburgh Magazine*, 2 vols, ed. Thomas C. Richardson (Edinburgh: Edinburgh University Press, 2008/12), vol. 2 (2012).

Hogg, James, *Familiar Anecdotes of Sir Walter Scott* (New York: Harper and Brothers, 1834).

Hogg, James, *Highland Journeys*, ed. H. B. de Groot (Edinburgh: Edinburgh University Press, 2010).

Hogg, James, *The Pilgrims of the Sun* (1815), in *Midsummer Night Dreams and Related Poems*, ed. Jill Rubenstein, completed by Gillian Hughes with Meiko O'Halloran (Edinburgh: Edinburgh University Press, 2008), pp. 3–50.

Hogg, James, *The Shepherd's Calendar* (1829), ed. Douglas S. Mack (Edinburgh: Edinburgh University Press, 2002).

Hogg, James, *The Three Perils of Woman; or, Love, Leasing, and Jealousy, a series of Domestic Scottish Tales* (1823), ed. Antony Hasler and Douglas S. Mack (Edinburgh: Edinburgh University Press, 2002).

Horkheimer, Max, and Theodor W. Adorno, *Dialectic of Enlightenment: Philosophical Fragments* (1947), ed. Gunzelin Schmid Noerr, trans. Edmund Jephcott (Stanford: Stanford University Press, 2002).

Home, John, *Douglas* (1756), ed. Gerald D. Parker (Edinburgh: Oliver and Boyd, 1972).

Hume, David, 'Of Public Credit' (1752), in *Selected Essays*, ed. Stephen Copley and Andrew Edgar (Oxford: Oxford University Press, 1996).

Hume, David, *A Treatise of Human Nature* (1739–40), ed. David Fate Norton and Mary J. Norton (Oxford: Oxford University Press, 2000).

'Improvements', *The Examiner* (8 September 1811): 578.

'In our endeavours towards the reformation of our manners [. . .]', *The Castle-Douglas Weekly Visitor and Literary Miscellany*, 2.62 (21 January 1831): 74–6.

Irving, Edward, *The Last Days: A Discourse on the Evil Character of These our Times* (London: R. B. Seeley and W. Burnside, 1828).

Jack, R. D. S., 'Robert Burns: Poet of Freedom', *Scotia: American-Canadian Journal of Scottish Studies*, 6 (1982): 41–59.

Jarrells, Anthony, 'Provincializing Enlightenment: "Edinburgh" Historicism and the Blackwoodian Regional Tale', *Studies in Romanticism*, 48.2 (2009): 257–77.

Jeffrey, Francis, review of *The Cottagers of Glenburnie* by Elizabeth Hamilton, *The Edinburgh Review*, 12 (July 1808): 401–10.

Johnson, Samuel, *The History of Rasselas, Prince of Abissinia* (1759), ed. Thomas Keymer (Oxford: Oxford University Press, 2009).

Jonsson, Fredrik Albritton, *Enlightenment's Frontier: The Scottish Highlands and the Origins of Environmentalism* (New Haven: Yale University Press, 2013).

Jordan, Frank, 'Chrystal Croftangry, Scott's Last and Best Mask', *Scottish Literary Journal*, 7.1 (1980): 185–92.

Judson, Barbara, '"Sympathetic Curiosity": The Theater of Joanna Baillie', *Tulsa Studies in Women's Literature*, 25.1 (2006): 49–70.

Jung, Sandro, '"A Scotch Poetical Library": The Morisons of Perth, Print Culture, and the Construction of an Enlightenment Scottish Literary Canon', in Ralph McLean, Ronnie Young and Kenneth Simpson (eds), *The Scottish Enlightenment and Literary Culture* (Lewisburg: Bucknell University Press, 2016), pp. 185–208.

Kant, Immanuel, *Critique of the Power of Judgment* (1790), ed. Paul Guyer, trans. Paul Guyer and Eric Matthews (Cambridge: Cambridge University Press, 2000).

Kelly, Gary, *English Fiction of the Romantic Period 1789–1830* (London: Longman, 1989).

Kidd, Colin, 'Enlightenment and Ecclesiastical Satire before Burns', in Ralph McLean, Ronnie Young and Kenneth Simpson (eds), *The Scottish Enlightenment and Literary Culture* (Lewisburg: Bucknell University Press, 2016), pp. 95–114.

Kidd, Colin, 'North Britishness and the Nature of Eighteenth-Century British Patriotisms', *The Historical Journal*, 39.2 (1996): 361–82.

Kidd, Colin, 'Subscription, the Scottish Enlightenment and the Moderate Interpretation of History', *Journal of Ecclesiastical History*, 55.3 (2004): 502–19.

Kidd, Colin, *Subverting Scotland's Past: Scottish Whig Historians and the Creation of an Anglo-British identity, 1689–c. 1830* (Cambridge: Cambridge University Press, 1993).

Killick, Tim, *British Short Fiction in the Early Nineteenth Century: The Rise of the Tale* (Aldershot: Ashgate, 2008).

Lagrange, Joseph-Louis, *Mécanique analytique* (Paris: Chez La Veuve Desaint, 1788).

Leask, Nigel, 'Burns, Wordsworth and the Politics of Vernacular Poetry', in Peter de Bolla, Nigel Leask and David Simpson (eds), *Land, Nation and Culture, 1740–1840: Thinking the Republic of Taste* (Basingstoke: Palgrave Macmillan, 2005), pp. 202–22.

Leask, Nigel, *Curiosity and the Aesthetics of Travel Writing, 1770–1840: 'From an Antique Land'* (Oxford: Oxford University Press, 2002).

Leask, Nigel, *Robert Burns and Pastoral: Poetry and Improvement in Late Eighteenth-Century Scotland* (Oxford: Oxford University Press, 2010).

Lee, Yoon Sun, *Nationalism and Irony: Burke, Scott, Carlyle* (New York: Oxford University Press, 2004).

Lemke, Cordula, 'Nostalgic Ossian and the Transcreation of the Scottish Nation', in Dafydd Moore (ed.), *The International Companion to James Macpherson and The Poems of Ossian* (Glasgow: Scottish Literature International, 2017), pp. 52–64.

Lincoln, Andrew, *Walter Scott and Modernity* (Edinburgh: Edinburgh University Press, 2007).

Livesey, Ruth, *Writing the Stage Coach Nation: Locality on the Move in Nineteenth-Century British Literature* (Oxford: Oxford University Press, 2016).

Livingston, Alistair, 'The Galloway Levellers: A Study of the Origins, Events and Consequences of their Actions', MPhil dissertation, University of Glasgow, 2009.

Lockhart, John Gibson, *Peter's Letters to his Kinsfolk*, 3 vols (Edinburgh: Blackwood, 1819).

Lukács, Georg, *The Historical Novel* (1937), trans. Hannah Mitchell and Stanley Mitchell (Lincoln: University of Nebraska Press, 1983).

Lumsden, Alison, 'Walter Scott and *Blackwood's*: Writing for the Adventurers', *Romanticism*, 23.3 (2017): 215–23.

Lumsden, Alison, *Walter Scott and the Limits of Language* (Edinburgh: Edinburgh University Press, 2010).

Lyell, Frank Hallam, *A Study of the Novels of John Galt* (Princeton: Princeton University Press, 1942).

Mackenzie, Henry, 'Unsigned Essay in *The Lounger*, 9 December 1786', in Donald A. Low (ed.), *Robert Burns: The Critical Heritage* (London: Routledge and Kegan Paul, 1974), pp. 67–71.

MacKillop, Andrew, *'More Fruitful than the Soil': Army, Empire and the Scottish Highlands, 1715–1815* (East Linton: Tuckwell, 2000).

Mackinnon, William Alexander, *On The Rise, Progress, and Present State of Public Opinion in Great Britain, and Other Parts of the World* (London: Saunders and Otley, 1828).

Macleod, Innes (ed.), *Sailing on Horseback: William Daniell and Richard Ayton in Cumbria and Dumfries and Galloway* (Dumfries, 1988).

Makdisi, Saree, *Romantic Imperialism: Universal Empire and the Culture of Modernity* (Cambridge: Cambridge University Press, 1998).

Manning, Susan, 'Burns and God', in Robert Crawford (ed.), *Robert Burns and Cultural Authority* (Iowa City: University of Iowa Press, 1997), pp. 113–35.

May, Chad T., '"The Horrors of My Tale": Trauma, the Historical Imagination, and Sir Walter Scott', *Pacific Coast Philology*, 40.1 (2005): 98–116.

McCracken-Flesher, Caroline, '*Pro Matria Mori*: Gendered Nationalism and Cultural Death in Scott's "The Highland Widow"', *Scottish Literary Journal*, 21.2 (1994): 69–78.

McCracken-Flesher, Caroline, 'The Sense of No Ending: John Galt and the Travels of Commoners and Kings in "The Steam-Boat" and "The Gathering of the West"', in Regina Hewitt (ed.), *John Galt: Observations and Conjectures on Literature, History, and Society* (Lewisburg: Bucknell University Press, 2012), pp. 73–92.

McCue, Kirsteen C., 'George Thomson (1757–1851): His Collections of National Airs in their Scottish Cultural Context', PhD dissertation, University of Oxford, 1993.

McDiarmid, John, *Picture of Dumfries & Its Environs* (Edinburgh: John Gellatly, 1832).

McGann, Jerome J., *The Romantic Ideology: A Critical Investigation* (Chicago: University of Chicago Press, 1983).

McGill, Meredith L., *American Literature and the Culture of Reprinting, 1834–1853* (Philadelphia: University of Pennsylvania Press, 2003).

McGinty, Joseph Walter, 'Literary, Philosophical and Theological Influences on Robert Burns', 2 vols, PhD dissertation, University of Strathclyde, 1995.

McGinty, J. Walter, *Robert Burns and Religion* (Farnham: Ashgate, 2003).

McIlvanney, Liam, *Burns the Radical: Poetry and Politics in Late Eighteenth-Century Scotland* (East Linton: Tuckwell, 2002).

McKeever, Gerard Lee, '"All that I choose to tell you is this": Improvement Confronts the Supernatural in Hogg's Short Fictions', *Studies in Hogg and his World*, 25–26 (2015–16): 30–44.

McKeever, Gerard Lee, 'Burns's Tales of "Aloway Kirk" and Romantic Short Fiction', *Scottish Literary Review*, 8.2 (2016): 19–35.

McKeever, Gerard Lee, '"Simplicity, Rightly Understood": Improvement in the Collaboration of Robert Burns and George Thomson', in Alex Benchimol and Gerard Lee McKeever (eds), *Cultures of Improvement in Scottish Romanticism, 1707–1840* (London: Routledge, 2018), pp. 74–91.

McKeever, Gerard Lee, 'Tam o' Shanter and Aesthetic Cultural Nationalism', *Studies in Scottish Literature*, 42.1 (2016): 31–48.

McKeever, Gerard Lee, '"With wealth come wants": Scottish Romanticism as Improvement in the Fiction of John Galt', *Studies in Romanticism*, 55.1 (2016): 69–94.

McLean, Ralph, 'Hugh Blair and the Influence of Rhetoric and Belles Lettres on Imaginative Literature', in Ralph McLean, Ronnie Young and Kenneth Simpson (eds), *The Scottish Enlightenment and Literary Culture* (Lewisburg: Bucknell University Press, 2016), pp. 137–51.

McLean, Ralph, Ronnie Young and Kenneth Simpson (eds), *The Scottish Enlightenment and Literary Culture* (Lewisburg: Bucknell University Press, 2016).

McNeil, Kenneth, 'Time, Emigration, and the Circum-Atlantic World: John Galt's *Bogle Corbet*', in Regina Hewitt (ed.), *John Galt: Observations and Conjectures on Literature, History, and Society* (Lewisburg: Bucknell University Press, 2012), pp. 299–321.

Mee, Jon, *Romanticism, Enthusiasm, and Regulation: Poetics and the Policing of Culture in the Romantic Period* (Oxford: Oxford University Press, 2003).

Mellor, Anne, 'A Criticism of Their Own: Romantic Women Literary Critics', in John Beer (ed.), *Questioning Romanticism* (Baltimore: Johns Hopkins University Press, 1995), pp. 29–48.

Mellor, Anne K., 'Joanna Baillie and the Counter-Public Sphere', *Studies in Romanticism*, 33 (1994): 559–67.

Mellor, Anne K., *Mothers of the Nation: Women's Political Writing in England, 1780–1830* (Bloomington: Indiana University Press, 2000).

Miller, Dan, 'Contrary Revelation: "The Marriage of Heaven and Hell"', *Studies in Romanticism*, 24.4 (1985): 491–509.

Miller, Thomas P., *The Formation of College English: Rhetoric and Belles Lettres in the British Cultural Provinces* (Pittsburgh: University of Pittsburgh Press, 1997).

Millgate, Jane, *Walter Scott: The Making of the Novelist* (Toronto: University of Toronto Press, 1984).

Moir, David Macbeth ['Delta'], 'An Autumn Walk', *Blackwood's Edinburgh Magazine*, 28 (December 1830): 941–2.

Moore, Dafydd, *Enlightenment and Romance in the Poems of Ossian* (Aldershot: Ashgate, 2003).

Morris, Michael, *Scotland and the Caribbean, c.1740–1833: Atlantic Archipelagos* (New York: Routledge, 2015).

Morrison, Robert, 'John Galt's Angular Magazinity', in Regina Hewitt (ed.), *John Galt: Observations and Conjectures on Literature, History, and Society* (Lewisburg: Bucknell University Press, 2012), pp. 257–80.

Mudford, William, 'The Silent Member, No. IV: Voting by Proxy', *Blackwood's Edinburgh Magazine*, 28 (July 1830): 47–62.

Muir, Edwin, *Selected Poems*, ed. Mick Imlah (London: Faber and Faber, 2008).

Murdoch, Alexander, and Richard B. Sher, 'Literacy and Learned Culture', in T. M. Devine and Rosalind Mitchison (eds), *People and Society in Scotland: Volume I 1760–1830; A Social History of Modern Scotland in Three Volumes* (Edinburgh: John Donald, 1988), pp. 127–42.

Murray, Julie, 'Governing Economic Man: Joanna Baillie's Theatre of Utility', *ELH*, 70.4 (2003): 1043–65.

Myers, Victoria, 'Joanna Baillie's Theatre of Cruelty', in Thomas C. Crochunis (ed.), *Joanna Baillie, Romantic Dramatist* (London: Routledge, 2004), pp. 87–107.

Nairn, Tom, *The Break-Up of Britain*, 2nd edn (London: Verso, 1981).

Nash, Andrew, 'The Cotter's Kailyard', in Robert Crawford (ed.), *Robert Burns and Cultural Authority* (Iowa City: University of Iowa Press, 1997), pp. 180–97.

Newman, Steve, 'Localizing and Globalizing Burns's Songs from Ayrshire to Calcutta: The Limits of Romanticism and Analogies of Improvement', in Evan Gottlieb (ed.), *Global Romanticism: Origins, Orientations, and Engagements, 1760–1820* (Lewisburg: Bucknell University Press, 2015), pp. 57–77.

Newte, Thomas [William Thomson], *A Tour in England and Scotland in 1785, by an English Gentleman* (London: G. G. J. and J. Robinson, 1788).

O'Connell, Helen, *Ireland and the Fiction of Improvement* (Oxford: Oxford University Press, 2006).

O'Halloran, Meiko, *James Hogg and British Romanticism: A Kaleidoscopic Art* (Basingstoke: Palgrave Macmillan, 2016).

O'Halloran, Meiko, 'National Discourse or Discord? Transformations of *The Family Legend* by Baillie, Scott, and Hogg', in Sharon Alker and Holly Faith Nelson (eds), *James Hogg and the Literary Marketplace: Scottish*

Romanticism and the Working-Class Author (Farnham: Ashgate, 2009), pp. 43–55.

Oliphant, Margaret, *Annals of a Publishing House: William Blackwood and His Sons*, 2 vols (Edinburgh and London: William Blackwood and Sons, 1897).

Overton, W. J., 'Scott, the Short Story and History: "The Two Drovers"', *Studies in Scottish Literature*, 21.1 (1986): 210–25.

Owenson, Sydney, Lady Morgan, *The Wild Irish Girl* (1806), ed. Kathryn Kirkpatrick (Oxford: Oxford University Press, 1999).

Paine, Thomas, *Rights of Man, Common Sense and Other Political Writings*, ed. Mark Philp (Oxford: Oxford University Press, 2008).

Peterkin, Alexander, *A Review of the Life of Robert Burns, and of Various Criticisms on his Character and Writings* (Edinburgh: Macbedie, Skelly and Muckersy, 1815).

Phillipson, Nicholas, 'The Scottish Enlightenment', in Roy S. Porter and Mikuláš Teich (eds), *The Enlightenment in National Context* (Cambridge: Cambridge University Press, 1981), pp. 19–40.

Phillipson, N. T., and Rosalind Mitchison (eds), *Scotland in the Age of Improvement: Essays in Scottish History in the Eighteenth Century* (Edinburgh: Edinburgh University Press, 1970).

Pittock, Murray (ed.), *The Edinburgh Companion to Scottish Romanticism* (Edinburgh: Edinburgh University Press, 2011).

Pittock, Murray (ed.), *The Reception of Sir Walter Scott in Europe* (London: Continuum, 2006).

Pittock, Murray, *Scottish and Irish Romanticism* (Oxford: Oxford University Press, 2008).

Plotz, John, 'Hogg and the Short Story', in Ian Duncan and Douglas S. Mack (eds), *The Edinburgh Companion to James Hogg* (Edinburgh: Edinburgh University Press, 2012), pp. 113–21.

Pope, Alexander, *Windsor-Forest* (1713), in *Poetical Works*, ed. Herbert Davis with an introduction by Pat Rogers (Oxford: Oxford University Press, 1978), pp. 37–50.

'Preface', *Edinburgh Review*, 1 (1755), pp. i–iv.

Pritchett, V. S. (ed.), *The Oxford Book of Short Stories* (Oxford: Oxford University Press, 1981).

Radcliffe, David Hill, 'Imitation, Popular Literacy, and "The Cotter's Saturday Night"', in Carol McGuirk (ed.), *Critical Essays on Robert Burns* (New York: G. K. Hall, 1998), pp. 251–79.

Regan, John, *Poetry and the Idea of Progress, 1760–1790* (London: Anthem Press, 2018).

Regan, Shaun (ed.), *Reading 1759: Literary Culture in Mid-Eighteenth-Century Britain and France* (Lewisburg: Bucknell University Press, 2013).

Richards, Eric, *Debating the Highland Clearances* (Edinburgh: Edinburgh University Press, 2007).

Richardson, Alan, *Literature, Education, and Romanticism: Reading as Social Practice, 1780–1832* (Cambridge: Cambridge University Press, 1994).

Roberts, Daniel S., '"The Only Irish Magazine": *Early Blackwood's* and the Production of Irish "National Character"', *Romanticism*, 23.3 (2017): 262–71.

Robertson, William, *The History of Scotland during the Reigns of Queen Mary and of King James VI till his Accession to the Crown of England: with a Review of the Scottish History Previous to that Period*, 2 vols (1759) (London: Jones, 1827).

Robertson, William, and William H. Prescott, *History of the Reign of Charles the Fifth; with an Account of the Emperor's Life after his Abdication*, 2 vols (London: Routledge, 1857).

Rohrbach, Emily, *Modernity's Mist: British Romanticism and the Poetics of Anticipation* (New York: Fordham University Press, 2016).

Rowlinson, Matthew, *Real Money and Romanticism* (Cambridge: Cambridge University Press, 2010).

Ruskin, John, *The Stones of Venice*, 3 vols (London: Smith, Elder and Co., 1851–53).

Schoenfield, Mark, 'Family Plots: Land and Law in John Galt's *The Entail*', *Scottish Literary Journal*, 24 (1997): 60–5.

Scott, Patrick, 'Describing the Kilmarnock: Printing, Publication & Later History', in Allan Young and Patrick Scott, *The Kilmarnock Burns: A Census* (Columbia: University of South Carolina Libraries, 2017), pp. xxi–xxxvi.

Scott, P. H., *John Galt* (Edinburgh: Scottish Academic Press, 1985).

Scott, Walter, *Chronicles of the Canongate* (1827), ed. Claire Lamont (Edinburgh: Edinburgh University Press, 2000).

Scott, Walter, 'General Preface to the Waverley Novels, January I, 1829', in *Sir Walter Scott On Novelists and Fiction*, ed. Ioan Williams (New York/London: Barnes and Noble/ Routledge and Kegan Paul, 1968), pp. 409–27.

Scott, Walter, *Guy Mannering* (1815), ed. P. D. Garside (Edinburgh: Edinburgh University Press, 1999).

Scott, Walter, *Ivanhoe* (1819), ed. Ian Duncan (Oxford: Oxford University Press, 1996).

Scott, Walter, *Redgauntlet* (1824), ed. Kathryn Sutherland (Oxford: Oxford University Press, 1985).

Scott, Walter, *The Shorter Fiction*, ed. Graham Tulloch and Judy King (Edinburgh: Edinburgh University Press, 2009).

Scott, Walter, *Waverley; or, 'Tis Sixty Years Since* (1814), ed. Claire Lamont (Oxford: Oxford University Press, 1986).

'Severus', 'On different Species of National Improvement, particularly in Scotland', *Scots Magazine and Edinburgh Literary Miscellany* (August 1808): 598–601.

Sharp, Sarah, 'Hogg's Murder of Ravens: Storytelling, Community and Posthumous Mutilation', *Studies in Hogg and his World*, 23 (2013): 31–40.

Sher, Richard B., *The Enlightenment & the Book: Scottish Authors & Their Publishers in Eighteenth-Century Britain, Ireland, & America* (Chicago: University of Chicago Press, 2006).

Sherman, Stuart, *Telling Time: Clocks, Diaries, and English Diurnal Form, 1660–1785* (Chicago: University of Chicago Press, 1996).

Shields, Juliet, *Sentimental Literature and Anglo-Scottish Identity, 1745–1820* (Cambridge: Cambridge University Press, 2010).

Sibbald, James, '*Poems, chiefly in the Scottish Dialect.* By Robert Burns, Kilmarnock', *The Edinburgh Magazine, or Literary Miscellany* (October 1786): 284–5.

Simmons, Claire A., '"Feudal Days": John Galt's Ambivalent Medievalism', in Regina Hewitt (ed.), *John Galt: Observations and Conjectures on Literature, History, and Society* (Lewisburg: Bucknell University Press, 2012), pp. 169–97.

Simpson, Kenneth G., 'Ironic Self-Revelation in *Annals of the Parish*', in Christopher A. Whatley (ed.), *John Galt 1779–1979* (Edinburgh: The Ramsay Head Press, 1979), pp. 64–91.

Sinclair, Sir John (ed.), *The Statistical Account of Scotland 1791–1799, Volume I: General*, ed. Donald J. Withrington and Ian R. Grant (Wakefield: EP Publishing, 1983).

Sinclair, Sir John (ed.), *The Statistical Account of Scotland 1791–1799, Volume IV: Dumfriesshire*, ed. Ian B. Cowan (Wakefield: EP Publishing, 1978).

Sinclair, Sir John (ed.), *The Statistical Account of Scotland 1791–1799, Volume VI: Ayrshire*, ed. John Strawhorn (Wakefield: EP Publishing, 1982).

Slack, Paul, *The Invention of Improvement: Information and Material Progress in Seventeenth-Century England* (Oxford: Oxford University Press, 2015).

Slagle, Judith Bailey, 'Evolution of a Writer: Joanna Baillie's Life in Letters', in Thomas C. Crochunis (ed.), *Joanna Baillie, Romantic Dramatist* (London: Routledge, 2004), pp. 8–26.

Slagle, Judith Bailey, *Joanna Baillie: A Literary Life* (Madison: Fairleigh Dickinson University Press, 2002).

Smith, Adam, *An Inquiry into the Nature and Causes of the Wealth of Nations* (1776), ed. R. H. Campbell and A. S. Skinner, 2 vols (Oxford: Oxford University Press, 1976).

Smith, Adam, *Lectures on Jurisprudence*, ed. R. L. Meek, D. D. Raphael and P. G. Stein (Oxford: Oxford University Press, 1978).

Smith, Adam, *The Theory of Moral Sentiments* (1759), ed. Knud Haakonssen (Cambridge: Cambridge University Press, 2002).

Smout, T. C., *Nature Contested: Environmental History in Scotland and Northern England since 1600* (Edinburgh: Edinburgh University Press, 2000).

Smout, T. C., 'Problems of Nationalism, Identity and Improvement in later Eighteenth-Century Scotland', in T. M. Devine (ed.), *Improvement and Enlightenment: Proceedings of the Scottish Historical Studies Seminar, University of Strathclyde 1987–88* (Edinburgh: John Donald, 1989), pp. 1–21.

Sorensen, Janet, 'Alternative Antiquarianisms of Scotland and the North', *Modern Language Quarterly*, 70 (2009): 415–41.

Sorensen, Janet, *The Grammar of Empire in Eighteenth-Century British Writing* (Cambridge: Cambridge University Press, 2000).

Spadafora, David, *The Idea of Progress in Eighteenth-Century Britain* (New Haven: Yale University Press, 1990).

Stafford, Fiona, *Local Attachments: The Province of Poetry* (Oxford: Oxford University Press, 2010).

Stafford, Fiona, 'Plain Living and Ungarnish'd Stories: Wordsworth and the Survival of Pastoral', *The Review of English Studies*, 59.238 (2008): 118–33.

Stafford, Fiona, 'The Roar of the Solway', in Nicholas Allen, Nick Groom and Jos Smith (eds), *Coastal Works: Cultures of the Atlantic Edge* (Oxford: Oxford University Press, 2017), pp. 41–60.

Steven, Maisie, *Parish Life in Eighteenth-Century Scotland: A Review of the Old Statistical Account* (Aberdeen: Scottish Cultural Press, 1995).

Stevenson, William, 'On the Reciprocal Influence of the Periodical Publications, and the Intellectual Progress of this Country', *Blackwood's Edinburgh Magazine*, 16 (November 1824): 518–28.

Stewart, David, *Romantic Magazines and Metropolitan Literary Culture* (Basingstoke: Palgrave Macmillan, 2011).

Stewart, David, 'Romantic Short Fiction', in Ann-Marie Einhaus (ed.), *The Cambridge Companion to the English Short Story* (New York: Cambridge University Press, 2016), pp. 73–86.

Strange, William C., 'The Fire Argument in The Jolly Beggars and The Cotter's Saturday Night', *Studies in Scottish Literature*, 17.1 (1982): 209–17.

Swaim, Barton, *Scottish Men of Letters and the New Public Sphere, 1802–1834* (Lewisburg: Bucknell University Press, 2009).

Tarlow, Sarah, *The Archaeology of Improvement in Britain, 1750–1850* (Cambridge: Cambridge University Press, 2007).

Taylor, William, *The Military Roads in Scotland* (Newton Abbot: David and Charles, 1976).

Thomson, George (ed.), *A Select Collection of Original Scotish Airs [. . .]* (London: Preston, 1793).

Thomson, James, *The Seasons* (1726–30), ed. James Sambrook (Oxford: Clarendon Press, 1981).

Thompson, E. P., 'Time, Work-Discipline, and Industrial Capitalism', *Past & Present*, 38 (December 1967): 56–97.

Thordarson, Thorvaldur, and Stephen Self, 'Atmospheric and Environmental Effects of the 1783–1784 Laki Eruption: A Review and Reassessment', *Journal of Geophysical Research*, 108.D1 (2003): 1–29 [AAC 7].

'To the Editor of the Political Herald; Reply to A. S. on Improvements in Scotland', *The Political Herald, and Review*, 18 (1786): 416–21.

Towsey, Mark R. M., *Reading the Scottish Enlightenment: Books and their Readers in Provincial Scotland, 1750–1820* (Leiden: Brill, 2010).

Trumpener, Katie, *Bardic Nationalism: The Romantic Novel and the British Empire* (Princeton: Princeton University Press, 1997).

Tuchman, Gaye, with Nina E. Fortin, *Edging Women Out: Victorian Novelists, Publishers, and Social Change* (London: Routledge, 1989).

'Urbanus', 'On the Progressional Improvement of Mankind', *The Edinburgh Magazine, or Literary Miscellany* (June 1801): 439–44.

Virgil, *The Aeneid*, trans. Frederick Ahl (Oxford: Oxford University Press, 2007).

Voltaire, *Candide; ou l'Optimisme* (Paris: la Sirène, 1759).

Walker, Carol Kyros (ed.), *Walking North with Keats* (New Haven: Yale University Press, 1992).

Watkins, Daniel P., *A Materialist Critique of English Romantic Drama* (Gainesville: University Press of Florida, 1993).

Whatley, Christopher A., '"It Is Said That Burns Was a Radical": Contest, Concession, and the Political Legacy of Robert Burns, ca. 1796–1859', *Journal of British Studies*, 50.3 (2011): 639–66.

Wheatley, Kim, *Romantic Feuds: Transcending the 'Age of Personality'* (Farnham: Ashgate, 2013).

Wickman, Matthew, *Literature After Euclid: The Geometric Imagination in the Long Scottish Enlightenment* (Philadelphia: University of Pennsylvania Press, 2016).

Wickman, Matthew, 'Of Tangled Webs and Busted Sets: Tropologies of Number and Shape in the Fiction of John Galt', in Maureen N. McLane (ed.), *Romantic Numbers, Romantic Circles Praxis Series* (April 2013), <https://www.rc.umd.edu/praxis/numbers/HTML/praxis.2013.wickman. html> (accessed 27 June 2019).

Wickman, Matthew, *The Ruins of Experience: Scotland's 'Romantick' Highlands and the Birth of the Modern Witness* (Philadelphia: University of Pennsylvania Press, 2007).

Williams, Raymond, *The Country and the City* (London: Chatto and Windus, 1973).

Williams, Raymond, *Culture and Society, 1780–1950* (1958) (New York: Columbia University Press, 1983).

Williams, Raymond, *Keywords: A Vocabulary of Culture and Society* (1976), rev. edn (London: Flamingo, 1983).

Williams, Raymond, *Marxism and Literature* (Oxford: Oxford University Press, 1977).

Wilson, John, *Lights and Shadows of Scottish Life: A Selection from the Papers of the Late Arthur Austin* (Edinburgh: Blackwood, 1822).

Wilson, John, 'On the Genius and Character of Burns', in D. O. Hill, John Wilson and Robert Chambers, *The Land of Burns: A Series of Landscapes and Portraits Illustrative of the Life and Writings of The Scottish Poet*, 2 vols (Glasgow, Edinburgh and London: Blackie, 1840), vol. 2, pp. vii–clviii.

Wilson, John, 'The Radical's Saturday Night', *Blackwood's Edinburgh Magazine*, 6 (December 1819): 257–62.

Wilson, John, 'Some Observations on the Poetry of the Agricultural and that of the Pastoral Districts of Scotland, Illustrated by a Comparative View of the Genius of Burns and the Ettrick Shepherd', *Blackwood's Edinburgh Magazine*, 4 (February 1819): 521–9.

Winter, James, *Secure from Rash Assault: Sustaining the Victorian Environment* (Berkeley: University of California Press, 1999).

Winter, Sarah, 'Scottish Enlightenment Concepts of Equity in the Nineteenth-Century British Novel', in Ralph McLean, Ronnie Young and Kenneth Simpson (eds), *The Scottish Enlightenment and Literary Culture* (Lewisburg: Bucknell University Press, 2016), pp. 245–68.

Withrington, Donald, 'What was Distinctive about the Scottish Enlightenment?', in Jennifer J. Carter and Joan H. Pittock (eds), *Aberdeen and the Enlightenment: Proceedings of a Conference Held at the University of Aberdeen* (Aberdeen: Aberdeen University Press, 1987), pp. 9–19.

Wollstonecraft, Mary, *Original Stories from Real Life, with Conversations, calculated to Regulate the Affections, and Form the Mind to Truth and Goodness* (London: J. Johnson, 1788).

Wollstonecraft, Mary, *A Vindication of the Rights of Men with A Vindication of the Rights of Woman and Hints*, ed. Sylvana Tomaselli (Cambridge: Cambridge University Press, 1995).

Womack, Peter, *Improvement and Romance: Constructing the Myth of the Highlands* (Basingstoke: Macmillan, 1989).

Wood, John, 'Plan of the Towns of Dumfries and Maxwelltown from Actual Survey' (Edinburgh: T. Brown, 1819), NLS EMS.X.009, <http://maps.nls.uk/view/74400022> (accessed 27 June 2019).

Wordsworth, Dorothy, *Recollections of a Tour made in Scotland A.D. 1803*, ed. J. C. Shairp (Edinburgh: Edmonston and Douglas, 1874).

Wordsworth, William, *Lyrical Ballads*, 2nd edn, 2 vols (London: T. N. Longman and O. Rees, 1800).

Zenzinger, Peter, 'Low Life, Primitivism and Honest Poverty: A Socio-cultural Reading of Ramsay and Burns', *Studies in Scottish Literature*, 30.1 (1998): 43–58.

Index